WHERE THE PAST BEGINS

WHERE THE PAST BEGINS

A WRITER'S MEMOIR

AMY TAN

4th ESTATE · *London*

4th Estate
An imprint of HarperCollins*Publishers*
1 London Bridge Street
London SE1 9GF

www.4thEstate.co.uk

First published in Great Britain in 2017 by 4th Estate
First published in the United States by Ecco, an imprint of
HarperCollins*Publishers*, in 2017

1

'One of the Butterflies' by W. S. Merwin taken from *The Shadow of Sirius*
(Bloodaxe Books, 2008) and reproduced by permission of Bloodaxe Books.
www.bloodaxebooks.com

'The Breaker of Combs' was first published in *Zyzzyva*, October 2016.
'The Unfurling of Leaves' was first published in *Allure* magazine, November 2005,
titled as 'A Natural Woman.'

Amy Tan asserts the moral right to be identified
as the author of this work in accordance with the
Copyright, Designs and Patents Act 1988

A catalogue record for this book is
available from the British Library

ISBN 978-0-00-758554-0 (hardback)
ISBN 978-0-00-758555-7 (trade paperback)

Designed by Suet Yee Chong

Printed and bound in Great Britain by
CPI Group (UK) Ltd, Croydon, CR0 4YY

MIX
Paper from
responsible sources
FSC **FSC C007454**
www.fsc.org

This book is produced from independently certified FSC paper
to ensure responsible forest management

For more information visit: www.harpercollins.co.uk/green

For Daniel Halpern,
suddenly and finally,
our book.

Slipstream

[From the journal]
2012

You think you are oceans apart when it is really only
a slipstream that you fell into by accident or inattention.

CONTENTS

WHERE THE PAST BEGINS

In my office is a time capsule: seven large clear plastic bins safe-guarding frozen moments in time, a past that began before my birth. During the writing of this book, I delved into the contents—memorabilia, letters, photos, and the like—and what I found had the force of glaciers calving. They reconfigured memories of my mother and father.

Among the evidence were my parents' student visas to the United States, letters from the U.S. Department of Justice regarding their deportation, as well as an application for citizenship. I found artifacts of life's rites of passage: wedding announcements, followed soon by birth announcements, baby albums with tiny black hand-prints and downy locks of hair; yearly diaries; the annual Christmas letters with complaints and boasts about the children; floral-themed birthday and anniversary cards; a list of twenty-two people who had given floral contributions for my father's funeral; and condolence cards bearing illustrations of crosses, olive trees, and dusk at the Garden of Gethsemane. There was also a draft of a surprising mature-sounding letter that I had written to serve as the template my mother could copy to thank people for their sympathy.

Perhaps the most moving discoveries were the letters to me from my mother and the letters to my mother from me. She had saved mine and I had saved hers, even the angry ones, which is proof of love's resilience. In another box, I found artifacts of our family's hard work: my mother's ESL essay on becoming an immigrant and her nursing school homework; my father's thesis, sermons, and his homework for a graduate class in electrical engineering; my grade school essays and my brother Peter's history compositions; the report cards of Peter, John, and me, from kindergarten through high school, as well as my father's college records. In different files, I recovered my father's and mother's death certificates. I haven't come across Peter's yet, but I found a photo of him in a casket, his sixty-pound body covered by a high school letterman jacket, but with nothing to conceal the mutilation of his head by surgeries and an autopsy. So now I have to ask myself: What kind of sentimentality drove me to keep that?

Actually, I never throw away photos, unless they are blurry. All of them, even the horrific ones, are an existential record of my life. Even the molecules of dust in the boxes are part and parcel of who I am—so goes the extreme rationale of a packrat, that and the certainty that treasure is buried in the debris. In my case, I don't care for dust, but I did find much to treasure.

To be honest, I have discarded photos of people I would never want to be reminded of again, a number that, alas, has grown over the years to eleven or twelve. The longer I live the more blurry photos I've accumulated, along with a few sucker punches from people I once trusted and who did the equivalent of knocking me down to be first in line at the ice-cream truck. Age confers this simple wisdom: Don't expose yourself to malarial mosquitoes. Don't expose yourself to assholes. As it turns out, throwing away photos of assholes does not remove them from consciousness. Memory, in fact, gives you no choice over which moments you can erase, and it is annoyingly persistent in retaining the most painful ones. It is extraordinarily faithful in recording the most hideous details, and it will recall them for you in the future with moments that are even only vaguely similar.

With only those exceptions, I have kept all the photos. The problem is, I no longer recognize the faces of many—not the girl in the pool with me, or three out of the four women at a clothes-swap party. Nor those people having dinner at my house. Then again, I have met hundreds of thousands of people in my sixty-five years. Some of them may have even been important in my life. Yet, without conscious choice on my part, my brain has let a lot of moments slide over the cliff. While writing this memoir, I was conscious that much of what I think I remember is inaccurate, guessed at, or biased by experiences that came later. If I were to write this same book five years from now, I would likely describe some of the events differently, either because of a change of perspective or worsening memory—or even because new evidence has come to light. That is exactly what happened while writing this book. I had to revise often as more discoveries appeared.

I used to think photographs were more accurate than bare memory because they capture moments as they were, making them indisputable. They are like hard facts, whereas aging memory is impressionistic and selective in details, much like fiction is. But now, having gone through the archives, I realize that photos also distort what is really being captured. To get the best shot, the messiness is shoved to the side, the weedy yard is out of the shot. The images are also missing context: the reason why some are missing, what happened before and after, who likes or dislikes whom, if anyone is unhappy to be there. When they heard "cheese," they uniformly stared at the camera's mechanical eye, and put on the happy mask, leaving a viewer fifty years later to assume everyone had a grand time. I keep in mind the caveat that I should question what I see and what is not seen. I use the photos to trigger a complement of emotional memories. I use a magnifying glass to look closely at details in the black-and-white images in sizes popular in the 1940s and 1950s— squares ranging from one and a half to three and a half inches. They document a progression of Easter Sundays after church and the annual mauling of Christmas presents, which were laid underneath scraggly trees or artificial ones, in old apartments or new tract homes. Some of these photos refuted what I had believed was true, for example, that our family owned no children's books, except one, *Chinese Fairy Tales,* illustrated by an artist who made the characters look like George Chakiris and Natalie Wood from *West Side Story.* A photo of me at age three shows otherwise: I am mesmerized by the words and pictures in a book spread open in my lap. In other photos of that same day, there is evidence of presents of similar size waiting to be ripped open. I had not known this when I wrote the piece "How I Learned to Read." But it all makes sense that I would have had books given by family friends, if not by my parents. As a writer, I'm glad to know that my grubby little paws were all over those pages.

I came across many photos of me from the ages of one to five looking flirtatiously photogenic: perched in the crook of a tree, looking up from a wading pool, holding a cup with two hands, giving myself a hug, or grinning at the bottom of a playground slide. My father was an amateur photographer with a prized Rollei camera. He was no doubt giving me suggestions on how to arrange myself, praising me for remaining still, and telling me how pretty I looked, words I would have taken as a reward of love not given to my mother or brothers.

The oldest and rarest photos are in large-format albums. After seventy years, the glue has flaked off the bindings and the rusty rivets have lost their heads. The paper corner brackets that held the photos in place have fallen off, and the photos lie loose between thick black pages. Some of the studio photos taken over a hundred years ago are the size of postage stamps, which was why I did not realize they were of my grandmother until six years ago, when I placed a magnifying loop over the sepia images.

One album holds photos my father took of my mother when they became secret lovers in Tianjin in 1945. He had arranged an artful collage: a large photo of my mother is in the center and smaller ones of himself surround her, as if to say that she is the center of his universe. My father also took many photos of Peter, the firstborn. I found multiple copies of the same photos, suggesting he sent them to friends or handed them out at church. My younger brother, John, received short shrift. Very few are of him alone.

By the early 1960s, my father stopped taking artfully posed photos with his Rollei. He switched to a Brownie camera for snapshots at birthday parties or when relatives or family friends came a long distance to visit us. There are fewer photos of my brothers and me when we were no longer cute and huggable; our limbs had elongated and turned knobby and our faces were sweaty, pimply, and darkened by the sun. In one, I am wearing white cat's-eye glasses. My hairstyle looks like an explosion of black snakes, the aftermath of a novice beautician's first attempt at giving a perm. My nose is bulbous, my cheeks are balloons, and my legs are thick and shapeless. That was how I saw myself. I browse through more images, seeking clues of the start of illness in our family. In one of the last photos of my father, he appears to have aged a great deal in just one year. His face looks tired and puffy. He has lost half of his eyebrows, which makes him look less vivid. After he died, there were few posed photos, not even for Lou's and my wedding, aside from a dozen snapshots taken by friends and family members with disposable cameras. How lucky I am that my father, the amateur photographer with his prized Rollei camera, left behind such a rich pictorial history of our family.

In another bin, I found my first attempts at fiction writing, starting at the age of thirty-three. I saw layers of abandoned novels from over the last twenty-seven years, distressing pages I had not looked at since the awful day when I knew in the hollow of my gut that the novel was dead and that no further revisions or advancement of the narrative would save it. I had long since gotten over being heartsick about them. Nowadays, I let go of pages much more easily. That's a necessary part of finding a story. Yet I had my trepidations about rereading those abandoned pages. When I did, I saw again the flaws that doomed them. But I was also happy to remember those fictional places where I had lived for months or years, while sitting long hours at my desk. I was still interested in the characters and their personalities. There is much in these stories I am still fond of. I never lost them. They are there, but just for me.

I took out a random assortment of childhood memorabilia and felt fond and strange emotions handling these objects that had once meant so much. I was aware that my fingerprints overlay those I had left as a child. There was residue of who I was in these objects. I was the girl who secretly wanted to be an artist. At eleven, the drawing of my cat lying on her back was the best I had ever done. At twelve, the best was a portrait of my cat soon after she was killed. I saved my brother's scrawled science project notes on the care, feeding, breeding, and deaths of his guinea pigs. I kept his Willie Mays baseball mitt, which is no longer pliable. I kept two naked dolls with articulated joints whose eyes open and close, but not in synchrony, giving them a drunken cock-eyed expression. I remembered why I kept the pink WHILE YOU WERE OUT message slip on which the high school secretary had written that my brother Peter was doing well after brain surgery. I thought then that if I threw it away, he would die. So I kept it, but he died anyway.

This past year, while examining the contents of those boxes—the photos, letters, memorabilia, and toys—I was gratified to learn that many of my childhood memories were largely correct. In many cases, they returned more fully understood. But there were also shocking discoveries about my mother and father, including a little white lie they told me when I was six, which hugely affected my self-esteem throughout childhood and even into adulthood. The discoveries arranged themselves into patterns, magnetically drawn, it seemed, to what was related. They include artifacts of expectations and ambition, flaws and failings, catastrophes and the ruins of hope, perseverance and the raw tenderness of love. This was the emotional pulse that ran through my life and made me the particular writer that I am. I am not the subject matter of mothers and daughters or Chinese culture or immigrant experience that most people cite as my domain. I am a writer compelled by a subconscious *neediness to know,* which is different from *a need to know.* The latter can be satisfied with information. The former is a perpetual state of uncertainty and a tether to the past.

The original idea for this book had nothing to do with excavating artifacts or writing about the past. My editor and publisher, Daniel Halpern, had suggested an interim book between novels, based on some of the thousands of e-mails I bombarded him with during the writing of *The Valley of Amazement*. I thought it was a bad idea, but he convinced me otherwise with reasons I no longer recall but likely included words any writer would like to hear over a glass of wine: "compelling," "insightful," "easy to pull together." I plowed into the e-mails to see what might be usable. The earliest were the e-mails we exchanged after we met for the first time over drinks to discuss the possibility of working together on my next novel. My e-mails were not carefully composed. They were dashed off with free-form spontaneity, a mix of rambling thoughts off the top of my head, anecdotes of the day, and updates on my dogs and perfect husband. In contrast, Dan's e-mails were thoughtful and more focused on my concerns, although they also included notes about Moroccan cuisine. He sometimes responded to my offhand remarks with too much care, thinking I had expressed serious wringing of my soul. After six months of wading through our e-mails, I knew I had been right from the start. This was a bad idea for a book. The e-mails would not add up to an insightful book on anything to do with writing. It could serve as a paean to procrastination. I now faced writing a real book.

Unlike those e-mails, I could not write whatever came to mind for a book and consider it good enough to show. Normally, it would take me a week to produce a page that I felt was good enough to keep. Upon rewriting the book, that page and those surrounding it would be cut. While crafting my sentences, I would be aware that an editor expects that a submitted manuscript will be clean, polished pages. [*ed. note: Not this editor.*] My awareness of this fact would lead me to revise endlessly and self-consciously, steamrollering over characters and the freshness of scenes until they were flat and moribund. That had been a major reason each novel had taken longer to finish. After a year of trying a mushy bunch of other ideas, I finally came up with a plan. What had enabled me to write those thousands of e-mails was spontaneity. If I applied that to writing a book, I would be able to finish quickly. I would not think too far ahead about what to write; I would simply write wherever my thoughts went that day and allow for impulse, missteps, and excess. Revision and excision could happen later. To ensure spontaneity, I made a pact with my editor: I would turn in a piece, fifteen to twenty-five pages every week, no excuses. [ed. note: *I should add, I told my author that any pages beyond the required fifteen would not go as a credit for the next installment. We also agreed on some vocabulary that could not be used during the march toward completion. They were:* chapter, essay, memoir *(which became my secret),* finished manuscript, the new book, *and* deadline. *The pieces of prose became known as* cantos, *harmless enough when writing prose.*] Since I would have no time to revise, Dan would need to understand that he would receive true rough drafts, written off the top of my head, and thus, they would contain the traits of bad writing, garbled thoughts, and clichés. To minimize self-consciousness, I asked that Dan not provide comments, good or bad, unless he thought I was veering seriously off track and writing a book he would be insane to publish. [ed. note: *Which I have never done.*]

What editor would not be happy to be the enforcer of such a plan? What sane writer would not later realize that schedule to be ulcerating and impossible? [ed. note: *Honestly, it didn't seem that onerous to me.*]

Even so, I did not miss a deadline, except one. The last. [ed. note: *Technically, she was always a day late, using the excuse of PST, to protest her PTSD.*] It was the Monday after the 2016 presidential election, and I felt lost, unable to focus. For the last piece, I chose the only subject that was relevant to me at the moment: the election and how my father would have voted. When I finished, I had both a book and an ulcer.

I wrote more than what is in this book. Free-form spontaneity had given rise to a potluck of topics and tone. Some were fun, like my relationship to wildlife and, in particular, a terrestrial pest from Queensland, Australia, a newly identified species of leech, *Chtonobdella tanae,* that bears my name. I also wrote a piece on the magnificent short story writer Mavis Gallant, our conversations over ten years of lunches and dinners in Paris, the last one spent in her apartment, where I read aloud to her for hours after a lunch of blinis and smoked salmon. I also considered using a few pages of cartoons—doodles drawn when I was bored at a conference—which I called "a graphic memoir of my self-esteem." In the end, as the shape of the book emerged, Dan and I agreed on the ones I should keep. I had only one concern: what remains might give readers the misperception that I am cloistered in a lightless room with buckets of tearful reverie. There is reverie, but the room is surrounded by windows and is so bright I have to wear sunscreen when I write.

Since this is an unintended memoir, I thought it would be appropriate to include writings from my journals. I gleaned entries that reflect the spontaneity and seeming randomness of ideas that characterize how I think. They are also in keeping with the nature of the other pieces in this book. I call the longer, anecdotal entries from my journals "interludes." I call the shorter entries "quirks." They are quirky thoughts from the top of the head, or quirky things I have seen or heard, or quirky remnants of dreams. For writers, quirks are amulets to wonder over, and some have enough strangeness in them to become stories.

I added two other pieces that reflect fairy-tale qualities of the fiction I loved to read as a child. They are taken from the heartbreaking bin of abandoned novels. Both are prologues. The first, "The Breaker of Combs," has become this book's prologue. It captures the mythic past I grew up with and broke from before returning to it as a writer. The second, "Language: A Love Story," takes flight from my earlier obsession with linguistics when I was a college student. I got as far as a doctoral program before I realized that academia had killed my excitement for linguistics and had instilled anxiety over how to distinguish myself from the other doctoral students. The linguistic principles cited in this rhapsody are likely out-of-date and incorrect. But I have kept it pretty much as I drafted it twenty-five years ago. I had a special interest in Manchu at the time, a near-extinct language with a wonderfully imagistic and onomatopoeic lexicon. It, too, carries the essence of myth, having once been the language of the Manchus that ruled China. The language was already headed to extinction before the Qing was overthrown in 1911. While revising this prologue for this memoir, I learned from an amateur genealogist that my DNA suggested the possibility of a Manchu ancestor. Of course it does. The Manchu of my book is also the Manchu of my past. Imagination is enough to make it so. You just have to look back. The title of this memoir, *Where the Past Begins,* comes from the last line of that story. Dan suggested it. I had not even remembered writing it.

Although I gave up on the idea of a whole book of e-mails between my editor and me, I realized their relevance to this book while writing a piece about my mother's letters. In personal letters, my mother expressed herself differently. She began with events of the day and would then relate a particular situation, which led her to question what had actually happened. That eventually led to tangents, then a looping curlicue line of further thoughts, until she was galloping toward obsession. Only the end of a sheet of paper brought her written thoughts to a halt. I recognize that I do the same in my e-mails, except there is no limit imposed by a sheet of paper. I realized also that e-mails are different because they lend themselves to confession, philosophizing, profanity, and vulnerability. They are intimate because they are not words that would be said to many. They require trust and familiarity. In other words, these e-mails contain the attributes of memoir. Dan's original suggestion [*ed. note: She is referring to the imposed exercise, I believe.*] gave birth to this book.

I am intermittently aghast that everything I have written will actually be an open book. I am contradictory in my need for privacy to write about what is private. That was why I had wavered over whether to include the e-mails. But when I told a number of writer friends what the original premise for this book had been, they all said they would have liked to read that book. Believe me, no one could have endured a whole book of them. [*ed. note: I did.*] But I have selected enough to show the beginning of a writer-editor relationship and the ensuing conversation over the book I was trying to write.

If you have ever wondered how messed up a writer's drafts can be, you'll find consolation or encouragement in reading "Letters to the Editor." If you have ever wondered how writers and editors work together, these e-mails would not be the best example. I don't think most writers would have dropped in on their new editor as often as I did to chitchat by e-mail about any old thing, including the loss of my mind that had once enabled me to write. Most editors would not have answered rambling e-mails with such diplomacy and kindness when the obvious answer to each e-mail should have been a firm suggestion that I cease using my fingers to tap out e-mails and apply them to finishing my much-delayed novel. He always made it seem like he would be happy to know more about what was on my mind.

For inspiration, patience, and guidance, I dedicate this book to my editor, Daniel Halpern.

THE BREAKER OF COMBS

My aunties once told me a story about the Breaker of Combs, an old woman who everyone shunned, except during the worst kind of tragedies. That's when she was asked to break the comb of a ghost who was loved too much: a baby boy or a faithful husband, a scholar son, or a beautiful fiancée.

One family we knew called her when the wife hanged herself with the length of her own hair. Her daughter, who was to be married that year into a good family, discovered her mother's body and cut her down. Then the family found them both, mother and daughter, one dead, one clinging, both with their eyes popped open. My aunties said long after the mother was buried, the girl wandered around the house with her tongue hanging out, gagging with grief.

When the Breaker of Combs arrived, she told the father to bring out the dead woman's comb, the one the daughter had used to sweep through her mother's hair every night. The old woman inspected the comb, a fine piece of golden jade, with many sharp teeth and the body of two phoenixes for a handle.

"As everyone knows," began the old woman, "when a daughter

combs her mother's hair, she receives through its roots all her mother's mistakes and sorrows."

Then the old woman passed the comb over the girl's head three times, and wiped it clean on a long white cloth. She tied the cloth into three large knots and commanded the girl with the hanging tongue to unravel them one by one.

When the first knot was undone, the Breaker of Combs cried, "We have loosened the girl's connection to her mother's past." When the crying girl untied the second knot, the woman said, "We have let go of the mother's connection to her daughter's present." When the third knot was undone, the Breaker of Combs announced, "Now the dead woman has no ties to this girl in this world or the next." And as the girl began to wail loudly, the old woman laid the jade comb on the open cloth, picked up a stone hammer, and broke the comb into many pieces.

The girl instantly became quiet, all her grief shattered forever, just like that. Her grateful family sent the old woman away with one gold ingot and several extra coins, begging her never to speak of this tragedy again.

That was all my aunties told me, but that's not the end of the story. I heard what really happened. That young girl took the jagged pieces of the comb and cut off her own long hair, short as a boy's. Then she ran away, joined the Communists, and never combed her hair again.

I

IMAGINATION

CHAPTER ONE

A LEAKY IMAGINATION

From an early age, I believed I had an extra amount of imagination. I did not come up with that assessment on my own. Many people had told me that. They said I had artistic imagination because I could draw a cat that looked like a cat and a horse that looked like a horse. They praised me for drawing a house with a door that was proportional to the people who stood next to it. They admired the tree next to the house, its thick trunk and smaller branches populated with tiny green leaves. They thought I was creative for putting a bird in the tree. People stared at my drawings, shook their heads, and said I had a wonderful imagination.

At first I wondered why others could not do what came naturally to me. All you had to do was draw what was there in front of your eyes, be it a real cat or a cat in a photo, and after you had drawn it a number of times, it was easy to draw it from memory. I was so good at drawing that by age twelve I was asked by my piano teacher to give his eight-year-old daughter drawing lessons in exchange for my piano lessons. I probably gave the girl instructions like these: *The eyes should be drawn in the middle, between the nose, and not on the forehead the way you have it. Just draw it the way it is.*

Fufu, drawn by me at age twelve.

I later learned that a good eye is not the same as a good imagination. My high school art teacher, an artist himself, wrote that conclusion on my final semester report card: "Has admirable drawing abilities but lacks imagination or drive, which are necessary to a deeper creative level." The comment was sharply wounding at the time. He did not say I needed to use *more* of my imagination. He simply said I *lacked* it—that and depth.

After my last year in high school, I did nothing further with my artistic inclinations, save the occasional sketch and doodle. I do know that had I continued, I would not have gone in the direction of abstract art. Even today, I am often puzzled by abstract art—those ten-foot-high paintings with a minimal dot of color or squiggles. At museums, my husband and I turn to each other and jokingly utter the words of cultural philistines: "And they call that art!" I now remember there were several afternoons in class when my art teacher instructed us to create a drawing using only colored shapes. Whatever I did, that was likely what sealed his opinion that I had no imagination or depth, at least not for the complexities of abstract art, which I now recall was the kind of art he made.

I recently took up drawing again when I joined a monthly nature journaling class, which has as much of an emphasis on journaling as plein air sketching. I began by drawing birds. Once again, I heard the same compliments from friends and family: that I have a good eye. I can draw a bird that looks like a bird. This time, however, I recognized that my abilities stop there. I can draw a *likeness,* but I can't easily create backgrounds more complicated than a branch with a few leaves. I can't add a new context—falling buildings or a melting ice cap—or anything else that would enable the figurative drawing to represent an idea, say, global warming through the iris of a raven. As it turned out, everyone in the class had a good eye and a number of them were especially skilled and also imaginative. Our teacher, a naturalist artist and author, told us anyone can learn to draw, a view I've heard expressed by numerous artists since then. You can acquire techniques—like how to block out the shape of your subject, to use the negative space around a figure to see its shape, to use shading to represent the anatomical structure of birds, amphibians, and large mammals. You can play with a mix of watercolors, gouache, and graphite. You can get by perfectly well with just a pencil and journal book, or you can feed your artistic needs by draining your savings account buying mechanical pencils, blending tools, gel pens, a set of twelve soft and hard graphite pencils, a good brand of watercolor pencils, then an even better brand of watercolor pencils, an embossing tool, watercolor brushes, watercolor brushes with built-in reservoirs, sketchbooks and then really good sketchbooks, zoom and macro binoculars, a spotting scope, a field research bag for carrying your sketch kit, plus a portable stool for sitting in the field for hours. You have to practice daily to make certain skills intuitive—for instance, foreshortening and shadows related to the direction of the light. You need the right shape of the whole creature before you draw an eye. I can't help it, though—I like to draw the eye early on and correct it later. I like that the bird is eyeing me suspiciously as I draw it.

Now that I've been drawing every day, I have come to realize the larger reason I was not destined to be an artist. It has to do with what does *not* happen when I draw. I've never experienced a sudden shivery spine-to-brain revelation that what I have drawn is a record of who I am. I don't mix watercolor paints and think about my changing amalgam of beliefs, confusion, and fears. I don't do shading with thoughts about death and its growing shadow as the predicted number of actuarial years left to me grows smaller. When I view a bird from an angle instead of in profile, I don't think of the mistaken views I have held. With practice, I will become better at drawing the eye of a bird or its feet, but I can't practice having an unexpected reckoning of my soul. All that I have mentioned—what does *not* happen when I draw—*does* occur when I write. They occurred in the earliest short stories I wrote when I was thirty-three. Then, as now, they are revelations—ones that are painful, exhilarating, transformative, and lasting in their effects. In my writing, I recognize myself.

Drawing will continue to grow as a pleasurable activity. I enjoy the practice and patience it requires. I love the sensuous feel of graphite sliding across paper. I was excited by my discovery two days ago that watercolors are not flat swashes of pigment; they create mottling, shading, and other interesting effects that suggest texture and depth. I am delighted by the final outcome. Is it a good likeness? Does it show signs of life? I was humored by my childish pride when someone on Facebook made a comment on my first watercolor of a coot, a bird with a white bill and black body: "You did a good job of capturing its essence." She knew it was a coot.

I have also found ways in which nature journaling is very much like fiction writing. It requires me to be curious, observant, and inquisitive. I have to continuously wonder over what I am seeing and remove the usual assumptions. Wonderment has always been my habit, even before I knew I was a writer. It still is today. When I was on Robben Island in South Africa, for example, I noticed four orange-eyed oystercatchers on the shore, evenly spaced and perfectly aligned. They simultaneously dipped their beaks into the sand, looked at us, then dipped again—all with the precision of an avian troupe of Radio City Rockettes. What was going on? I mused over the possibilities, some of them rather far-fetched—that this was similar to the instinct that "birds of a feather flock together," and by acting as a regiment with identical movements, they can be attentive to important incongruities in their environment, say, an osprey, or a bunch of gawking tourists with cameras clicking. Or perhaps it was a parasite or virus that caused some sort of zombie bird syndrome, similar to the zombie ants I saw in Papua whose brains sprouted a foaming parasitic fungus, which directed the ants to attach themselves to an ideally located leaf on the forest floor until the brain bursts forth with spores that would create a new generation of zombie ant masters. The next time I see this synchronized behavior, I will wonder again and come up with more guesses. When I do nature sketching, I am trying to represent what I see, what is true to a particular species of bird and its behavior. My observations and questions have to do with what might be factually true, which I could discover only by asking an ornithologist. But in writing fiction, the truth I seek is not a factual or scientific truth. It has to do with human nature, which is tied to my nature. It is about those things that are not apparent on the surface. When I set out to write a story, I am feeling my way through a question, often a moral one, and attempting to find a way to capture all its facets and conundrums. I don't want an absolute answer. When writing fiction, I am trying to put down what feels true. Even though the story may not ostensibly be mine, it contains knowledge based on my personal history. It is my experiences that have coalesced into a situation that holds sad irony or horrific clarity. I want to bring forth what I cannot see, what is not there, or is there but nearly indiscernible because the million pieces that make up its whole are scattered all over the place, and extend from past into present. While writing I allow my brain to circumnavigate all the possibilities, but I am not confined to one conclusion. No truth is permanent. Irony is not an intractable fact. Imagination is fluid in flowing to any alluvial ditch of emotions, personal idiosyncrasies, or memories that appear when the flood subsides.

If my curiosity is innate, it has been greatly enhanced by involuntary apprenticeship to my mother and her school of wonderment. She questioned everything, from fishy odors to fishy explanations, both of which pointed to a faulty character. She saw significance in coincidences, and coincidences in just about any juxtaposition of events. On one occasion, it was my saying a word—so ordinary I can't recall what it was—at the same time that the head of a rose in a vase fell off its stem. My mother stared at me and said, "Are you my mother?" My grandmother had killed herself in 1925, and the idea that I was her reincarnation made me queasy. I insisted I wasn't her mother, yet I wondered if I might be. How would a person know who she had been in a past life? You don't journey from one lifetime to the next with luggage tags. "You don't have to hide," my mother said. She continued to give me odd looks throughout the day. "Why you say you bored?" she asked at one point. "My mother said that, too." She wondered aloud if I was her karmic punishment for not showing her mother enough concern. My mother's brand of wonderment combined curiosity, nosiness, hypothesis, loose opinion, suspicion, seeing what you believe, and seeking what you hope, including miracles, and the reincarnation of your mother into the form of your bad American daughter.

Coincidences abound in my life as well. Just an hour ago, as I was writing the above paragraph, my keyboard switched midsentence to writing only in Chinese characters. I cannot read or write Chinese. My immediate reaction was "hackers," and not "karmic retribution." I checked for signs of illegal log-ins, changed my password, reconfigured my settings, printed out current drafts, and rebooted my computer. After a hair-raising forty-five minutes, my computer was once again a monolingual speaker of English. I still don't know why the unwanted translation happened. But I do allow it might have been a little joke played on me by my mother. I would have preferred something less exciting, like a beheaded rose.

Nature sketching will remain an important part of my life and not simply because of the wonderment it inspires. It allows me to regard imperfection as normal. Fiction writing, on the other hand, does not allow me to ever feel satisfied with what I've done. If I thought to myself that a draft of anything I wrote was "good enough," let alone, "great," that would be the sign of a neurological disorder (one of my mother's early signs of Alzheimer's disease was her lack of concern over an increasing number of dings and dents on her car). When I draw, however, I allow myself to be as sloppy as I want. If I draw birds that are too large and clumsy to fit onto the limits of the paper, I buy a bigger drawing pad. When the next drawing is too big for the new pad, I cut off the crown or tail or wings, and it need not be in an artistic fashion. I once gave a curlew an overly curved bill so that it would fit on the page. It made the curlew look like it had gotten its bill stuck in an electrical socket. I have drawn many free-form arrangements of feathers that would never enable a non-helium-propelled bird to fly. I once unintentionally drew the optical illusion of a branch passing in front of a bird and exiting from behind. I see the imperfections and laugh. They're hilarious. I post my drawings on the Nature Journal Facebook page. I show them to my husband and friends. I foist them on strangers with the eagerness of a woman showing off photos of her scowling grandkids. I am the girl I was in kindergarten who said to my parents: "Look what I did."

I might even show my drawings to my former art teacher. He and I maintain a yearly Christmas correspondence that includes updates on our health, the books we've read, and the museums we've visited. I'll send him a drawing or two and remind him about the

Fresno, 1952: The poor minister, his frugal wife, and growing family.

comment he made on my report card when I was seventeen. I'll tell him I'm glad I failed to become an artist.

A t the age of eight, I learned I had a knack for writing, one with financial benefits. I had written an essay on the assigned topic "What the Library Means to Me" and won in the elementary school division. The prize was an ivory and gold tone transistor radio. There was a reason I won. I wrote what I knew the librarians and supporters of a new library wanted to hear: I was a little kid who loved to read, that I loved the library so much I had donated my life savings (eighteen cents) so that a new library could be built. I knew to mention my age and the amount of my estate. I already had very good intuitions about what pleased people, that is, I knew how to be calculating.

Yet there is something in that library essay that I would later recognize as an early glimmer of my imagination and my disposition as a writer. It lies in sentences from the middle of the essay: "These books seem to open many windows in my little room. I can see many wonderful things outside." That was the sign: rooms and windows as a metaphor for freedom and imagination, one being the condition for the other. And there was also the fact that I liked to be alone in my little room. Throughout childhood, my little room—or rather, the little rooms of many successive houses from birth to seventeen—became my escape hatch from my parents' criticism, where I was safe from scrutiny. I was in a time machine propelled by the force of a story, and I could be gone for hours having adventures with newly sprung skills—breathing underwater with a goddess, answering riddles posted by sages disguised as bearded beggars, riding bareback on a pony across the plains, or enduring cold and starvation in an orphanage. Gruel was delicious, like Chinese rice porridge. I found companionship in *Jane Eyre,* a girl who was independent minded and brave enough to tell her hypocritical aunt that she was unkind and would go to hell. Jane Eyre taught me that loneliness had more to do with being misunderstood than being alone.

Throughout most of my school years, I submitted to expectations and gave the appearance that I had conformed. I was a compliant writer, dutifully putting forth what I thought teachers and professors wanted to read. In grade school, good writing was largely directed to punctuation, spelling, grammar, and penmanship. The words and sentences with errors were circled in red. I tended toward sloppiness and the second-language learning errors of my mother's speech—"I love to go school." Only a few essays received any comments other than "Watch your spelling." I unearthed a report card from the seventh grade, which showed that my lowest grade was for English and the next lowest was for Spanish. (I'm glad to report that these grades did not dissuade me from receiving my B.A. in English and M.A. in linguistics.) In college, I wrote essays according to what I knew my professors wanted to read: themes on social class and the cultural shape of the ideal, or the impossibility of avoiding moral complicity as a soldier in battle. I once deviated from the formula for an essay on Hemingway's *The Sun Also Rises,* which I disliked for reasons I can no longer remember. But I vividly recall the professor sitting on the edge of his desk, facing the class, and reading aloud my essay, without identifying me as the writer. He delivered each sentence in a mocking tone and would pause at the end of each paragraph to refute what I had said. He angrily concluded, "This student knows *nothing* about great literature and has no right to criticize one of our greatest American writers." Thereafter, I did not write essays that offered a true opinion of what I had thought of any book. I became a facile writer, a compliant one. Based on that criterion, I wrote well.

After I quit my doctoral program in linguistics, I seldom wrote much beyond reports on children I had evaluated for speech and language delays. On occasion, I penned gloomy thoughts, a page or two in loose-leaf binders, some in a journal book. A few years ago, I found some of those outpourings. They had the same kind of glimmerings I had found in my library essay—the metaphors. They were not remarkable; in fact, some were overworked or reaching. But I was excited to see that they contained two common characteristics: dark emotion and a reference to a recent experience. I had used those metaphors at age twenty-five, when I felt I was still young but world-weary. I was impatient to be done with mistakes and bright promises. I wanted to acquire a few wrinkles to show I was not a baby-faced innocent. My worries were too numerous to keep track of on two hands—my fear that I was not suited to the job I had taken, my preoccupation with the recent murder of a friend, the expectations of marriage, my mother's constant crises, our financial hardship, and much more, which combined with my inability to articulate what I needed emotionally. When I tried, I was hyperbolic. After a trip to the beach, I wrote in my journal that I was like a sea anemone that retracted when poked and was unable to differentiate between what was benign and what intended to do me harm. After taking photos at a party on the anniversary of a friend's murder, I grew despondent thinking about the flat surface of my existence; nothing stood out as better or more meaningful. I wrote that my life was "like a series of Polaroid snapshots, those stopped-time, one-dimensional images on chemically altered paper that served as the stand-in for tragic and trivial moments alike." I later wrote that I was wasting my time doing things that were as aimless as shooting silver balls in a Pachinko machine, and for a reward of more silver balls, which I could use to play endlessly in a simulacrum of success. And then I bemoaned my use of metaphor as a bad habit and avoidance problem. Why couldn't I say what I needed instead of being the martyr of cooperation?

My emotions today are not as dark as those of a twenty-five-year-old. But the metaphors still consist of a similar mix of moods and recent experience. They do not follow the definition of metaphors learned in school—one thing being similar to another based on traits, like size or movement. They are not like those packaged homilies, e.g., the early bird gets the worm. Instead, they are often linked to personal history, and some of those autobiographic metaphors are ones that only I would understand. They arise spontaneously and contain an arc of experience. In effect, they are always about change between moments, not about a single moment, and often about a state of flux that leads to emotional understanding of something from my past. Those that are clearly linked to personal history could be described as *autobiographic metaphor*. Here's an experience taken from my journal, which I have not yet used for its metaphoric imagery, but which is rich enough to produce one.

> *I was swimming in open water, eye to eye with a twenty-five-foot-long whale shark on my right, within touching distance, so close I could see the velvety details of the white spots on its taupe body. As I drifted back to admire the pattern, I felt a light tap on my back and thought I might have bumped into Duncan or Lou until I saw a wall of spots loom up on my left, and all at once I found myself cradled in the small wedge between the velvety bodies of two behemoths. I was so euphoric over the magnificence of what the three of us had created—a primordial womb, a secret place—that I never considered I might have been instantly crushed between them until the sharks slowly swam past me and disappeared into the fathomless deep blue of open water, leaving me alone and unprotected.*

In rereading this anecdote, I recognize the emotions as those I have felt with infatuation during my youth. I recall being attuned to every detail of my lover, feeling the euphoria of our specialness, being unmindful of danger, until I was left suspended with uncertainty over the safety of my heart. Of course, the two experiences—infatuation and whale sharks—differ greatly in the actual degree of danger. The chances that you will get hurt are extremely high with infatuation and they are unlikely with sharks, as I discovered after swimming with them for five days. They remained curious and extraordinarily gentle. One was considerate enough to wait for me whenever I tired and could not swim fast enough to keep up.

The best metaphors appear unexpectedly out of the deep blue by means of intuition and my infatuation with nuance.

When I wrote my first short story, I used the image of a gardenia. The story concerned a woman who was struggling to understand the sudden death of her husband. It was heavily influenced by my own emotional experiences with the sequential deaths of my older brother, Peter, and my father. When my brother died, flowers arrived at our house, offerings of condolences in the form of carnations, chrysanthemums, roses, asters, lilies, and gardenias. My father had been the guest minister of many churches, and their clergy as well as the church members had all prayed for the needed miracle. Their floral outpouring of sympathy lined our kitchen counter and dining room table. Some were set on our coffee table in the living room. A similar variety of flowers arrived at our house when my father died six months later. I recall the colorful array of flowers and their mingled scent. I remember thinking about the cost of all those flowers. My parents rarely bought flowers. They were an unnecessary extravagance. The condolence flowers wilted within the week, but we kept them until the petals fell off and the stems rotted and smelled like dead flesh. Life is fleeting. You can't hang on to it. That was the meaning of those flowers.

I had once thought gardenias were the best flowers. They had a heavy perfume, creamy white petals, and thick glossy leaves. A wristlet of gardenias was the coveted flower of high school proms. But after my brother's funeral, I no longer liked gardenias. Their beauty and scent belied their purpose as the messenger of grief. When gardenias arrived after my father died, the smell was nauseating.

In my story "Gardenias," I used the imagery of a room choked full of gardenias. The dark green leaves were viewed as stiff and sharp enough to cut tender skin. Their heads bowed as they died and the creamy white petals turned brown at the edges and curled like the fingers of corpses. That was indeed the image I had of them, which was why the smell of them had become as repulsive. They were the same odor of the rotted stems, the odor of dead bodies. Those flowers became the imagery of grief I could not express as a teenager hiding in my room. In the end, my metaphor broke under the burden of meaning so much that I had to abandon the story. But the heart of it—the nature of grief—remains mine.

I read an article today on the findings of a study on visual imagery, which gave me an insight on why I like to both draw and write. MRI imaging was done on the brains of twenty-one art students and twenty-four nonartists as they drew a likeness of an object before them. The findings showed that the artists' brains were clearly different, the most interesting being a greater density of gray matter in the precuneus of the parietal lobe, where visual mental imagery is processed. The researchers said no conclusions could be drawn as to whether the extra padding of gray matter was present at birth. But, if that was the case, it would suggest that some degree of artistic skills are innate. The scientists affirmed that exposure to art activities most certainly plays a role, as does the "environment"—for example, having an art teacher who says you have a good imagination. So now I wonder: Did my drawing proclivities in childhood increase my aptitude for the visual and emotional imagery I would later use in my writing? If I draw a bird a day, can I increase the gray matter in the precuneus and further enrich my metaphoric brain? With age, the normal brain loses cells at a faster clip, taking with it the names of common gizmos, the items you were supposed to buy the next time you were at the pharmacy, and the best way to get from your house to that place where you're going to do the you-know and that's why you can't be late. I would like to sock away extra stores of gray matter for a rainy day.

The study made me realize something about the way I write. When I see a visual image in my mind as a scene, I try to capture it in words. The process shares some similarity to drawing a bird. I look at what I imagine, I sketch it out in my story, and I do constant revisions as I try to capture it more clearly. The imagery I see is somewhat like looking through a virtual reality headset, in which I can turn myself 360 degrees to have a complete sense of the visual

*Drawing of a crossbill eating grit inspired by a photo by
ornithologist and friend Bruce Beehler.*

imagery around me. That imagery may be incomplete at first. The
lawn has been planted, but the flowers haven't bloomed. I need mosquitoes to show up before it feels real. I put myself in the imagery
and I walk through rooms, sit in the garden, and stroll down the
streets. I look at every detail of rooms I imagine. If it is not there, I
conjure it up. I inhabit the room and experience the noises, smells,
and personal details. I work toward emotional verisimilitude in all
the details of experience—the way it happened, even though this is
something that in reality has never happened. The "good eye" that
enables me to draw the likeness of a cat is the "mind's eye" that enables me to write a scene based on the imagery in my head. I sense
the good eye and the mind's eye are linked. I don't have to wait for
scientific research to tell me whether that's true.

I once did a TED talk on the subject: Where does creativity hide?
I did not understand the question or its intent. So I focused my
remarks on my own writing, my particular area of expertise, as it
were. I traced my origins as a writer to some mysterious confluence
of my unknown innate abilities with early life experiences, especially
trauma, which had led to the kinds of stories I am drawn to write.
The talk I gave went over well enough, but I was not satisfied with it.
In fact, I hated the talk. I had never explained what I thought creativity was, and that's because I could not wrap my mind around that

huge boggy box of a concept. It was like being asked those impossible metaphysical challenges, such as, "What is thinking?" While answering, you are thinking about how you are thinking. How do you even begin to parse the vast notion of creativity and isolate the elements and processes as they relate to writing? I kept seeing creativity as a neurological version of a Rube Goldberg contraption, in which one word triggers a thought, which leads to a question, and then three guesses, and some "what if" scenarios, which then plunk you into a continuum of interactions hither and yon.

And then one day, quite by chance, I learned something about the way I think, which in turn told me something else about the way I write. I was at a social gathering of scientists, artists, musicians, and writers. A researcher from a university did a short presentation concerning a potential cure for AIDS. He was on a team that had extracted a piece of DNA from a man who had a rare genetic mutation that made him immune to the AIDS virus. The scientific team engineered a molecular structure, known as zinc finger, which could hold the proteins with this DNA mutation. This was then transplanted into the immune system of a patient dying of AIDS. The patient became not only free of the virus but also immune thereafter. During the break, I talked to a molecular biologist, a pioneer of zinc finger. I asked him how the transplanted DNA proteins had made this possible. Did it change the virus, kill it, or did it alter something in the cells of the immune system that made it impossible for the AIDS virus to attach? He said it was more like the latter. When trying to understand scientific concepts beyond my grasp, I often resort to metaphors. I asked: "So it's sort of like pouring oil over a boat to keep Somali pirates from getting on board." He was taken aback. "Yes," he answered, "but how did you think of *that*?"

I, in turn, was taken aback by his question and realized my example was indeed rather odd. I could only answer that I looked for ways to understand things through metaphor. "But why oil and pirates?" he asked. And I answered, "Why zinc finger? How did you come up with that?" His answer was logical: the structure resembled five fingers and had to do with the interaction of zinc ions.

Later I thought more about our exchange. Why indeed had oily pirates surfaced out of a sea of metaphoric possibilities? Why had I not used, say, cowboys trying to capture greased pigs at a county fair? Something about the image felt familiar, but tracing its source was like doing detective work in disintegrating dreams. And then the connection snapped into place.

A few months before, I had been at a friend's ranch in Sonoma. It was a hot summer day, and about five or six of us were sitting in lounge chairs next to a small irregularly shaped pool. Proximity to water may have led us to recall a woman who spoke recently at a conference about her solo voyage halfway around the world. That naturally progressed to the recent rash of pirates hijacking boats. Then someone recalled a terrible story in which Somali pirates boarded a yacht and killed all four passengers. That led us to muse what we might have done to keep pirates from climbing onto a boat we might be on. Guns? Someone joked: We're from Marin County. We wouldn't have guns. We threw out more hypothetical solutions—in fact, they had to do with things you might have on board that could be thrown—kitchen knives, boiling water, fishing tackle. I then proposed my solution—barrels of engine oil poured over the surface of the boat, which would cause the villains to slip and fall back into the water. I pictured it clearly—a slick black coating, along with a bunch of now empty oil drums rolling toward the pirates to deliver the hilarious coup de grâce that cartoon characters use to elude the villains. Months after coming up with this antipirate solution, it emerged instantly as a match for my guessing how a raft of DNA proteins keeps the AIDS virus from interacting with other cells. Although a barrel of oil and a scaffolding of ions and proteins are far from similar in appearance, the patient and the passengers share something in common. They are terrified and helpless, facing imminent death and thus desperate for someone to bootstrap a solution, be it someone's DNA mutation or a greasy ship hull.

So much of my understanding of myself comes together through metaphoric imagery. One thing is like another. It is not the physical likeness. It is the emotional core of the situation, the feeling of what happens. If you do a Venn diagram of the metaphoric imagery and the situation at hand, the overlap is emotional memory. It has its own story, a subconscious connection to my past. I know it is subconscious because it comes out without my thinking about it. Its revelation is often shocking to me, as if I were seeing the ghost of my mother, bringing me a sweater she had knit for me when I was five. "Look what I did," she says. I recognize the feeling and what it means. This is why writing is so deeply satisfying to me. Even if the pages I've written prove to be unusable for the novel—and that often happens—I have still had the experience of using memory and intuition to write a story. I have found more intersections with the different points of my life. They create a map to meaning, taking me to origins and back again. I can see the pattern of early expectations and promise, and how death threw the patterns and religious beliefs askew, how a pronouncement that I had no imagination was both believed and ignored. Through writing, I dive into wonderment and come up with corpses, whale sharks, pirates, and the head of a rose.

Despite my fluidity in conjuring up imagery, writing the actual narrative is a laborious and confounding experience tantamount to conducting an orchestra of ghosts or being the caterer for a wedding reception full of thieves and drunks. The narrative comes in halting steps, lurches in a new direction every hour or drifts away. The first chapter is written ten times and will eventually be entirely discarded. The story is hobbled by doubt and piecemeal revisions, and for a good long while, the story is so flimsy I fear it will collapse. The little room is the storeroom of memorabilia: boxes of old diaries, both mine and my father's visas, fake certificates, letters pleading mercy, report cards, WHILE YOU WERE OUT messages, thousands of old photos of family and unknown people, aerograms written in Chinese, address books, birthday cards, baby announcements, wedding cards, sympathy cards, letters of recommendation, my homework, my brother's homework, my father's homework, my mother's homework, angry letters, acceptance letters, and the memories of things I lost, as well as those childhood souvenirs I'm sure I kept but cannot find—the great assortment of my life. As I struggle to capture what I mean, the right word I know so well is on the tip of my tongue, and so is the right idea, but as soon as I remember that word, phrase, or idea, another elusive set takes its place. I must do this repeatedly until I find enough of them to fill a novel. The process of writing is the painful recovery of things that are lost.

The characters arrive with stiff personalities or histrionic ones. They will remain caricatures until I can truly feel them. At several points in the writing, I will realize I have embarked on an impossible task. I will have fewer than a hundred pages, always fewer than a hundred, and they are all bad. I will be seized with paralyzing existential dread that I will never finish this book. Who I was an hour ago no longer exists. This is not writer's block. This is chaos with no way out. The metaphoric connections have been cut. The wonders are gone. The worst has happened. I am no longer a writer. And then, after another five minutes of self-flagellation, I start writing again.

When I took my first writers workshop, I heard someone talk about the continuous dream. The essence was this: once you set up your story, you should step into it and write as if you are living in that fictional dream. The result would be a story that would make readers feel that they, too, were in a seamless story, a dream. I believed that the continuous dream was a normal state that most writers went into, a state of higher awareness. It happened to me from time to time, but in spurts, and not as often as it should. I was new to writing fiction, and I believed that in time, my continuous dreams would become more continuous. While trying to minimize the noise of construction work in an adjacent building, I discovered that listening to music could keep me immersed in the mood of a scene for longer periods of time. But I still had to create the scene, characters, and basis for the story. Music could not fix flaws. Nor was music successful in keeping external distractions from reaching me—the phone, faxes, and what would happen to my privacy after I was published. I was naive—unaware that heaps of self-consciousness awaited me. After my first book was published I found my groove far less often than I did ruts. Each book since then has been increasingly difficult to write. The more I know about writing, the more difficult it is to write. I am too often in a self-conscious state that excludes the intuitive subconscious one. I need to stop rereading each sentence I write before I continue to the next. You can't write a novel one sentence at a time.

Distractions vie with self-consciousness as the reason novels-in-waiting languish from neglect. I have learned to say no to events, to parties, to seeing friends from out of town, to providing comments on books about to be published. But none of the strictures I put on my time are able to hold tight when there is a family emergency, or when a friend has just received a bad diagnosis. None of it works when I hear the piteous screams of my little dog, which was what he emitted the other night. I came out of the land of continuous dreams and ran to him. After loving his teddy bear, my little dog was unable to retract his penis into its protective sheath. The sight of that problem was much bigger for such a little dog than I would have ever imagined possible—had I even imagined it. Imagine my four-pound Yorkie as a miniature stallion. It was appalling to me, his noncanine mother. I quickly looked up information via the Internet and found the prognosis and the treatment: if the situation was not immediately handled—literally handled—my little dog would risk infection, even amputation. I got out the olive oil. I put on the examining gloves. An hour later, he was fine. I was not. That's the kind of distraction I'm talking about, ones I must handle immediately, no matter how well or poorly my writing is going.

To get away from distractions, I once tried an artists' colony. While I can work perfectly well on an airplane, I discovered that in this haven for industrious artists, I could not begin. The room was oddly arranged, with two twin beds and three metal desks lined against the walls, a configuration that made me uncomfortable. It was bad feng shui, and I would be out of harmony if I did not change it. The beds had orange bedspreads, which I also found disturbing. I spent the entire first night moving furniture around. The next morning, I bought new bedspreads. I then discovered that the room faced the rising sun and cast a glare on my computer screen. The room was muggy and I had to sit right next to a large fan and anchor my pages so they did not blow away. I then couldn't work because the unoccupied room next to mine became the meeting place for extra-marital affairs. Its trysting sets of industrious writers, musicians, and painters banged the bedstead against the common wall without self-consciousness or consideration of my peace of mind. I bought better earphones and listened to louder music. I left the artists' colony with twenty pages. My inability to write actually had nothing to do with the room. It was a beautiful room. Those orange bedspreads were not impediments to my writing. I was. I had imagined I was supposed to do great work in that room where Eudora Welty and Carson McCullers had also stayed. With their good works in mind, I found it hard to begin. I was too self-conscious of what I was supposed to produce, and thus I avoided writing altogether.

I read a study recently on creativity and the brain, which gave me insight into my difficulties writing. MRI imaging was done on the brains of jazz pianists who play by improvising, which is, in essence, composing on the fly, a high level of spontaneous creativity. The results showed that when the jazz pianists were improvising, their brains were not *more* engaged, but *less,* in particular, in the frontal lobes. In nonscientific terms, the frontal lobes keep you under control so that you appear to be a rational, well-socialized human being. They keep you from telling your boss he's an asshole or taking off your clothes in public simply because it's warm. Whenever I meet people who are not aware how asinine they come across, I suspect their frontal lobes have suffered decay. The frontal lobes, I am guessing, are the center of self-consciousness and self-censorship. Somehow, jazz pianists are able to put that state of control on standby. One jazz pianist described improvising as complete freedom.

When I write, I'm certain my frontal lobes are very much in active mode. The self-censors are busy. The wellspring of doubt and worry are overflowing. The standards of perfection are polished and on display. I imagine a look of deep concern on my editor's face when he reads the manuscript. I think I have a brain disease. I suspect the gray matter in my precuneus is becoming a bit threadbare. My need to avoid complacency has trapped me. It has had an ill effect on my writing. It is time to put away the imagined critics, the ones who said, "Lacks imagination or drive, which are necessary to a deeper creative level."

Like those jazz pianists, I, too, have also had nonstop improvisational flights. I know exactly what they feel like. They have occurred at least once with every work of fiction, both in short stories and novels. They come as unexpected openings in portals that enable me to step into the scene I am writing. I am fully there, the observer, the narrator, the other characters, and the reader. I am clearly doing the writing, yet I do not know exactly what will happen in the story. I am not planning the next move. I am writing without hesitation and it feels magical, not logical. But logic later tells me that my writing was freed because I had already set up the conditions that allowed my frontal lobes to idle in neutral. Most of the logistics of time, place, and narrative structure had been established. There was less to decide, because there was less to eliminate. What was left was for me to say what happens next, letting emotions and tension become the momentum driving the story forward. If I can push out my inhibitions, I will have access to intuitions, and with that come the autobiographical metaphors I have garnered over a lifetime. The imagery arrives without my consciously choosing it. The narrative knows intuitively where to go.

I cannot tell you the exact mechanics of how this happens. That would be tantamount to trying to deconstruct the arrival and contents of any stream of thought or emotions. But I do sense that the mind has an algorithm of sorts for detecting possible interactions of visual imagery, language, and emotion that can form autobiographic metaphors. Those combinations are not haphazard. There are patterns and parameters. It may be similar to chemistry. The brain is, after all, a busy hive of chemical interactions of oxygen, metals, hormones, and the like. Maybe each image has a valence—a potential for bonding with intuitions and emotions to form metaphoric compounds. Perhaps narrative tension is the electrically charged state that attracts pairings of words to thought, words to emotions, molecules of meaning.

I do know that the more tension I feel in the story, the further I am pulled forward—once close to fifty continuous pages in a twelve-hour period. That run occurred during the writing of my third novel, the same one I had been trying to write the year before at the artists' colony. By then I knew what was at stake for the narrator—the disappearance of a woman who may or may not have been her sister. I felt the same urgency and tension in thinking about the impending disappearance of my mother, who had just been diagnosed with Alzheimer's disease. The stakes were doubled when my editor Faith Sale was diagnosed a month later with Stage IV cancer. She was like a sister to me. I had no excuse to delay the book and keep it from her. I rented an apartment in New York City, near where Faith lived. Like the room at the artists' colony, the apartment was too sunny, the desk was not aligned according to the dimensions of the room. I put a plastic table and chair inside a lightless butler's pantry, and I started writing at 6:00 P.M. My mind was clear. There was no hesitation, no puzzling over plot points. I wrote in a state of elation, not knowing how much time was passing. When I finished, I opened the door and gasped to find the sun rising at dawn. Twelve hours had gone by. That day I gave the completed manuscript to Faith. The words I wrote that night were the ones that were published.

Looking back, those fifty pages seem like a miracle to me. I have never been in a similar fugue state since, neither in length nor intensity. In writing about this now, I realize what can free the mind of self-consciousness: uncertainty and urgency, and in the case of my third novel, the urgency was the combination of terror and love. Uncertainty and urgency moved the story forward in other novels. These days, those uninterrupted passages last for only a few paragraphs or at most, a few pages. They almost always arrive as the ending of a chapter or the novel—when the narrator and I reach a point where we recognize what this confluence of thought, emotion, and events has led to. As I continue to write, I don't know what will happen, and yet I do. It is inevitable, like déjà vu moments, experienced as familiar as soon as I write them, the revelation of my spiritual twin—the intuitive part of me made conscious.

That was what I sensed while writing *The Joy Luck Club*. When the metaphoric understanding came, I felt astonishment similar to what I experienced when I emerged from my spell in a lightless room to find the sun rising at dawn. In the story "Scar," I had not anticipated that imagery that was both violent and painful would also be emotionally freeing.

> Even though I was young. I could see the pain of the flesh
> and the worth of the pain.
>
> This is how a daughter honors her mother. It is *shou* so deep
> it is in your bones. The pain of the flesh is nothing. The pain
> you must forget. Because sometimes that is the only way to
> remember what is in your bones. You must peel off your skin,
> and that of your mother, and her mother before her. Until
> there is nothing. No scar, no skin, no flesh.

This was unexpected understanding from a place in the brain where metaphoric imagery is not governed by logic but exists as a sensation of truth steeped in memory, the twin to intuition.

Spontaneous epiphanies always leave me convinced once again that there is no greater meaning to my life than what happens when I write. It gives me awareness so sharp it punctures old layers of thought so that I can ascend—that's what it feels like, a weightless rising to a view high enough to survey the moments of the past that led to this one. Too soon, that feeling dissipates, and I am hanging on to contrails as I come back down to a normal state of mind—the one that requires me to write in the more laborious, conscious, preplanned way, all the while hoping I will soon have another intuitive run in which the pieces join, lose their seams, and become whole.

Has my imagination worked this way since birth? What enables me to draw a bird that looks like a bird? When did I start noticing that one thing is emotionally like another? When did emotion and imagery start colluding with velvety sharks?

Whatever imagination is, I am grateful for its elasticity and willingness to accommodate whatever comes along, for giving me flotillas of imagery circumnavigating a brain that finds emotional resonance in almost anything. I just have to let go of self-consciousness for it to spill out freely, as if all I am doing is listening to music.

CHAPTER TWO

MUSIC AS MUSE

I 've never played any of Rachmaninoff's music on the piano. Had I tried, any one of his pieces would have killed me with its demands for polar-opposite dynamics, acrobatic articulation, and cool concentration while evoking the extremes of human emotions at inhuman speed. While I have always liked music that takes me into dark thoughts, Beethoven's *Sonata Pathétique* was about as gloomy and as difficult a song as I was able to manage. In comparison, I thought Rachmaninoff's music was over the top on a psychopathology scale. It sounded like the voice of a hysteric who warbles between pledges of undying love and threats of suicide. Minor struggles become catastrophes, hopes bubble into delusions, and blame turns to vengeance, ending with someone's ancestral home being burned to the ground. This music would have been ideal for accompanying the moods of my mother.

And then, about fifteen years ago, I fell in love with Rachmaninoff's music. I found it hard to believe I had ever found fault with it. Age probably had much to do with my changing musical tastes. Over the years, I've accumulated plenty to reflect on: chest-ripping joy, strange fortune, disembowelment by betrayal, and love cratered deeper by the loss of far too many, including my mother. Rachmaninoff's music has become a wonderfully sympathetic companion. My fingers remain still. I am the listener, ready to take the emotional path into a story.

I used to think that everyone saw stories in music. But when I learned this was not true, it was like discovering that people don't see a story when they read words, that it is only mental understanding. I'm not saying that music should contain story narratives. It's more that I can't stop them from emerging freely, which, sad to say, is not what normally happens when I write novels. Writing requires conscious crafting, and the more conscious I am of *how* I write, the clumsier my sentences come out. The more effort I expend, the less imagination is available. In contrast, when I experience stories in music, it's effortless—and that's because I am not composing. I'm simply the listener, and through my imagination I can wander far into a field of sound. The experience is fun, even exhilarating, but I could never use either the process or the output for a novel. My imagination is oblivious to craftsmanship and focus. The story may have holes and inconsistencies. The character may morph several times. The storyline may be chaotic, predictable, or even maudlin. But I can't improve this spontaneous story any more than I could adjust the weirdness of dreams during sleep. They are simply what my mind went to in the moment—the freely formed melodic reveries guided by the emotions I feel in music.

In recent years, I've noticed an increasing need for reverie for some portion of the day. I feel this most acutely when I am on book tour and must talk, answer questions, and be a scintillating conversationalist from morning to night. I reach a point when my mind no longer wants to hear myself talk nor monitor the intelligence or truth of what I'm saying. It wants to take leave of orderly thoughts and the common sense to not mention sex and drugs in front of a general audience with young children. If I ignore the need to silence myself, I eventually feel mentally claustrophobic, as if I'm on a crowded elevator that stops at no floor.

I find reverie in drawing, or sitting in the garden on a sunny day when birds are hopping about. I find reverie in watching fish in an aquarium. And there are also melodic reveries, which are slightly different from other forms. The stories I see in music allow my mind to stretch—much in the same way one might stretch a muscle that is cramped. By allowing my imagination to run with the music, it acts as a purgative in clearing my mind of cluttered thoughts. No matter where I am in the world, music is the bringer of reverie. It is not simply pleasure. It is essential.

I don't see full stories with every piece of music. If the song is only a page or two, a scene and mood may appear, but when the music stops, the scene will, too. That's the case with Schumann's songs in *Scenes from Childhood,* which I played when I was eleven or so. Now, just as then, the songs evoke a scene, a child, and her moods. "Pleading Child" was a girl pouting and tugging at her mother's skirt to buy her a doll. "Perfectly Contented" was the same child, dancing with her new doll. I liked the songs well enough, mostly because they were easy to learn, but I did not identify with the conniving child. Only one song from that album felt true to the way I felt: "Traumerei," which simply means "dreaming" in German. I grew up thinking it meant "trauma," or "tragedy," and that the song expressed perpetual heartache. That is still the way I hear "Traumerei." If "Pleading Child" had been followed by "Traumerei," I would have imagined not just the girl trying to wangle a doll from her mother but also the transformational event that followed: a mother and father kneeling at the bedside of their recently deceased child, who is now holding her coveted doll, posthumously given. The emotions in "Traumerei" signaled the end of childhood, and at age eleven, when preadolescent hormones were kicking in, that song was perfect for me.

Larger pieces—sonatas, symphonies, fantasias, concertos, and the like—are long enough to carry me into a narrative covering the vicissitudes of life. The stories they evoke are harrowing. They follow bad maps and sudden hairpin turns. Happiness, hard work, and Christian intentions go plummeting off cliffs. These turbulent melodic stories don't reflect my current life. I'm a fairly happy person. I worry only a bit out of habit, which is why I make lists. I'm prone to petty irritations, like everyone, and only occasionally do I wish I knew voodoo to make certain people wake up mooing like cows. Yet the music I choose for melodic stories are not what I would characterize as happy. They are dramatic and strong enough in emotion to knock loose self-control. The composers whose music provides that emotional range are the "Romantics"—from Beethoven, Shubert, Mendelssohn, and Schumann to Chopin, Mahler, Debussy, Saint-Saëns, Fauré, Rimsky-Korsakov, early Stravinsky, and, of course, Rachmaninoff. The romanticism of their music should not be confused with tunes suitable for marriage proposals. The music I am the most drawn to is more freely driven by the story, and comes with full orchestrations and dynamic extremes, which impart the emotional sweep I love by literally sweeping from one section of the orchestra to another, violins to cellos, to woodwinds, to percussion, and onward. The dark mood in music serves as momentum. You see dark clouds and sense rain may come, and it does, with gale force winds. The narrative moves forward in bad weather. People run for cover to escape lightning. If it's sunny and people are happy, less happens. People sit down for a picnic, followed by a long nap.

When the music is played with the full orchestra, I experience the story omnisciently. But the point of view is fluid and can switch to a first-person narrator when the melody takes on the voice of a solo instrument. And the instrument I love most is the piano. It can hold the world in two hands and evoke practically anything, from landscapes, battles, and county fairs, to parishioners in a large church or a single penitent praying on calloused knees for love or mercy.

The time period and setting in the story is anchored to the nationality of the composer and the period in which the music was composed. With Rachmaninoff's music, for example, the story location is what you would find in a folktale in a pre-Bolshevik Russia. My imagination is peevishly stubborn about the time and the parameters of setting. Opera directors are able to relocate nineteenth-century operas into twenty-first-century parking lots and Laundromats, while also freshening up the social or political context. My conscious attempt to change that setting would be as successful as my contriving a novel about a family of athletes in Greenland. Forcing a different context would take me off reverie and into the conscious role of a writer. If I have to push my mind to go in a certain direction that is not intuitive, it can no longer imagine freely. It's more like a committee throwing out ideas for a whiteboard marketing strategy.

As the listener, I don't have to work, but I am not passive either. It is similar to what happens when I read. Once the story captures my senses, I am no longer conscious of the act of reading words. I am *in* the story. So it is with music, except that, unlike reading, the melodic story is not precast. It is suggested by mood. I have found that both stories and music use motifs as recurring patterns that evoke an idea, an emotion, or a memory. The motifs are subtle—unlike the elaborately embroidered symbolism of the scarlet letter that Hester Prynne wears over her heart, or the sled named Rosebud that Citizen Kane calls for on his deathbed. I may not notice elements as motifs when they are mixed in with everything else in a story. It could be a view of six mountains. It could be a single word said by a character. In music, it could be a diatonic passage, a fast tempo, or an echo of the melody played in bass clef. What makes them motifs is not simply that they recur. It has to do with my recognizing where and when they recur, as well as what precedes and what follows them. In a story, the significance of six mountains depends on someone seeing them for the first, second, or third time. The significance of a broken cartwheel depends on having characters who are deterred from reaching their destination. The significance of these motifs is a relationship, singly and together, which grows as I continue to recognize it in all its variations. When I recognize the motifs, what once seemed random or ordinary now has an interesting and possibly deepening pattern, which is also intuitive knowledge. The act of recognizing intuitive knowledge at a particular moment is the epiphany. It's the whole thing, not the pattern alone. The pattern itself quickly becomes hindsight that is quickly on its way to becoming a homily, e.g., a view of six mountains changes according to how fast you want to go past them. Through subtle change, both fiction and music can reveal what is different and what is connected: disillusionment that becomes reconciliation with the past; altruism that becomes betrayal by necessity. These nuances of emotional truth can be caught in a single line of text or a short passage of notes. I can feel it within a blunt word or the abrupt resolution of a chord.

M y tendency to see stories in music was probably influenced by the soundtracks of cartoons I saw as a child. They were scored to correspond to actions in a plot—the xylophone and pizzicato notes on violins matched Wile E. Coyote's tiptoed steps as he set up a trap for Road Runner. A slide of notes on the bassoon suggested Elmer Fudd had come up with a devious plan to foil Bugs Bunny, and a downward slide of notes on the violin let you know it wasn't such a good idea after all. During childhood, cartoons were a great way to listen to classical music. They still are. Bugs Bunny plays songs by Liszt and Chopin. Elmer Fudd sings "Kill the Wabbit" to Wagner's "Ride of the Valkyries." Carl Stallings, who orchestrated all the Loony Tunes cartoons, should get unending credit for intro-

Christmas 1959. In matching pajamas: John, five; Peter, nine; and me, seven.

ducing generations of kids to classical music. I rank *Fantasia* as the pinnacle of musical cartoon mastery for creating stories out of the music of different composers, including Stravinsky's *Rite of Spring,* Tchaikovsky's *The Nutcracker Suite,* and Mussorgsky's *Night on Bald Mountain.* The composers were inspired by a folktale, heroic myth, or poems. In "Night on Bald Mountain," darkness suffocates a small village and specters of death float up like crematory ashes. Heavy stuff for little kids with eyes wide open to uncensored imagination.

There was yet another way that music released stories for me. It came from the sheer boredom of practicing the piano one hour a day—the same prelude, rondo, or sonata, and the same mistakes. I had to remain fully attentive to sharps and flats, tempo and tone, pedaling and fingering—all the mind-numbing work that was conducive more to inspiring hatred of music than reverie. The piano was a daily reminder of failure, a fact reinforced by my mother, who called attention to my lack of progress and enthusiasm. I eventually discovered that when emotions accompanied the music, it was much easier to remember the dynamics of the piece. If a story came with the music, it was always about me, whatever happened recently, be it discord in the home or an unrequited crush. I felt angry when playing *forte* in the first movement of Beethoven's *Sonata Pathétique.* I felt unruffled happiness when the music flowed in *adagio cantabile.* Self-pity always came in *crescendo* surges, and lonely tears ebbed in *diminuendo* until there was stillness, silence, and death. The music was mine, both mistakes and emotions.

I had a rare opportunity to see how film scores are composed. During the film adaptation of *The Joy Luck Club,* I was given the titular role of coproducer, which, I happily discovered, required no meetings but allowed me to tune in to the creation of the music for the different scenes. Early on, the composer, Rachel Portman, sent us one of the motifs that would recur throughout much of the movie, with variations for each scene. The motif was a short phrase of notes on a pentatonic scale, the five-note scale typical of Chinese music. It was the foundation for building the music in the opening, and it was transformed for other scenes. It could change into a darker mood of war, or a lonelier, heartbreaking one of a mother's grief. It was as if this motif was the heart and voice of one character and the signature moment from her past that revealed the pattern of her life, one she recognized but her daughter did not.

The music for our film had all the characteristics of fin de siècle romanticism: songlike melodies based on emotion, lush orchestrations, and extremes in the dynamics. The tone and melody followed what was happening in each scene, and so closely that the music could alternately serve as subconscious memory or to express what was felt but was more powerful left unsaid. Instead of a mother saying, "I ache for my daughter the way my mother ached for me," the poignant motif from a scene in the past could express the complications of love, when present and past merged. Whatever had been nearly forgotten could be recalled by one of the motifs. Cue up the violins for the mind-reeling vortex into the past. Or let it simply be silence. We intuit things in so many combinations of our senses, and sometimes we forget silence. In music, silence is deliberate. When I finally heard the completed music Portman had orchestrated for each scene, I was weeping with the opening credits. That was not surprising. I am often brought to tears at the symphony or opera. But in this case, I wasn't the only one who was visibly moved by Portman's music. The director and coscreenwriter had the same tearful reactions, and that made us ecstatic. If you can move an audience to tears, they willingly give themselves to you. There is art, purpose, and manipulation in film music.

Because film music is deliberately composed for mood in scenes and characters, I find it ideal accompaniment while writing a novel. It serves both practical and synesthetic purposes. I discovered the former when I was working on my first novel, *The Joy Luck Club*. The house next to ours was undergoing renovation, and each day, starting at 8:00 A.M., jackhammers would start up, blasting the concrete in a basement just ten feet from where I sat in my basement. Since childhood, I've had an impressive ability to tune out my surroundings, much to the annoyance of my parents, and sometimes, my husband. I can be in a crowded room and still read or write, as long as nobody tries to engage me. My ability did not extend to jackhammers. I eventually solved this problem by listening to music through headphones. While I could still hear the noise, I was able to choose the music as foreground, what I paid attention to. The jackhammers became the background. Volume alone did not determine my focus. Over the next few days, I made a serendipitous discovery: Each morning, when I put on the headphones and played the same song, the music transported me not just back to writing but *into* the scene. My brain had imprinted the music and scene as inseparable. I had stumbled upon a form of self-hypnosis for writing. Over the next few months, I customized the songs to the scenes, and as jackhammers gave way to drilling, then banging, tapping, and sanding, I went from listening to *The Firebird* suite to selections of what my husband described as New Age gooey music. Those were the precursors to soundtracks.

Music continues to be the best way to keep me seated in the chair and writing. Even so, it still takes me years to write a book. I have many distractions in life, a growing list. I went through a period in which I played brainwave entrainment programs—music combined with binaural tones for brain wave frequencies associated with wakefulness, relaxation, creativity, and dreaming. If I had wanted, I could have customized music tracks and brain wave patterns for "calm reflection," "anger relief," "brainstorming," and even "euphoria." Imagine it—a human jukebox of moods. But I couldn't do it. That degree of brain manipulation reminds me of the film *Invasion of the Body Snatchers*. Individual personality and self-will are replaced with standard-issue outer space aliens.

I still use music to write scenes. I am embarrassed to admit that I actually have playlists titled "Joyful," "Worried," "Hopeful," "Destruction," "Disaster," "Sorrow," "Renewal," and so forth. I choose one track and play it for however long it takes me to finish the scene. It could be hundreds of times. The music ensures that emotion is a constant, even when I am doing the mental work of crafting the story, revising sentences as I go along. It enables me to return to the emotional dream after my focus has been interrupted by barking dogs, doorbells, or my husband bringing me lunch (what a dear man). Even when no one else is home, I put on headphones. It has the psychological effect of cutting me off from the world. It dampens sensory distractions and emphasizes the aural sense, the one needed for listening to the voice of the story. I take off the headphones when dinner is ready. I put them back on after dinner or the next morning. The emotional mood is still there. The hypnotic effect takes hold: when I hear the violins, I'm back in a cramped, cold room in China. Auditory memory has become the story's emotional memory.

I'm particularly drawn to film scores composed by Alexandre Desplat and Ennio Morricone, both known for lush orchestrations in the tradition of romanticism. The solos are often poignant and serve as thoughts of an individual character. They do the same for a character I am creating for a novel. While writing *The Valley of Amazement,* the track "Wong Chia Chi's Theme," from Desplat's score for the film *Lust, Caution* took me and my narrator seamlessly into the languorous life of a first-class courtesan house. It opens with an ominous tone set by cellos and bass, and then the piano comes in, just the right hand, playing the simple melody. Those are the internal emotions of a woman who is isolated, frightened, and losing resilience. She moves forward into danger, and now two hands play the melody in octaves, recalling a parallel moment from the past. For another scene, I chose the opening theme from Desplat's score for *The Painted Veil* to simulate a nervous mood on a long journey to an uncertain future. I listened to "Gabriel's Oboe" from Morricone's soundtrack for *The Mission* as the spiritual complement to exultant relief and joy at the end of the journey. That particular piece was later rerecorded for another album, but instead of the oboe solo, Yo-Yo Ma plays the melody on cello, and his rendition is especially good for expansive emotions related to spiritual revelation, epiphanies, infatuation, and betrayal. A slight change in tempo, key, and bowing technique conveys how falling in love is similar to falling into an abyss.

I've become more discerning about my selections over time. One of my favorite pieces fell out of favor when it was used in the film

Master and Commander. The movie was quite affecting, so much so that afterward, whenever I heard Ralph Vaughan Williams's "Fantasia on a Theme by Thomas Tallis," I pictured a drowning sailor fruitlessly waving his arms in a stormy sea as a majestic ship sailed away. I cannot write to pop, hip-hop, rap, or rock. They have throbbing beats that do not match contemplative moods. Any song with a singer doesn't work for me—even if it is the most tragically beautiful of opera arias sung in Italian. I can still see the singer, and he or she does not belong in my story. I would not be able to listen to a gavotte or waltz unless I was writing a scene that includes gavotting or waltzing in a seventeenth-century castle. Although I am a devotee of bebop jazz, I cannot listen to it when I write, not even a piano solo. By its nature, improvisational jazz is unpredictable and wonderfully quirky. I hear its music as a personality with strong opinions. I need to be my own version of quirky when I write. The opinions I hear in my head have to be my own.

My favorite Rachmaninoff piece is the Concerto No. 3 in D minor, the "Rach 3," as it is known among my friends who are as rapturous about it as I am. It is in my top five. I read that it was Rachmaninoff's favorite, too, and for reasons I wish I knew. I believe it was written when he was anguished that he could not return to Russia. But what did he want to return to? That's what is in the music. Did he feel that it was musically more interesting? The melody seizes me by the third measure and becomes emotional circuitry. There are days when I play the concerto on auto-repeat and listen to it all day, even when I am not writing. I love this music so much I have five recordings, including the scratchy one in which Rachmaninoff plays Rachmaninoff, and at such speed I imagine his fingers whipping up winds that blow the audience's hair askew. His performance of the first movement takes a little over ten minutes, whereas most pianists cover it in about sixteen or seventeen. Was that the tempo he had intended? I read speculation that Rachmaninoff's large hands, ones that could span thirteen keys, enabled him to play faster, and thus he did. But what musician, let alone composer, allows hand size to serve as the basis for tempo? Another hypothesis pointed to pure commercialism: a 78 rpm record could accommodate no more than a ten-minute performance. Someone else suggested that Rachmaninoff played faster because the derrieres of most average symphony-goers could not remain seated for a full concert played at normal tempo. I prefer to believe that these are apocryphal tales whose origins lie in gripes and rumors spread by conductors and musicians who could not keep pace. I want to believe that what shapes any composition and its performance is a deeper and intuitive sense of beauty and not the lowest common denominator.

The recording of the Concerto No. 3 that I love best is by the London Philharmonia, conducted by Esa-Pekka Salonen, with Yefim Bronfman on piano. I have seen Bronfman play live on the symphony stage. I once nearly leaped out of my chair with an odd feeling of fright and ecstasy, as his fingers tread through low bass notes and then crashed against them. He can also play with astonishing delicacy. In one passage of the Concerto No. 3, I always sense a millisecond of held breath between notes that feels like the missed beat that sends a heart into palpitation.

Yesterday, I listened to the Concerto No. 3 again and took notes by hand on the story I saw. I wanted to understand how my imagination plays freely with music. When the song ended, and I looked at my notes, I saw that the story had many cartoonish and fable-like qualities. But I did not think the character was my familiar. She is unstable, needy, in constant crisis, and exhausting to be around. If my husband has a different opinion, he has yet to tell me. The story bears some similarities to Anna Karenina and Madame Bovary—a female heroine with a fatal flaw when it comes to disregarding everything, including society, for the sake of passion. The character in this story does a lot of internal wailing. I would not want to read that in a novel or hear a real person go on and on like that. But in music, the excess is wonderful. There are sudden gaps in the narrative. The male character is nearly nonexistent. If this were judged by the standards of a novel, it would be viewed as overly dramatic, soppy, and a little too easy in what happens at the close of those victorious chords. As private reverie, I found it emotionally whole, a complete story. It was a crazy wild ride and I could actually see a little bit of my younger self in there.

So here is how the story played out. I've given a name to the character, Anna, although in my imagination she does not need one because I am the first-person narrator. The approximate times are based on Bronfman's performance. The comments in brackets denote what I think are the origins of the imagery.

00:00 The orchestra opens with an ominous undercurrent. The piano melody enters soon after, a simple, clean diatonic played in octaves. Anna, a young maiden in a cloak, is alone, trudging up an incline on a countryside road. Today is different, she tells herself. Her life is about to change. She is sure of it. She hopes. She is uncertain. She fears she may be disappointed or rejected. She must resist this nauseating hope. But when she reaches the crest, she sees the town on the other side of an open valley. [In my mind, it looks very much like the Land of Oz on the other side of a vast poppy field.] Her lover is waiting. Anna shrugs off the weight of fear and races forward with such determination she feels as if she is barely touching the road. [I see her walking as Neil Armstrong did on the moon.] She recognizes what has eluded her all her life—the knowledge that there is no greater meaning than to fulfill desire. Buoyed by this realization, her dress fills like a balloon and carries her toward love.

1:00 As Anna draws closer to the town, dark thoughts arrive and confuse her. She thinks about the wretched dark days when she existed with nothing to desire. She pictures in her mind the lonely life she has in a large lifeless house with white walls and tall ceilings. The rooms are nearly empty. Splayed books in white covers lay scattered on the floor. She had read each halfway through before throwing them down in disappointment. They did not tell her the reason she is alive. She has roamed for years from one room to another, calling to God to tell her why she deserves such loneliness, then cursing because she receives no answer. She has no memories of life with others, not even her parents.

2:10 As Anna walks toward her lover, she recalls the moment she knew her life would change. Yesterday, her loneliness had become unbearable, and to avoid succumbing to madness, she flung herself out the door and set on the road with only rage as her compass. A dark forest, a black sea—what did it matter? She was trudging along this same road, hurling invectives to God, when she saw a young man coming from the other direction. They exchanged quick glances, and just as they were about to walk past each other, they both stopped and openly stared at one another. By merely looking into his eyes, she knew what had imprisoned her all these years: she had never known *what* to desire. She had desired only the absence of loneliness when she should have desired the *presence* of love. She had desired to escape from madness. She should have desired to find passion. One desire had blocked the other. With that realization, Anna is freed from oppressive loneliness. She can see now that fate brought this young man to her. As she stares, he enters her soul through the portals of her eyes. [This is probably an amalgam of every Prince Charming–type cartoon I've ever seen—wordless stares and sighs somehow yield portentous meaning.] She and the young man have perfect understanding—and that is why he does not speak aloud. That is how intimately he knows me, she thinks. He knows I have always loved him, since the birth of eternity. She realizes something even more shocking: *he* has always loved *her*. He desires her love now as fiercely as she desires his. Without words, they make a vow: to meet the next day and express their love in all ways possible. And now, today, they will be able to speak to and touch each other for the first time.

2:50 Anna arrives at the tall gates of the village and finds herself in the town square, where streets radiate out like spokes. She does not know which to take. But before she becomes overly distressed, she discovers that her shoes know where to take her. She swiftly walks down one empty street to another. The houses seem empty and lifeless until curtains twitch, revealing the faces of busybodies. When she rounds one corner, she sees three stern-looking women in white caps and aprons scrubbing clothes. They stop their work and conversation to stare at her with a disapproving scowl. She is sure they know why she has come. She straightens her shoulders and walks erectly, casting off their opinions. She tells herself she won't allow these loveless women to deter her. They envy me, she says to herself. But now her feet have grown heavy. It's as if she is pushing through knee-high mud. To force herself to continue, she remembers the near-insanity of loneliness. She cannot go back. By remembering her lover's face, she will find determination. She summons up the memory of their meeting, of his eyes locking on hers, making her blind to these women's taunting faces. But now she cannot remember what color his eyes are. Once again, each step forward is weighted with certain disaster. Why can't she remember his face— the one that freed her cramped heart to grow with desire? It is still growing right here on this street. It has grown into a heart so bloated with desire it might kill her. She can feel it pushing into her throat, choking her. She is about to turn back when she hears her inner voice ask: What use is self-respect if there is nothing else to live for? She had nearly gone mad with pride and propriety. She might have killed herself if it weren't for his love. She throws off thoughts of scandal and wraps desire around her like a warm protective cloak. Newly found passion guides her once again, and each step grows lighter. Soon she is at her lover's door. Her life, at last, is about to change. It is the end of loneliness.

4:05 Anna walks in. The dwelling is humble, the sort of place where a wood carver or young artist might live. She wonders, what does he do? Perhaps he descends from aristocrats who have become impoverished, like her family. [Impoverished daughters of aristocrats are a staple of fairy tales and nineteenth-century novels.] The ceiling is low and the room is small. A table and plank benches are set before a stone fireplace in the middle of the room. At the other end of the room is a narrow cot, where her lover is sleeping, dreaming of his impatience to see her. A square window facing the empty streets throws a slant of light on his face, this handsome youth. His hair is so blond it is nearly white, his face is pale, his eyelids and nostrils are a translucent pink, his nose is long, and his chin is small. It is obvious he is an aristocrat, a Russian princeling, unaccustomed to work, with a mind fit for noble purpose. She is eager to see the color of his eyes again.

She throws off her cloak and warms herself by the fire. The glow from the hearth makes the entire room rosy. In the past, she never gave a thought to her appearance. But in this soft light, she knows she is radiantly beautiful. She is about to call to him when he awakens and rushes over to embrace her. His possessive gaze and caress remove all doubts that she has made the right decision in following desire. He has healed her, and only then does she realize she has been ill. He has warmed her, and only then does she realize her bones have been cold. She sees in his eyes that she truly is beautiful. She has astonished him. In the flickering light, his eyes appear to be gray, then pale blue, turquoise, ice blue, and silver. He leads her to his bed, a low cot covered with a blanket of rabbit skins. As soon as she lies down, she casts off shyness and her clothes immediately follow. No one has ever touched her skin. His hands know this. They murmur and whisper nonsensical words. She cries, knowing his whispers are about her, that he is telling her about the dimensions of his love. She cannot make out exactly what he is saying and will have to ask him to repeat it later—although perhaps she already knows. After all, their thoughts and feelings are identical. The exquisite sensations of their bodies are identical. She exults aloud: *These moments together have already been enough for a lifetime of dreaming.*

As if her thoughts had been an incantation, the spell is broken. Their time together is over. [Shades of Cinderella, the plot driven by a mindless keeper of time.] He looks at her sadly. He seems to be telling her with his eyes. *Time still divides us, but now we have eternity.* They unwrap arms and legs, and from one body they are again two. She is instantly cold. He bids farewell, and when she steps out, she sees that it is early morning. The night passed as if it had been only a few moments before falling asleep.

6:17 Anna walks home, light-headed, still caught in the dream. The old ache of loneliness is gone. She can hardly remember how she once felt. She has a destination now, a reason to live. When she reaches home, she sees how dingy the rooms are, how cavernous and yet constricted the place feels with its small chambers and long hallways. How had she been able to bear it for so long? She wants to go to him this instant and tell him what she has suffered and what he has changed. Why did she leave him in the first place? She cannot recall his saying it was time for her to go, not in words. Perhaps he had wanted her to stay and was wounded in thinking she had made the decision to leave him. She should return to him now. But then she remembers his shuddering groan. He believed they should savor desire and not be consumed by it all at once. He is right. She will wait and come to him when he cannot bear to be without her, when he, too, feels life is meaningless without desire. Warmth will always be at the other end of the road and she now knows how to reach it.

6:55 The simple diatonic melody begins. Anna is once more on her way to her lover. She looks older. It is evident that years have passed. Her step is not quite as lively. The incline feels steeper. This is simply a journey to get to where she needs to be. It starts to rain and the road soon becomes muddy. She slips several times. She considers whether to turn back. She still desires him, but when she returned home yesterday, she wondered why desire was still there when it should have been fulfilled long ago. Her mind holds so many worries it is hard to think clearly about any of them. She does not know his name. He does not know hers. She had reasoned that it did not matter because they knew each other in more important ways. But how? She never asked him. She never asked that of herself. They have spoken only in grunts and gasps, the language of desire.

A wind comes up and rain beats faster and washes over Anna's face like a waterfall, making it difficult to see. She is frightened. She cannot go any farther. In the distance she sees a hunched figure coming from the opposite direction. She soon realizes it is an old woman without the cover of a cloak. The woman's unbound hair streams down her face like long moss. Her once fine dress is soiled, ripped at the armholes. The hem is shredded. She is a wretch of misfortune, Anna thinks, the daughter of a respected family who would now pull up her skirts for the promise of a penny. The old woman laughs, as if she had heard Anna's unspoken insult. She shakes her head and throws Anna a pitying look. Anna is furious that this lowly harlot would pity her. A moment later, she is startled to see that the woman, although haggard, is not old at all. She could be her age, and in fact, they look so much alike they could have been twins. They have the same long dark hair, wide-set gray eyes, and a mole on the right cheek. Even the dresses would be identical if the whore's were not dirty and hers were not clean. When she looks down at her dress, she sees for the first time a black oily spot, then another and another. She instantly feels cold, so brittle with cold her spine might snap. The beggar woman does not exist, she tells herself. It is worse. She is the malevolent twin of her imagination who has been waiting to be recognized. Anna tries to calculate how many years have passed since she began these repetitive journeys to her lover's bed. How many mornings did she rise and leave the narrow cot with him still dozing? It must be thousands. Her skin must be worn thin from so many rubbings. She is afraid to look. Over the years, she refused to let questions about him into her mind. Yet she still felt tormented by small doubts: that he did not love her as much. Or that he did not even exist. The first time she had that thought, she immediately turned around on the road and rushed back to the village. On her way there, she noticed that the road had grown longer and steeper. When she reached his home, she peered through the window and saw him sleeping as usual. She was tempted to rap the window and see his delight that she had returned so soon. But then, as usual, she thought it was best to not interrupt his dreams of desire for her. She simply returned home.

But now, since meeting the wretch on the road, she cannot stop the worries. Does he still desire her? Is his desire the same as what he had for the harlot? Was that why the woman gave her a pitying look? What a brainless fool she has been. She should have banged on the window and broken the pane, then reached in and shaken him to make him speak. Does he, too, believe desire for her is life's meaning? Who else has he desired? What does he do besides satisfy himself with her body? Her malevolent twin is delighted she has doubts.

His incomprehensible groans and grunts were not promises of love, she tells Anna. They were lusty profanity in a foreign language. You saw him only between the hours of dusk and dawn? You had eyes for only what lay at the end of the road and not what surrounds you. Anna looks around her. The woman is not there. Who is speaking to her? She sees the trees around her are dead. How long have they been that way? She sees them as an omen. Love is withering, not just his, but hers. Soon she, too, will resemble the stiff dead trees she passes, their leafless branches clawing upward for more sky. [Shades of anthropomorphic trees in *The Wizard of Oz*.]

She turns around to go home. But she cannot. The more she resists, the stronger the wind blows against her.

10:30 In the past, she could do nothing but succumb to the delusion that he loved her. There is no delusion now. Knowledge is a murderer. She knows now she will not increase the small amount of happiness she receives from her lover. It does not accumulate but disintegrates as soon as she is on the road walking home. Her love for him will always remain gnawing desire. The old argument arises: if she refuses it, she will have nothing. She will be empty. She struggles to retain the vaporous illusion of love. No longer able to decide, she lies on the road and allows herself to be buffeted by the storm. She does not protect herself from the wind. She has already given up self-will. She will soon become a ghost of desire riding a beggar's back. Why not end it now—but which, her life or her desire?

12:45 The storm ends. It has purged doubt, and she is grateful she has survived. She finally understands that her resistance to desire had only made desire stronger. Each time she had thought of turning back, desire surged and became fear, a madness that clawed at her until she pushed through her lover's door again and lay on his bed. In the morning, he had let her out onto the streets where the laundry women could see her. She would then take the road home, carrying her useless satchel of self-knowledge. She had emptied her mind for him. She had welcomed him to use her body as a receptacle. She had asked for nothing. She would have done that until she disappeared—body, mind, and senses. Holding on to this terrible realization, she now turns around to go home. She pushes against strong winds. With each step, the road behind disappears.

13:17 Anna is home. The rain is nearly over. She finds calm for the first time being alone in her house. The arguments in her head are gone. In the past, she would have been frightened by quiet and loneliness. But now she knows she can leave her house whenever she wants. She does not need a destination based on desire. She walks outside and for the first time, she sees beauty in the landscape, in the slope of a small hill, in an enormous tree whose canopy is lit so brightly by the sun it looks like a veil of gold. This tree has always been there, and she now recognizes it as a place where she once sought refuge in a thunderstorm. She runs to the tree and climbs up to its crook. The leaves brush her skin. She sees the bright blue sky through the branches. There are so many ways to see sky. She spots a fat blue bird that sings to her. There are so many ways to see blue. Loveliness is unexpected. It comes without being asked for. How had she not known this? She looks out and sees the spire of the church of the village, the dark clouds moving toward it. And then the spire punctures the clouds and dark rain pours.

15:50 The simple diatonic melody returns. Anna is walking along the road again. Her pace is steady. She is confident. She will see him, her delusion of desire. For so many years, she had seen herself transformed in his lustful gaze. She had believed that the passion in his eyes had emanated from him, when in reality it had simply been her own reflection and longing. Without her desire, he will be empty. Without her passion, he does not exist. Without her shame, the scowling women become myth. They were all part of her delusion to make desire appear more important than it was. And with that realization, the road before her vanishes.

That is the end of the first movement. There are two more movements. And that is good, because the story of this woman does continue beyond a vanished road.

For the last thirty years, I've harbored a secret desire to compose music. I've had dreams that I already have. I hear it, my music, and am composing simultaneously with it being played by a full orchestra. The music is romantic in form. The song is lyrical. The strings play, the reed instruments come in, then the piano solo. The emotions are deep and wide. I know the themes of revelation. I see the partially written score before me, pages three feet wide and four feet tall. I am writing the score for all the instruments, in bars stacked atop each other. I sweep my hand over the paper and the notes appear. But then I wake and realize there is no score and that I lack the skills to transcribe even a note of what I heard. Yet I still feel a residual sense of wonder that the music came to me so easily. I'm frustrated that I can do nothing to retain it. And perhaps that is because there was nothing to retain.

The dreams of music are like the recurring dreams of a secret ballroom—an enormous unused room always found at the back of a house, past the dining room, or through a door in the laundry room. In the dream, I always wonder why I never noticed the room before. It could have solved my need for additional space for books or for a larger study or a painting studio. In one version of the dream, the ballroom is at the back of a third-floor Victorian apartment where I lived in the 1970s. In another, it is accessed via a cave in the yard of a ramshackle cottage where I lived when I was a student at UC Berkeley. There are three more dream houses, all different, but the ballroom is the same. It was once grand but now has plaster debris on the floor and chipped French blue paint on the walls, all easily fixed. Sometimes there is a smaller room beyond the ballroom. It is a mess, filled with construction materials, mops, buckets, saws, hammers, and a big concrete washbasin holding half-filled cans of paint. These are the materials I have to use to repair the ballroom. It is an enormous task. In some dreams, I am able to clean up the mess in a day and hold a dinner party at night. In other dreams, I decide to put off fixing up the room. I sweep the floor, then leave the house and discover I actually live in another house and the place I just left is a house I lived in twenty years ago and forgot I still owned. I'm flabbergasted. How could I have forgotten I own a house? I wonder how much it would fetch on the real estate market today.

These are the words I can use when I wake up to retain memory of the ballroom. I cannot use words to retain the music once I wake up. I don't have the musical ability to take it with me. It lives in its own language—all except one tendril of music, which I managed to capture. As soon as I woke, I used my cell phone to record myself humming part of the dream melody before it disappeared. I played it back. It was a somber tune, almost baroque in quality. When I listened to it a month later, it did not seem like anything I would have devised. I concluded that the tune I hummed was vaguely familiar because it was a song from my past, a hymn from childhood, or any of the thousands of songs I've heard at symphonies or on the radio. It could be a passage from a soundtrack. Or perhaps it was a fugitive melody from someone else's dream.

I have not given up on the idea that the music I hear in dreams can come alive in the waking world. I have had other things come to me in dreams. Cats that dip their tails in inkwells and write as instructed until one kitten has an accident. That became the children's book *Sagwa, the Chinese Siamese Cat*. I dreamed of a full moon party on a boat, during which a little girl falls into the water and becomes lost. When she is found, she is a different person. That became the children's book *The Moon Lady*. I dreamed the idea for making the narrator of a novel the ghost of my mother, who had just died. She suggested in the dream that she could serve as the omniscient guide to tourists on holiday in Myanmar, and per her wish, she became the voice in the novel *Saving Fish from Drowning*. All sorts of solutions to small plot problems have come through somnolent delivery. The best dream arrived two years ago: it was an entire novel—the setting, the narrator, other characters, the situation that leads to the narrative, accidents and bad timing, the other characters and their roles, a backstory in China, a family tree, the complications, even small scenes. When I woke, I wondered if it was the gibberish that is understandable only in dream logic.

While it was still in my head, I wrote it down, as much as I could remember. Ten pages. Then I read what I had written and it all made sense.

The actual writing will still be daunting. It gets harder with each novel. I will have to relearn my craft, overcome the same doubts, untangle the narrative from long detours, or take whichever detour is the story I should tell. I will also find the right music to accompany the scenes as I write them. I am thinking it might even be some of the music that I have yet to dream. It doesn't have to be a full orchestral piece—let us not be delusional. A simple motif would be enough, just four measures of it spun out into a melody that I could play on the piano in the clear voice of the right hand. It would require only a modest dream to deliver a motif barely hanging by a thread of intuition. I will hum it and capture it with a recorder, then transcribe the notes I hear onto a sheet of music. I will play freely with the motif, trying out variations, then transcribing five, the most emotionally resonant—onto sheet music. I will play that melodic motif a hundred times until it is engrained as emotional memory, as part of me. I will play that motif a thousand times for the novel that I have already dreamed I would write.

Souvenir from a Dream

SAN FRANCISCO, JANUARY 8, 2002. *In my dream about a former era, I was writing lyrics to a song, and when I woke, the lyrics were still in my mind. So I wrote them down. If was as if I had stepped out of a dream that took place in the 1920s and came back with a souvenir. Do these lyrics actually exist? Or did I truly dream them up? Maybe next: a flapper dress.*

Two can can-can
—Toucan can't.
Two can can-can
—Toucan can't.
If I can can-can
You can can-can
Then two can can-can.
Shall we dance?

Two lips will kiss.
Tulips wilt
Two lips will kiss.
Tulips wilt.

If I may kiss you?
No, you can't kiss me.
Two lips will kiss.
Two lips won't.

Let's be a twosome.
No, that's too soon.
Let's be a twosome.
No, that's too soon.

If I take one step
You can take one step
We two can two-step
Right up the church steps.

CHAPTER THREE

HIDDEN GENIUS

According to my parents, you could be a genius and not even know it if you were lazy. You had to work hard and push yourself to do what was difficult and that's how you would know how strong your brain was. If you did only what was easy, you would be like everyone else. I had the impression as a child that my lazy brain was like a flabby muscle. If physical exercise could turn skinny weaklings into musclemen, mental exercise could do the same for my brain. And then, if I was indeed a genius, everyone would know this and I would be called a prodigy. "If Peter can do it," they would say, "you can do it."

Peter was eighteen months older than I was and had been born a genius, destined to do great things in life. I heard my parents say that to me, our relatives, and to family friends. Whether he truly was a genius, I can't say, since he died when he was sixteen, too young to fulfill the promise foretold. Nonetheless, I don't remember a time in childhood when I didn't believe that my parents' boasts about him were based on fact. At the end of the first grade, he was promoted to the third, and, according to my parents, he was still more advanced than the other children. He learned everything quickly and had great powers of concentration. He devoted many days toward making a map of South America using different kinds of dried beans—Argentina was black-eyed peas, Brazil was lentils, Chile was yellow split peas—so many countries, so many beans. My parents displayed his South America on the mantels of our different homes, and only now do I wonder what became of that centerpiece of parental pride.

Peter never bragged that he was smarter. When I could not do whatever he was doing, he helped me. He taught me how to catch a ball with a mitt, how to throw a newspaper, how to ride a bike hands free, how to climb over a fence or under barbed wire, how to breed guinea pigs, how to collect baseball bubble gum cards, and how to look up words in a thesaurus. He taught me *Mad* magazine jokes, the names of the most popular songs, and how to spy on our neighbors when they were having a fight. Whatever game he was playing, he let me play. He was Davy Crockett in his fake coonskin cap. I was the Indian maiden. When he received a Lionel train set for Christmas, he assembled the control box and connected the electrical wires. He let me help by connecting the tracks and setting up the plastic scenery. In high school, he ran for treasurer, so I ran for secretary. He let me read his books, the primers in grade school, and later, the novels in high school.

Oakland, 1955. Playmates: Peter, five, and me, three.

I always believed he was better in everything and always would be, and not simply because he was eighteen months older. It was because of what my parents said about Peter, openly commenting on his brilliance. Just the other day, I found my first grade report card and saw what my father had written to my teacher. His praise of me was offset by his higher praise of Peter, an opinion that has remained since childhood as indelible in my mind as the ink in his note.

Amy used to have a sense of inferiority over her brother's out-shining intelligence. This report gives her a big boost in her morale. She will need our constant encouragement as well as yours to keep her stride in such a high-spirited rhythm.

I actually don't recall feeling inferior to Peter, at least not in a painful way. I simply accepted that he was smarter. I suffered no sense of inadequacy around other children my age. My parents and theirs would compare us in various ways. I weighed nine pounds and eleven ounces at birth, destined from the start to be the reigning champion for years in the categories of height, weight, and the speed in which we outgrew shoes. And I remained the heavyweight among the skinny children of family friends all the way until my first year in college, when I was diagnosed with a thyroid disorder and rapidly lost thirty pounds once I was treated. Last year, I winced when my parents' friends told me with good humor about the many boasts they endured hearing whenever our families gathered together for dinner: "Peter is a genius," or "Amy's teacher said she reads with great expression."

From a child's point of view, I thought that how I was judged each day determined how much love I would receive. A smarter child would be better loved, but so would a sicker one. I remember that I competed for expressions of love—for special attention that came in the way of smiles, or being invited to watch my mother get ready for a party, or standing balanced on the soles of my father's feet, or being given an early taste of whatever special dish my mother was cooking. I was deemed lovable for quietness, neatness, good manners, and a happy face. I was more lovable when I was feverish but not when

I threw up, more lovable if I did not cry when a needle went in my arm, but not so lovable when I had scraped my knee doing something forbidden. One time I won the cooing praise of my mother for simply going to bed early without being told to do so. To remain praiseworthy I pretended to be asleep. I pretended so well, my mother turned off the light and closed the door, and then I sat up in tears, listening to other children laughing and shouting in the other rooms. I would draw pictures to win praise from teachers, especially when starting at a new school. I recall my shock and disappointment that the drawing of another kindergartner had been selected to hang in the principal's hallway display window. Her drawing was terrible. It looked like she had scrawled on the paper with crayons stuck up her nose. My drawings were realistic, meaning: the people had feet and the houses had doors.

During childhood, I believed there were times when my mother disliked me, even hated me. Love was not constant. It varied in amount. It was removable. My insecurity about love was no doubt amplified by my mother's threats or attempts to kill herself whenever she was unhappy with my father, her children, or her lot in life.

The good parent today may think it's terrible for a child to live with uncertainty. But how can any parent prevent impressionable children from wondering where they stand in comparison to others? There are a hundred ways children are judged every day, from the moment the household awakens—how noisy the child is, how quickly or slowly the child eats breakfast or ties his or her shoes. And, as a parent, you cannot ensure popularity on the playground or how a teacher grades your child. You can't change birth order and the fact that your brother was the firstborn son and the sole object of affection of newly besotted parents, and that he would later be regarded as your leader and protector. When my younger brother came along, like many middle children, I was jostled about in an evolving and changeable position in the new family order. The day John was born, I sat on the stoop in new Chinese pajamas embroidered with a hundred children, waiting anxiously for my mother to return to me. A family friend tried to soothe me and coax me into playing with her daughter. I would not budge from my spot on the stoop, the place where my mother had left me.

My little brother, John, who was nicknamed "Didi," received love whenever he cried. He cried when his photo was taken, or when he was seated apart from our mother. He would cry when Peter and I would not let him play with our toys. He was not required to follow in Peter's and my fast-paced footsteps. No overt demands or comparisons were made that might cause him to have a sense of inferiority. He was not told he should aim to become a doctor. Where were the impossible goals, the anxiety-inducing predictions? "Whatever will be will be" was my parents' plan for him. They were never lackadaisical about anything to do with Peter or my education—or about anything, for that matter. But Didi could do no wrong. When my parents caught him eating gum he had peeled off the sidewalk, Peter and I were to blame for not watching him more carefully. When he broke our toys or stole our Halloween candy, our parents said that we should have shared instead of being selfish. Our parents unintentionally seeded Peter's and my resentment toward our younger brother. Didi always got us in trouble, and we avoided him as much as possible.

My mother told me when I was an adult that she and my father treated John differently because they felt guilty that they spent relatively little time with him. They neglected him, she said. With Peter and me, they had been fully devoted from the start of our lives. They took us to parks, pointed out errors, helped us with our homework, monitored our progress, accompanied us to the library, and gave us piano lessons. As the years went by, my father became increasingly busy. He was simultaneously a full-time electrical engineer, a graduate student, a substitute Baptist minister, and an entrepreneur who had the same aspirations of many Silicon Valley engineers in the 1960s who were starting their niche companies in a garage. My mother had a full-time job as an allergy technician and ran a home business selling wigs. They were too tired to goad yet another child to improve his grades and practice the piano. My father did not spend hours helping Didi learn all twelve multiplication tables in one night, as he did with me. He was not forced to learn calligraphy in the second grade, as I was, as a method for improving penmanship. They allowed him to watch cartoons for hours as he lay splayed across the sofa, wrapped in his ratty blanket. My parents simply wanted John to feel loved and happy in a more expedient way.

My resentment toward my little brother changed during the year both of us stood on the sidelines, largely invisible, during the twelve months when both Peter and my father were dying of brain tumors. Family, friends, ministers, and church members surrounded our parents, prayed for miracles, spoke to our comatose brother, listened to my father recite the latest doctor's report, sat with them in the hospital during each surgery, and laughed and cried as they recounted anecdotes of happier days. My mother saw every involuntary twitch of my comatose brother as meaningful. That year, they paid little attention to anything John and I did. He and I were equally neglected, equally criticized for not being helpful during crisis, equally buffeted by our mother's depression, equally uncertain about her sanity when she brought in teams of faith healers and karma adjusters. We were equally scared when our mother wondered if there was a curse that would kill all of us. Who was next? When we complained of headaches or stomachaches, we were hauled down to the hospital for tests. We did not know how to grieve. We could not be crazy like our mother.

John and I survived that year of failed miracles. With my father gone, we stopped saying prayers at the dinner table. Our mother's will to live collapsed and surged, from day to day. She would weep and ask aloud, "Why did this happen?" and then count out the imagined reasons. At other times, she was seized with a manic outpouring of ideas for our future—a restaurant, a souvenir shop, going to Taiwan so John and I could learn manners and to speak Chinese, or moving to Holland, simply because it was clean. Only we understood all the ways our family had fractured and why our mother would never heal. It was both natural and necessary that John and I became compatriots who could depend on each other for the rest of our lives.

Easter 1959: In the park after church.

My parents loved their children so much they wanted us to have the best opportunities an immigrant family could find. That required having the best models for success. One was Albert Einstein, who had also been an immigrant. I can't imagine my parents truly believed we could be as smart as Einstein. But why not aim high and then fail just a little? That was their thinking. The only glimmer of Einstein they saw in me was his well-known trait of daydreaming and ignoring those around him. They had read a story that when Einstein was off in his own little world, his mind was actually exploding with ideas. My mind was not. I was not paying attention.

There was another Albert—Dr. Albert Schweitzer, who had the best morals. He won a Nobel Prize for having gone into the jungles of Africa, where he risked life and limb to cure gaunt-faced children of terrible wasting diseases. My father, a minister, also cited him as one of the highest examples of a good Christian. Goodness would not have motivated me to be like Dr. Schweitzer. The magazine stories about his heroism included photos of his patients' crusted feet eaten away by leprosy. Dr. Schweitzer's work was not suitable for a child with precocious anxiety and a morbid imagination.

The other model of success was musical. Mozart was the standard-bearer for many ambitious parents, ours included. My mother told me that Mozart started composing when he was five. No coincidence that I was five when she said that. That was also when a luminous black piano, a Wurlitzer spinet, arrived at our house and took its place along the entire length of a wall in our small living room. The Wurlitzer transformed our lives all at once. Our parents told us that the piano cost a lot of money, and this made me believe we had suddenly become rich. My mother had always complained that we were poor, in part because we gave away so much money. My father tithed 10 percent to the church and also sent money to his brothers and their families, who were refugees in Taiwan. We were shown photos of their sun-browned faces to make us proud to be good-hearted children. We also had to take care of my mother's half brother and his family, who had left a life of wealth and privilege and arrived in the United States, unable to speak English, and unaccustomed to doing the kind of menial work that many Chinese immigrants had to do. They came during a time when my mother was attending nursing school and working part time in a hospital, a job that required her to empty bedpans, change soiled sheets, and wash people's bottoms. One time, she had to listen to a newborn baby cry unceasingly. It had been born without an anus, she said. They could not feed it. She heard that baby cry throughout her night shift. It was agonizing. The next night, it was still crying. The following night, she heard no crying. She told us horror stories like that to show how much hardship she had to endure for our sake. She spoke of her life being so pitiful she almost "could not take it anymore." When that expensive piano arrived, she was so happy I thought the pitiful days were over.

My mother warned us not to damage its perfect surface—no dings, dents, scratches, stains, or sticky fingerprints. The bench was also very expensive, she said, and we were scolded for sliding across with bare legs to make squeaky farting sounds. She became the detective who matched fingerprints to culprits. She was the terrifying interrogator when the first scratches appeared. *Who did this? Who?* When no one confessed, we were all sent to bed without din-

1955: Me at age three, posing for my father's Rollei.

ner. This instrument, so powerful and yet so fragile, was now our mother's most prized possession, and she let us know often that she and my father had sacrificed a great deal in coming to America so that we children could have a better life, which included learning to enjoy music.

I did not understand until I was an adult what she meant by "sacrifices." They were all that she had left behind in Shanghai, where she had had a life of privilege, starting from the age of nine, when her widowed mother married the richest man on an island outside of Shanghai. She went from being the honorable widow of a poor scholar to a wealthy man's fourth wife—one of his concubines, which made her a woman at the lower end of society. According to one version of clan history, her family had expected her to remain a widow, and thus she disgraced them all by remarrying. But had she not married, she would have had to depend on the largesse—or rather, the miserliness—of her opium-addicted older brother. Another version cast her as the victim of a rape by the rich man, which resulted in pregnancy. In less than a year, after she gave birth to a son, my mother's mother was dead. One side of the family said she swallowed raw opium to end her shame as a concubine. The other side related it as an accident. My mother believed a bit of both versions. She said that her mother found it unbearable that she had descended to being the lowly concubine in a household of other numerical wives. So she made the rich man promise that if she gave birth to a son, he would let her live in her own house in Shanghai. He agreed. My mother was the only one who heard the deal had been struck. She saw her mother's mood change in talking about their return to Shanghai. Life on the island was boring, she complained. But when the son was born, the rich man's promise evaporated. My mother witnessed her mother's fury when she learned she had been fooled. To teach her husband a lesson, she swallowed opium. She had only meant to scare him, my mother explained. Her mother never would have intentionally left her, her nine-year-old daughter, alone, an orphan. "She loved me too much to do that. She died by accident." But there were a few times when she acknowledged that her mother killed herself because "she could not take it anymore." Sometimes she felt the same, she would say.

My young mother remained in the mansion after her mother died. The rich man felt remorseful and posthumously revered his fourth wife as the mother of his son. In death, her position in the house was unassailable. The rich man promised to treat my mother as his own. He gave her a new name to reflect her official attachment to the family. He sent her to a private school for girls and paid for piano lessons. He bought her pretty clothes and a Bedlington terrier. My mother said that her stepfather was fond of her—he even let her eat with him, while everyone else had to sit at another table. Yet her feelings toward him remained conflicted. She blamed him for her mother's death—first, for making her his concubine, and second, for breaking his promise. I imagine she called him "Father" out of respect, but whenever she spoke about him to me, she did not describe him as either her stepfather or her mother's husband. She used his full name. She did not refer to the children of his other concubines as sisters or brothers. She referred to them by name and whichever number concubine was their mother. "The number two daughter of the number three wife." Although she lived in the mansion while growing up, she told me she never felt she belonged. She was the daughter of a concubine who had killed herself, who had cast a shadow on the house. Relatives reminded her that she was lucky she was allowed to live in that house since she was not blood-related to the rich man. My mother said they reminded her so often she knew they were saying she did not really deserve to be there. "I was alone with no one to love and guide me, like I did for you," she said. Without a mother to guide her, she did not recognize that the man who wanted to marry her was evil and would nearly destroy her mind.

I am guessing she was eighteen or nineteen when she married. She described herself as naive and stupid. He was the eldest of the second richest family on the island, a family of scholars. His father was the rich man's business partner. He had also trained to be a pilot, one of an elite team, which made him a celebrity hero with a status equal to a movie star. He was supposed to marry the rich man's eldest daughter, my mother said. It was to be an arranged marriage, the prestigious union of two wealthy families of high society. But the pilot wanted my mother, the prettier one, the daughter of the concubine who had killed herself. Everyone told her it was a good opportunity and she was lucky the man wanted her. "Why do you want to be pretty?" my mother said when I cried one day because I feared I was ugly. "Being pretty ruined my life."

As soon as they married, her husband told her he had no intention of giving up his girlfriends, one of whom was a popular movie star. He brought women home almost every night. "That bad man said I should share the bed with them," she said. "Can you imagine? I refused and that made him mad. *He* was mad? What about *me*?" "That bad man was also a gambler who spent my dowry. That bad man was no hero. He was a coward. During a big battle, many pilots died. But he turned his plane around and claimed he got lost." Over the fourteen-year course of their marriage, she gave birth to a son, three daughters, and a ten-pound stillborn daughter whose skin was blue. (That stillborn half sister lives in my imagination as an angry-looking baby the color of the sea.) When my mother's son died of dysentery at age three, my mother was in such despair over her life that she said as she cradled him, "Good for you, little one. You escaped." Even after she attempted suicide, her husband refused to let her go. She was his property. He could torment her, slap her, or put a gun to her head whenever she refused to have sex with him.

A few years ago, at a family dinner, a distant cousin I had never met said to me, "Your mother had many boyfriends in China." Another woman, also a stranger to me, said, "Many." They wore a look of bemusement. I was shocked by what they had just divulged, not just the information but also the humor they took in telling me this. Had my mother been alive, she would have been propelled into a suicidal rage. I wanted to defend her. Yet I was also guilty of wanting to know more. Was it true? Did she have lovers? If so, who were those men? Did they love her? Did she love any of them? I did not ask, and they said no more.

Knowing my mother, I could imagine her taking lovers to spite her philandering husband. She had never been passive in expressing anger. I could also imagine another reason: she felt she belonged to no one. She wanted someone to love her. I also knew for certain that she had one lover while she was still married: my father. They had met around 1939 or 1940 when they both took a boat leaving out of Hong Kong. An uncle, my father's brother, was on the same boat and gave me an account. My father was on his way to Guilin, where he worked as a radio engineer at a large radio factory, and my mother was going to Kunming, where her pilot husband was based. My uncle said sparks flew between my mother and father right from the start. He said she was beautiful and lively, and he wished that my mother had taken an interest in him instead of my father. Neither my father nor he knew at the time that she was married. Or, if my father had known, he did not share that with his brother.

Five years later, in 1945, my mother was in Tianjin with her sister-in-law, and she recognized the man coming toward her from the opposite direction. He was unmistakable—the downturned crinkle of his eyes, the wide snaggletooth grin, the wavy lock over his fore-head. My mother recalled their meeting as fate. If she had come one minute later, she would have been on a train with her sister-in-law, on their way to Yanan. By then, my father was working in Tianjin for the U.S. Information Service Agency as a ham radio engineer. He spoke perfect English, dressed smartly, and was admired by both American and Chinese men and women as charming, handsome, and good humored. He played gentle pranks and laughed a lot. "He could have married any woman," my mother emphasized. "They all wanted him, many mothers of many daughters. But he chose me." When they began their affair she was twenty-nine years old and he was thirty-one.

I have many photos of them taken during their early romance. The look in her eyes is unmistakable. She wears a shy smile in the afternoon, a radiant one in the morning. I do not know how long they lived together in secret, but I imagine from different clothes she wore in those photos that it was long enough to go from a cooler season to a warmer one.

My mother's husband, the celebrity war hero, was enraged that she had run away. He hired a detective, who put up her photo in every beauty salon. One day, when she walked out with her freshly styled hair, she was arrested and brought back to Shanghai. There she was put in jail in a common cell with prostitutes. The news came out in the gossip columns: the beautiful society girl who was unfaithful to her husband, the hero pilot. While she was in jail, awaiting trial, she attempted suicide. When she was told she could be released to go home before the trial, she said she preferred to remain in prison rather than risk being beaten by her husband. Even if she was released, where would she go? No one would have dared give her shelter, a relative told me. She had committed a serious crime and brought scandal on the family. Behind the scenes, the family of the wealthy man paid bribes to numerous people to ensure the charges would be dropped and that no more would be written in the gossip columns. She had no choice but to return to the home where her three daughters, husband, and his strong-

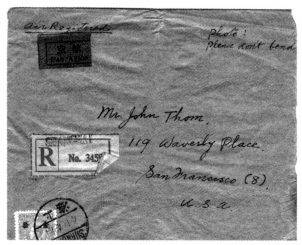

1949. Enclosed: The diploma belonging to Tu Chuan that my mother used for her student visa.

willed concubine awaited her. At times, when she could not bear her life, she went to live with other relatives. Her husband would position her daughters below her window, where they would cry for her, begging: "Come back, Mama!" My half sister Jindo told me she cried the loudest. My other half sister, Lijun, was only four, and she recalls that she did not understand what was going on, except that her mother was too upset to take care of any of them.

My father remained in Tianjin, where he eventually worked with the U.S. Army Corps. He had already received acceptance letters in 1944 to study in the graduate program at both MIT and the University of Michigan. But wartime had made it impossible to leave. In 1947, he was hired by the American Council on Economic Affairs. He eventually got a visa to the United States as an "official with the Council on Economic Affairs," and soon after he arrived, he applied for a student visa.

There are big holes in the history of their affair. At some point they made a pledge to one another. My father indicated on his passport that he was married. My mother said he did that to prove to her that they were married in spirit, even if not legally. They must have also discussed how my mother might make her way to the United

States. To prepare, she secured a bachelor's degree, not via the usual methods of matriculation, but with help from a relative who supplied her own diploma from the University of Shanghai. Their names were similar Tu Chuan, Tu Chan. My mother's application indicated her Chinese name was Chan. The discrepancy wasn't a serious problem. It was common for Chinese people to spell their names in English in several ways. My father variously spelled his "Thom" "T'om," and "T'an," before settling on "Tan." With proof of her undergraduate degree, my mother applied to a college in San Francisco, stating her intention to study for her master's degree in American literature. I once thought it was an odd choice, given her questionable English proficiency and lack of interest in novels. But I now think she had been clever in her choice. Had she said she wanted to study piano, the U.S. Consulate would have denied her a student visa, citing that she might as well stay in Shanghai and study at the prestigious Conservatory of Music. On the other hand, where should a student go to get a master's degree in American literature?

I don't know how my mother emotionally survived during the years she and my father were apart. But I have proof that she was wretched. A photo of her taken in 1948 shows her unsmiling face looking thin and slack. She weighed seventy pounds. Did my mother receive letters from my father during their time apart? Did her husband intercept them? I wondered if my mother ever gave up hope that they would see each other again. Did she imagine he might fall in love with another woman who was unencumbered by husband, children, and scandal?

In 1949, as the Communists were coming into power, the marriage laws changed. A man was no longer allowed to have multiple wives, only one. A woman could divorce. My mother seized the opportunity, and through a complicated ruse carried out with help from the rich man's family, she forced her husband to answer publicly if his concubine, the woman standing next to him, was his wife. The concubine stared at him and he confirmed that the concubine was his wife. My mother presented him with a document and once he signed it, she was legally freed.

In the last remaining days before the Communists took control of Shanghai, she sent a telegram to ask my father if he still wanted her. "Come immediately," he answered. The concubine was eager to see her go and told her she should leave the children for now, until she was settled. My mother boarded the last boat to leave Shanghai and went to Hong Kong, along with many others who believed they would not fare well under the Communists. She applied for her student visa at the U.S. Consulate in Hong Kong and must have encountered incredulity that she would be studying for a master's in American literature when her English skills were so poor. Lucky for her, the university sent a letter to the consulate stating that she would receive intensive English language refresher courses when she arrived, including "ear training" and the use of colloquial speech. A month later, she received her student visa. By then, she was impatient to reach her fate. She changed her mind about sailing to the United States, a trip that would have involved multiple stops before it reached San Francisco a month later. She bought a plane ticket for $700 on Philippine Airlines.

When she arrived in San Francisco, she learned that my father had not enrolled at MIT, as planned. I imagine he had been agonizing over the role he had played in the demise of my mother's marriage, in the criminal charges, the public scandal, and the loss of her children. He had been raised a Christian and followed the King James version of the Bible. In a written personal testimony, he said he felt he had become spiritually lost—like Saul in the desert—until he heard the calling from God to become a minister. He skipped MIT and enrolled in the Berkeley Baptist Divinity School.

My mother was hardly religious. She likely had no idea what kind of life she was headed toward. At first, she accepted her penurious conditions, washing her own dishes, cleaning house, and raising children without the help of a nursemaid. She bowed her head and closed her eyes when they prayed at mealtimes. Over the years, however, love was not enough to stifle complaints about certain sacrifices. Why should he tithe 10 percent of a $200-a-month salary as the minister of a Chinese Baptist church? Why should they live in a place

San Francisco, 1949: The bride who suddenly arrived from Shanghai.

the church had furnished with leftover furniture nobody wanted? I read about her unhappiness in my father's diaries—notations of arguments that lasted into the early morning. Before their third child was born, my mother's arguments over money led my father to give up his job as a minister to take up his earlier occupation as a slightly less impoverished engineer. He worked overtime and my mother attended night school—not in American literature—but in vocational nursing. They continued to send money to my father's brothers, who had fled Shanghai for Taiwan. My mother's half brother, the son of her mother and the rich man, was also a refugee in Taiwan. He had been so shocked in going from a princeling in Shanghai to a pauper in Taiwan that he literally went blind. His wife sold pieces of jewelry so the family could eat. When they wrote my mother and father to say they were at the end of their money and hopes of surviving, she and my father sponsored them and their children to the United States. My mother said she willingly did this, not simply because they shared the same mother, but out of gratitude for what his father had done to help her. In 1957, eight years after my mother left China, the two families moved into a duplex on Fifty-First Street in Oakland. Our family lived on the first floor and my uncle and his family lived above us. That was the year my mother was finally able to afford a piano, a washing machine, and a TV set.

I don't know what my mother would have listed as her sacrifices to give us a better life. Some of what she gave up was material: beautiful dresses and fur coats. Some had to do with her former lifestyle—having a maid, a driver, and a cook. She also had to give up habits, like smoking. She certainly had to give up pride, a lot of it, when she was no longer perceived as an articulate witty woman whose speech and writing were refined. In the United States she could not speak easily to anyone. Her English was poor, and most of the Chinese people she met in the United States spoke Cantonese, not Mandarin or Shanghainese. She had to give up her weekly visits to hair salons. By her early forties, her hair was shot with white. On weekdays, she came home wearing a white nurse's uniform and clunky white shoes. She would sit on the sofa and complain of "sour" legs. We did not know she once had a maid to massage her feet. In her forties, although she was still pretty, she became dowdy. She set her hair with curlers at night only before a social event, then dressed up in her silk satin Chinese dresses, sketched in her eyebrows, put on lipstick, and revived part of her former glamour.

So those were some of her sacrifices. They had nothing to do with us. We did not exist then. She made those sacrifices for love, to belong to someone. That need to be loved was so enormous that she did indeed make a terrible sacrifice: her daughters, ages four, seven, and thirteen. By leaving China, she had no way to retrieve them unless she returned on a one-way ticket and demanded her husband give her custody. She would have had no means to support them, but, in any case, he would have refused, out of spite, and not because he loved being a father. He was a monster; in later years, he would be convicted and sentenced to fifteen years of prison for raping schoolgirls, the friends of his daughters. My mother could not have known how far his mistreatment would go. She had no knowledge that her daughters were also being abused by the stepmother, the concubine.

The woman had a son she loved, but she resented raising my mother's children. She put them in closets. She pinched Jindo's inner cheek so hard her fingernail nearly cut all the way through the cheek. She forced Lijun to sit on a spittoon as a child's toilet and did not allow her to get off and when she finally did her bottom was infected from having been bitten by insects. She did not feed them adequate food, which led to Lijun developing rickets.

When the United States cut off relations with the Communist government, my mother would hear news of her daughters only occasionally via mail forwarded by those friends who lived in countries that still had diplomatic ties to China. The other day, I found a photo of Jindo in her early twenties, looking quite similar to my mother when she was young. The back was inscribed in neatly written Chinese: "For my dearest mother. I dream of you day and night." Did the message cause my mother anguish and guilt? I never heard my mother express remorse. She expressed resignation in various ways: "could not be help," "no choice," "cannot prevent it." It could not be prevented in other families as well—among friends and family. Those were the exigencies of being refugees. My mother's own brother and his wife left their newborn daughter with a poor farmer during the war, so that a crying baby would not alert the Japanese to the whereabouts of their group of young Communist revolutionaries. My uncle and aunt reunited with their daughter after seven or eight years. My mother did not reunite with her daughters until thirty years had passed, by which time they were older than she had been when she left them.

My mother and father did not tell their new friends in the United States about her prior marriage and the children still in China. My father did not confide in his mentors at the divinity school, although the reasons he joined the ministry probably had much to do with his sin for loving another man's wife. And they did not tell Peter and me, their American-born children, who were sick and tired of hearing our mother talk about a bunch of unknown sacrifices she made just so we could enjoy music.

At the piano, our mother had fast magical fingers. She sat erect and we stood on the sides watching. My father wore a love-struck look as he watched her play. What a talented wife! Her favorite pieces were Chopin etudes, polonaises, and, especially, the waltzes, which always roused my father to take my mother's hand and lead her to dance. She and my father were stylish dancers, the best on many a wedding dance floor, where they moved sinuously together, my mother turning up her heel when they paused on the upswing, my father dipping her backward as a finale. At home, he would sometimes take her in his arms and twirl her around the living room and down the narrow hallway, humming a tune like "The Skater's Waltz." At the end, he would lift her, all eighty pounds, and kiss her on the lips. She would always protest when she saw that her children were watching.

Every night, my brothers and I changed into our matching pajamas and joined our mother and father around the piano. She would play the old Christian standards my father loved so much: "Onward Christian Soldiers," "I Come to the Garden Alone," and "The Old Rugged Cross." My father would sing in the forceful voice of a Baptist minister. Peter, who was seven at the time, had already learned to read proficiently and knew many words in the hymns. I would draw my finger across the page, as if I could read, too, although I imagine now that the only words I recognized, if any, were those that were often repeated: *God, Jesus Christ, Holy, Lord, Amen.* The piano made my mother happy, or at least less prone to sudden storms of anger and unpredictable spells of brooding. That made us think the piano was a very good thing. But then my parents found a piano teacher. Our piano teacher, Miss Towler, was a white-haired gentle lady with a soft voice and old-fashioned manners. She lived with her mother, who liked to sit smiling in a wicker chair in the sunroom upstairs, where I waited when Peter had his lesson.

My mother promised we would love the piano as much as she did. "The more you practice, the faster you love." At first, we believed her. The lessons, we were told, were very expensive, five dollars a week *each* for Peter and me. This was yet another sacrifice they were making on our behalf. Our father had to work extra hours to pay for those lessons. And in return, we had to practice an hour a day. Only a terribly selfish child would not agree to do that—one hour a day, hardly anything. To adults, an hour may fly by before you know it. But for a child in kindergarten, that was the golden hour of after-school playtime, when you could finally shake off the restlessness that had accumulated during the school day then shriek and laugh as much as you liked. The afternoons were also when the greatest entertainment in the world came on the TV: *The Mickey Mouse Club*. We could not turn on the TV for the two hours when Peter and I were practicing. For one hour a day, 365 days a year, I sat on that expensive hard piano bench, moving my fingers and straining my eyes to read the sheet music.

Those lessons changed how my parents saw me. I became a lazy girl because I dawdled as long as possible before sitting down on the bench. I was a bad girl for lying about how long I had practiced. I was a careless girl because I made many mistakes and did not bother to conquer them. I was ungrateful when I did not smile and thank my parents for all they had sacrificed so I could enjoy music. There were many afternoons when I sat idly at the piano and stared out the window, watching my cousins run past, shrieking as they circled the house in a game of tag-you're-dead. I was a lump of self-pity on that piano bench.

Learning to play the piano was not as easy for me as it had been for five-year-old Mozart. Consider all I had to keep in mind. Count out the time and pay attention to the tempo. A whole note has a big hole in the middle—tap it out with your foot: one, two, three, four. Black notes that are linked by ropes move along more quickly. I banged out scales, imagining my fingers were tiny soldiers marching in circles. My piano teacher had taught me that each finger had an assigned number, one to five, the thumb being number one, and the pinkie being five. If I did not pay attention to the fingering, I might run out of fingers before I did notes. My fingers ran through the drills—up and down one octave and back, then two octaves and back, then three. Eventually, the octaves took on sharps or flats, and my fingers had to do gymnastic feats, twisting under or over each other to play the notes with even pressure and in time with the rhythm imposed by the tyrannical beat of a wooden metronome. My fingers always ached and I would bend them backward and pull on them, thinking I could stretch them to a length that would enable me to span the big chords without as much pain. How could I ever love something that stole my playtimes, tired my eyes, cramped my fingers, and made my parents yell at me for being a selfish, lazy child? You're smart, my parents said. It should be easy for you. All you have to do is try harder. If Peter can do it, so can you.

Even today, I find it mind-boggling that I was supposed to make sense of tiny notes on a sheet of music before I could even read words. My eyes had to dart between clumps of black spots on a page and convert them into finely tuned neuromuscular movements of the right and left hands. I marvel that very young children can play with both hands. Can they write different words simultaneously with their right and left hands? If they were forced to do so for an hour a day, would two-handed writing become a common teachable skill? How is it that very young children can moderate the loudness of their playing according to notations for *mezzo piano* and *piano, mezzo forte* and *forte*? I seldom see kids who can moderate the loudness of their voices at weddings and funerals. And what kid, barely out of toddlerhood, has had sufficient ceremonial and emotional experiences to play in the mood of a stately *largo*?

Training for our future profession began early. Peter and I were designated as entertainers at family dinners. Whenever guests came to our house, we would hear these dreaded words: "Show Uncle and Auntie what you learned." When we visited family friends who also had a piano, we would be pitted against their piano-playing children. Our family friends were Chinese, most of them U.S.-born and with strong ties to the Chinese community. If they spoke Chinese, it was Cantonese, which my father spoke, but not my mother. Many of those friends were members of an investment group they called The Joy Luck Club. They bought shares in stocks each month based on sound analysis, and if all went as planned, they would one day be wealthy. In a similar sense, piano lessons for their kids were an investment for future returns. Our five-dollar piano lessons would enable us to go from *plinkity-plunk* family night torture to concert performances at Carnegie. Aim high. Over time, models of success came along and we were told to practice harder so we could be like them. One was Van Cliburn, who beat the Russian pianist and won the cold war, so went the media hype. Aim high. Later we had to contend with the little Chinese prodigy Ginny Tiu, who regularly appeared on *The Ed Sullivan Show,* grinning and winking at the camera as she played impossibly fast tunes. See how she loves to play, my mother would say. Why don't you love it, too?

On piano nights with family friends, all the parents would busk for praise by giving the standard apology: "He just started and is not very good," or, "She doesn't practice hard enough," which we kids were supposed to prove to be completely false but failed to do so—all except a boy I will call Charles. He was older than most of us; I would now guess, ten or eleven. I recall that his head was shaped like a giant inverted pear, which made his facial features appear comparatively small and pinched. He did not wear a downcast face when seated on the piano bench. He appeared calm, even pleased to be asked to play. He needed no sheet music. His fingers simply burst into action and rippled across the keyboard. His body swayed naturally with the music and he made no mistakes, finishing with his hands suspended in midair as the last notes faded and were replaced by enthusiastic applause. We were doomed. After our mediocre performances, our parents would say, "Be like Charles. Practice hard!" Some adults would give Charles the standard exaggerated words of praise: "Another Mozart." Charles caused turmoil in many families.

We were all unwilling would-be prodigies, who endured being judged on a sliding scale of better or worse than others, depending on which kids came to these social dinners. I learned the emotions of competition—dread and despair, embarrassment and humiliation, shame and guilt, resentment, even hate, and the complex schadenfreude—joy over the discordant failures of others, followed by Christian fear that God knew I was mean in my heart. I hated expectations, the false praise of my parents' friends when I did badly, and I had a hard time accepting even genuine praise from my parents. Praise made me anxious. It was only temporary relief and it could be snatched away with the next song. At age six, the world was sorting itself into kids who were winners or losers, smarter or dumber, liked a lot or not at all. Where did I belong? My position was constantly in flux, and there were more ways to fail. Life had become serious, full of worries and feelings of self-pity that I was not allowed to express.

Around Christmas, a year after the piano lessons started, Peter and I learned our parents had signed us up to perform in a talent show at church. I received a beautiful new dress in stiff violet chiffon and patent leather shoes, which made me think the talent show might not be so bad. Miss Towler instructed me to smile at the audience before sitting down to play. She taught me how to do a grand curtsy, which I could make after playing, throughout the applause. I had to hold my skirt out wide, tap my toe on a flower pattern on the rug, and then sweep my leg out clockwise, dip down with eyes facing the floor, before looking up with a smile, then gracefully stand upright.

I knew the stakes were high and I practiced my song, a Bach minuet, for the full hour each day. I also practiced the curtsy. Through such rigor, I successfully memorized the piece. It started off in a minor key, which sounded sad to me, but later the key changed to a major mode, which made for a happy ending. So it seemed to me. Before departing for church, I played the piece flawlessly three times. I was all set, excited but confident.

By the time I arrived at the hall, my parents' nervous assurances that I would do well were making me nervous that I might not. For them, so much was at stake, the sacrifices, pride, good parenting. The auditorium was an enormous echoing space the size of a basketball court, crammed with hundreds of restless people sitting on squeaky folding chairs. The church members were predominantly white, but there were also about twenty Chinese people and their kids, who would also be competing in the talent contest. Actually, it was not billed as a "contest" but a "talent show," which carried the positive

American message that every child was a bright little star who could shine in his or her own galaxy. But I had not been raised in the ideology of American constellations. Each star would be shinier or duller than the others. Only one kid could be the very best, and one would be the very worst, the worst being equivalent to the dumbest and least liked. I could not be expected to be the very best. After all, I was only six and had been playing the piano for only a year, and many of the kids were older. My goal, as put forth by my parents, was to play better than other kids my age and perhaps slightly older. Aim high.

I sat in the front row with the younger kids and watched each of them take their turn on the stage. I do not recall the feats performed that day. But I'm sure they were the usual heartwarming acts one would have seen at talent shows of that era—baton twirling, ventriloquism, tap dancing, reciting "Hiawatha," singing "How Much Is That Doggie in the Window," or playing an instrument, like the violin, the song flute, or the piano. I remember my anticipation just before my name was called, the feel of my heart booming at a fast tempo all the way up into my throat. My mother's hands fidgeted with a wad of tissue. My father politely clapped with equal appreciation of each child's efforts.

When it was my turn, I walked in a daze toward an unfamiliar piano, a tall upright that was so unlike our dainty black spinet or the majestic Steinway grand at my piano teacher's home. It was unlike the short blond or walnut-colored spinets in the homes of family friends. In the past, the height of the bench had been adjusted with cushions or a thick phone book to enable my arms, wrists, and hands to be aligned over the keyboard. The bench I now sat in was too low, which made the keyboard too high. I could not ask anyone to change this. The piano also smelled funny, like the musty closet of a former house that we kids believed was haunted. I did not like the ivory keys. They had yellowed and looked like the bad teeth of old people.

When I began, my fingers moved mindlessly, touching the keys by habit. The keys did not feel right. The middle ones had worn-in dips, and some keys were stiff and others were loose, like a tooth that was about to fall out. The notes did not come out as I had practiced.

The pizzicato notes were too soft, then too loud. All at once, my fingers toppled over themselves and stopped. A mistake. The piano and audience were silent. I had already failed. I waggled a finger in search of the right key that would lead me forward. The problem was, I had memorized a whole song, start to finish, and not sections that would have allowed me to reenter at any point. There was no sheet music I could consult. Miss Towler was not sitting next to me to give me hints. I had no choice but to start over. My hands played mechanically and once again, I was aware that the keys looked like yellow teeth, that the bench was too low, that the notes were too loud, then too soft. And again, my fingers fell into a tangle in the same spot. I began again, this time pressing hard against the muffled keys, as if increased force and loudness could push me through this obstacle course. But now my fingers could not even get past the first two measures. Before I could begin again, I heard soft clapping, which grew into louder applause. This was not praise, but a signal that I was being dismissed and should leave the stage. I ran into a dark hallway, crying and shaking with terror. I had become a completely different girl—the dumbest. People would laugh at me the rest of my life. All the kids would be happy that I had failed. Worst of all, my mother and father would be furious. They would scold me for shaming them, for not practicing hard enough, for wasting their money on lessons. I wanted to disappear the way cartoon characters did. Before I could run off, I saw my mother and father quickly coming toward me. But when they reached me, I saw that they were not angry. They were smiling in a sad way. My mother held out her arms and I ran to her and buried my face into the folds of her skirt and cried hard. After a while, my father lifted me and gently told me that I did not need to cry anymore. That made me cry even harder. A few church members passing by patted my head and told me that trying was what mattered. And then I saw Peter. He stared at me with a solemn face then looked down, clearly embarrassed for me. I sobbed hard, gulping air until my lungs could not take in any more. In this hyperventilated state, as I flailed to breathe, people consoled me. "Shh, shh. No need to cry anymore."

At my next piano lesson, my teacher had me play the awful piece without looking at the sheet music. My fingers moved according to its new bad habit and were jammed at the same spot. She immediately saw the reason: incorrect fingering. It was simple to fix: with more attention to the fingering I would be able to play it perfectly the next time. But I knew that was not true. My fingers would betray me again, if not with this piece then with others. And there would be no next time. I would refuse. If I did not, I would again suffer public humiliation, which at age six was one of the worst feelings I had ever experienced. I told my parents I did not want to play the piano anymore. In fact, I declared I would never play again, and they could not make me.

Over the next fourteen years, I played an hour a day. During that time, the piano bench acquired many scratches and dents. My mother grieved over the first few and blamed us, her careless children. That is what I remembered and confirmed recently as true when I read my father's diaries. The bench continued to acquire chips and gouges, more as a result of being jostled from one new home to another. We moved often, and the piano remained the centerpiece in a succession of living rooms. I bore the sixty minutes with the same focus I had in completing homework or washing the dishes—as a chore. My parents continued to believe that one day I would love the piano, but they stopped using the word *prodigy*. I think they still held hopes I would become a concert pianist, perhaps only as a hobby. Aim high. Over the course of fifteen years of lessons, I went through a number of piano teachers, each with their particular tried-and-true teaching techniques. One woman made me curve my hand over a red apple so that I could play with preformed claws. Another teacher, who was a former conductor, pushed down hard on my right shoulder so I could feel the rhythm that my ear had stubbornly refused to recognize. None of them said I was unusually gifted. My mother had asked. Throughout grade school, I had to perform in piano recitals held in these different piano teachers' homes, with the youngest going first, the oldest last, and me always in the interminable middle, where the comparisons were greatest. As I grew older, I learned that if I expected to do badly, I suffered no stunning blow when I did. On one occasion, as I neared the end of a long rondo, I realized with surprise that I had played the piece perfectly—until my fingers crashed down on the final chord in a different key. In high school, I was the accompanist for the Girls Glee and once froze, unable to start playing "I Enjoy Being a Girl." The music teacher lifted his baton three times before he glared at me and commanded me in a tense voice to begin.

My mind drifted during my solitary hour of practice. Whenever my mother interrupted me, I shot back, "How can I concentrate when you're talking to me?" I used to imagine I was somewhere else. I saw scenes in my head, and they were shaped by the music—the ominous dark place signaled by the bass register in a minor mode, the full-chorded passages that led a royal procession, the pizzicato tiptoe forays into magical lands, the triplets dashing to a ball, a castle, the arms of a cartoon prince. The music was not just backdrop. It created the scenes in my head. I went to forests, and meadows, to a place underwater where maidens sang with floating hair. I saw through sidewalks, where there were jewels. The scenes were images from fairy tales. But the emotions were mine, and most of them wavered between hope and sadness. During the year my father and brother Peter were dying of cancer, I found refuge in gloomy music. I favored the largo funereal mood of Chopin's prelude op. 28, no. 4. It contained solitary despair and the usual realization that life led to a bad ending. Every three or four weeks, I would be given a new batch of songs to learn. Some contained emotions that suited me, others felt as mechanical as arithmetic. Before I could perfect them, I had to leave them behind and learn new ones.

During my sophomore year in college, I decided to drop my piano course. I was old enough to choose what I wanted to do in life and it had been clear for some time to both my mother and me that I would never be a concert pianist. My decision scared me. I was going to alter what had become part of me, the hated one honed by hard work and the burden of expectations. I had to acknowledge that fifteen years of piano lessons, tears, threats, and humiliation had led to nothing, and that, in effect, I had failed. My father had died three years before, and I was glad I would not see his disappointment when I made my announcement. I imagined my mother would cry. She would invoke my father's name. When I finally told her, I laid out the reasons I had to stop—that I needed the time to complete required courses, that it took too much study time to go across campus to the practice room, that walking at night was dangerous. She did not become angry, as I had expected she would, nor did she heap guilt on me for money wasted on lessons. She said that she had expected that I would one day stop. Instead of relief, I felt a strange sense of loss that I can only now surmise as shock that she had long given up seeing me as being better than I was. She had expected little of my younger brother. She had expected less of me than I had thought. She was sad, I could tell, and she added that she only hoped that one day I would enjoy music. I assured her that I already did.

My mother did not live long enough to see how much music would figure into my life. She would have been overjoyed to dress up and go with me to the symphony, to the opera, and perhaps even to a jazz concert. She would have discreetly bragged to people that I had written a libretto for an opera. "A true story," she might have said, "based on all my difficulties with my daughter. She was awful." She would have been pleased that I championed young musical geniuses, prodigies, who worked hard and loved to play music in front of audiences. To please her, I might have even sat down on occasion at the piano—a Steinway grand—to play a song I had practiced over and over again until I could play it with ease. I would have recalled with her all those terrible times when we argued over whether I had practiced long enough. We would have laughed.

I would have told her that music has been freed from my fingers. It could accompany me wherever I went, even into my imagination, into the privacy of my mind and emotions. It was what I shared with others, what we talked about at the end of a concert. I had learned to enjoy music. More than that, I loved it. It had become important in my daily life.

Last night I found my nemesis, the Bach Minuet in G Minor, which I had tried to play at the talent show when I was six. It was in a thin tattered book with yellowed pages, some of which had come loose. "First Lessons in Bach" the book said, "a study in accent and in obtaining a proper balance of tone." The first piece was the one I had memorized, a simple melody with two flats, fluctuating between sustained notes and dotted pizzicato ones. When I tried to play it, I was astonished that I had been required to learn this at such a young age. And then I reached the same spot where my fingers tumbled into one another fifty-nine years later, and did so again. As then, I had used the incorrect fingering, putting the third finger on the black key instead of the second. I attempted to play it correctly, but the childhood memory of that mistake, enforced by terror, made it hard to overcome. I was overly cautious when I reached the notes that I had failed to play. They contained so many emotions: the reason I had hated public performance for many years; the reason I hate being forced into any kind of competition; the reason that I play the piano only when I am alone. The reason why I hate to this day any kind of expectation placed on me, including those having to do with books I am writing. My stomach lurches at the thought of public scrutiny whether expectations were met.

I played the minuet for hours, trying to overcome an old habit and ingrain a new one. I went into memories of a church hall and its echoing sounds of applause, its odd-smelling piano, the cold folding chairs, the short bench, the loose-toothed ivory, the missing sheet music—all that kept me from moving forward. I eventually played it perfectly—again and again, until it was 2:00 A.M. and my fingers ached. I had overcome the mistake, and changed the habit. I remembered the folds of my mother's skirt where I had hidden my face and had sobbed because I had failed, and sobbed even harder when I realized I had already been forgiven.

REORIENTATION:
HOMER, ALASKA

[From the journal]

Homer, Alaska, June 9, 2005. We rowed several miles across Kachemak Bay, going past Gull Island and its mound of birds: kittiwakes, murres, corvids, puffins, cormorants, gulls, and pigeons of all sorts, tucked in crevices. At the peak, an eagle perched like a flagpole ornament. Any shift in its position set off shrill cries and wing beating of thousands of birds.

We reached an island where our host lived—a lovely rustic house with sheltered patios and a living room with an uninterrupted view of the bay. He took us on a short walk to a beach and mentioned some sort of churning tidal action that created a whirlpool effect. It had the power to open up and swallow entire boats. I'm probably not remembering this correctly. But it was enough to scare me. Alaskan tales.

He then told us about an occurrence in winter. A thin layer of fresh water spreads over the seawater and freezes. The sun's rays cut through the ice and break the seawater sheath into ice shards that resemble candles. When they collapse and slide into the water, they make no sound. But if the wind pushes those ice candles against the land, the pieces slide against and over the top of those before them, until they are jammed upright, like sparkling glass, and as they tumble row upon row, they make the sound of tinkling bells.

He invited me to come use the house as a writer's retreat. If you come in winter, though, you're stuck. You can't row back. I imagined how lovely it would be to spend a month or two writing in isolation, playing their piano, looking at birds, and listening to the ice candles. He said you might have to put your ear to the ice to hear it. It does not happen that often. You might have to spend five winters on this island cut off from Homer Sound, everything. Out there, if you screamed, no one would hear you.

II

MEMORY IN EMOTION

CHAPTER FOUR

GENUINE EMOTIONS

In October 2004, I began to wake up daily with a great sense of happiness. This had not been my normal mood first thing in the morning when multiple alarms disconnected me from dreams before they could warp away on their own.

When this happy morning mood started, my life was indeed full and happy, and I lacked only the time and discipline to do all that I wanted. Of course, I had an assortment of problems and annoyances, as does everyone, like having our car spray painted when it was parked on the street, or getting our house skunked when our windows were wide open and guests were about to arrive, or dealing with a few achy vestiges of Lyme disease, a chronic illness I managed with medication so that I was now well enough to finally have a writing brain again. In the overall assessment of life, those things that truly mattered—family, friendship, meaningful work, a home, and dogs—made my life a happy one. But it was still not normal for me—or anyone—to wake up and want to say out loud, "Top o' the morning to you!" What I felt was the kind of tipsy happiness that might accompany drunkenness, but without an alcoholic aftertaste. By noon, my mood settled into a less bouncy state. The garbage dis-

posal broke during preparations for a lunch for ten and that definitely
did not make me happy. By the next morning, the cycle began again.
I'm happy! When I told my husband about these odd feelings, he said,
"What's wrong with feeling too happy?"

Shortly after becoming too happy, I was at the airport, on my
way to Sun Valley, where I was scheduled to speak at a writers conference. At the airline counter, the representative told me that my
flight to Salt Lake City had been canceled. I asked for options. She
typed in long strings of code and told me that the next flight was in
an hour and a half. Great! But it was oversold. Oh. But if I could not
get on that flight, there was another flight. Perfect. But I'd have to
run to make my connecting flight to Sun Valley, which would also
be the last one for the day. I joked that I could always sleep in the Salt
Lake City airport. As it turned out, I did miss the connecting flight,
but I flew to Boise instead and took a bus to Sun Valley, which got
me to my destination only nine hours later than originally planned.
While doing the airport shuffle, not once did I feel angry or upset.
Even as it was happening, I thought it was surreal that I was so calm.
I should have at least felt worried, instead of being as complacent as a
cow in a field of endless grass.

I thought about what was different in my life and remembered I
had started a new medication to control temporal lobe seizures only
a week before. My seizure episodes had never been that debilitat-
ing. I did not have grand mal convulsions. In fact, for the most part,
they were entertaining sensory aberrations, and the only problem
was the stupor that immediately followed some of them; the brain
interprets a burst of excess electrical activity as the equivalent of not
having slept for three days, and thus shuts me down for about fifteen
minutes. One time, the people seated with me at a restaurant appeared to swing away from me and then back, as if they were on a
giant turntable. A few times, I saw Renoir paintings as big as life. I
saw low-budget alien creatures from a B movie. The most frequent
one occurred in the morning as soon as I awoke: an odometer, about
fifteen numbers long, spinning so fast the numbers disintegrated and
dripped like raindrops. I made it a game to call out the numbers as

they fell. Twenty seconds later, it was over. None of these sensory quirks held any meaning to me. They were not frightening or symbolic of anything in my life. (The renowned neurologist Oliver Sacks, who would later include my case in one of his books, confirmed that seizure-induced hallucinations are typically meaningless.) When I was diagnosed with epilepsy, my neurologist told me that the likely reason for the seizures was sixteen brain lesions in my brain, a souvenir of neurological Lyme disease. He showed them to me in an MRI scan. The lesions in the left temporal lobe were possibly irritating to the cortex, and from time to time, excess electrical activity gave rise to seizures. In prescribing the antiseizure medication, the neurologist warned that I should note any unusual signs, such as a spreading rash, which could be deadly. He had mentioned nothing about an outbreak of jolliness that could wax and wane throughout the day. I found the tissue-thin sheet of instructions and warnings that came with the medication, and read the tiny type that said this medication was also prescribed off label and at a lower dosage for clinical depression and bipolar disorder. In other words, my antiseizure medication was also a mood stabilizer. I suspected that it had tilted my already stable mood up and out of whack.

I have had bouts of depression in the past. They had occurred after big changes in my life, what should have been happy periods— including the unanticipated success of my first book, *The Joy Luck Club*. On the day my book was published, I cried. They were not tears of joy for a dream come true. I was afraid. I had never dreamed of having a novel published. I was too practical to have imagined a career as a fiction writer, and I was already making a good living as a freelance business writer. I owned a home and was married to a wonderful compatriot who shared my beliefs and values. But now there were early signs that my life was about to change in momentous ways. To counter the building excitement among my editor, publisher, and agent, I prepared for humiliation and a quick return to obscurity. I was overwhelmed with a sense that this book would upend the happiness I already had. Everyone expected too much, and I was certain I would fail. I refused to allow myself any pleasure from what was happening. Unexpected praise brought me back to those days in childhood when praise was followed by greater expectations, greater and greater hopes, and then came failure, humiliation, and disappointment from others. Praise, I had learned, was temporary, what someone else controlled and doled out to you, and if you accepted it and depended on it for happiness, you would become an emotional beggar and suffer later when it was withdrawn. Praise was given to me in heaping loads, and I had to emotionally push it away. When I received prizes, I gave dour acceptance speeches. One went something like this: The moon is more admired when it was full than when it was a sliver, and yet it is the same moon even when the perspective of others had changed. A book reviewer for the local newspaper wrote that I gave the most morose acceptance they had ever heard. Criticism was heaped on me as well—bad reviews, eviscerating ones. I overheard or had reported to me conversations about my inability to write a sentence, and that I did not deserve success, or that I was not really Chinese, comments made by people who I had once thought were my friends.

Serendipity, chaos, and drama ruled my life. I did not need a psychiatrist to tell me that my need for stability was related to a childhood in constant tumult, which had forced me to decide which was better: numbness or pain, acceptance or avoidance. I started antidepressants and found it dampened my sense of impending doom. Eventually I simply felt normal and could carry on with a life that would never be normal. Unlike the antiseizure medications, however, the antidepressants never once made me feel euphoric. If they had, I probably would not have discontinued them.

A few months after the happy effect started, I attended a holiday party of women writer friends. The conversation turned to a discussion of loyalty, and a friend related an example. When she was a child, she went to a dentist who had handled her family's dental care for years. Even after the dentist lost an arm in an accident, the family continued to use his services. Everyone at the party thought that was very touching. My friend said there was no question they should remain loyal, but as a kid she had felt uncomfortable when the dentist awkwardly leaned his armless side against her for balance while using his other hand to do a filling. This image was so startling that a giggle escaped before I could censor myself. My friend stared at me, as did others. I quickly apologized. I was shocked that I had found humor in a man's misfortune and a family's loyalty, but then I giggled again, and my attempt to suppress further laughter led to my snorting what I had been trying to hold back. The sound of those nasal farts then caused me to laugh so hard I was wheezing, nearly breathless, pausing only to whisper an apology to the guests for this regrettable lack of decorum. There were other episodes of unwarranted hilarity to come, and I eventually noticed something odd: a ticklish sensation around my ribs that accompanied irrepressible laughter. It caused me to bend over—literally doubled over with laughter.

More mood changes followed. One day, while focused on my writing, my two little dogs came bounding into my office, wagging their tails. They often did that. But this time, I felt a ticklish squeezing sensation in my heart—the pulling of a heartstring, you might call it. The idiom actually got it right. It was the physical equivalent of saying, "Aw, how sweet." I had felt that sensation before—but only on rare occasions, for example, when witnessing a touching moment at a wedding or a funeral, or in being surprised with an expression of deep affection. The problem now was the frequency of these heartwarming moments. Every time the dogs gave me a sassy look and wagged their tails, my heart twanged. The dogs wagged their tails a lot. Sometimes the ticklish sensations came one after the other and were disruptive when I was writing. A friend suggested I check with my doctor to ensure the sensation was not a symptom of incipient heart disease. I was certain it was not, since the effect only occurred in moments of endearment, and never when I was, say, angry or bored.

I eventually did some sleuthing on the Internet and pieced together a possible explanation: the tickle effect did not originate from within the heart. It was, in reality, a sensation transmitted by the vagus nerve, whose pathway runs from the temporal lobe and down areas of the neck, lungs, heart, and stomach. It is essentially the brain's emotional control center and can trigger all kinds of visceral reactions—otherwise known as autonomic responses, like trembling, fainting, low blood pressure, a fast heartbeat, butterflies in the stomach, nausea, gooseflesh, or the feeling that your blood is running cold—those "fight or flight" sensations that are simpatico with fear. It can blur judgment when you fall in love, feeding you a dopamine high that disables your ability to discern that the object of your infatuation may actually be, as your friends have been trying to tell you all along, a cheating, manipulative asshole. I guessed that my left temporal lobe, now chemically altered by antiseizure meds, had developed a hypersensitive sweet spot for cuteness and poignant situations and, fortunately, not for assholes. I should have been grateful to have so much sweetness and light in my life. However, I did not need to be reminded of that fact twenty times an hour. I had to knead my chest to rid myself of the wriggling worm sensations of vagus spasm overdrive.

My vagus nerve hit a low point when it began reacting to both genuinely heartrending moments and sappy ones. I felt the pang of poignancy watching two friends in their sixties exchange wedding vows. I felt the pang of poignancy seeing a Viagra commercial giving hope to seniors that sex does indeed follow dancing. My vagus nerve had a defective algorithm for recognizing genuine emotions. It wrung out tears for corny love scenes. It caused my eyes to flood when I was at funerals and heard eulogies for people I barely knew, which then caused people near me to think I had been especially close to the deceased. I became teary-eyed listening to the national anthem of any country whose flag was raised during televised Olympics award ceremonies. It could have been North Korea or other dictatorships—it didn't matter. I had become Pavlov's weeping dog.

I wondered every now and then how my altered brain might be altering my personality. I might soon become one of Hare Krishna's disciples, who beamed happiness as they chanted and tossed flower petals. If I smiled too much, people might think I was either stoned or smirking. I recalled an experiment done on the effect of smiling.

People who deliberately smile more often are quantitatively and qualitatively happier. Was it actually true that the musculature of the face can reconfigure the brain and increase happiness and lessen fear? Too much happy-go-luckiness could also become detrimental to my fiction writing. If I was such an easy sucker for contrived sentimentality, I might lose my sensitivity for the nuances of human nature, intent, and emotional truth. I would become a divining rod for schlock. I would become the literary embodiment of clichéd expressions and too many exclamation marks. I chuckled! I gasped! I sighed! I sobbed! I would gush to people: My dogs are just too cute. My husband is just so sweet. My best friend is just the greatest. Maybe the change had already started and it showed in my writing.

One of my friends suggested I stop taking the medication and switch to something else if my altered mood bothered me so much. I was reluctant to do so because this particular medication not only controlled my seizures fairly well but it had also dampened the pain of peripheral neuropathy in my feet. Both of those things were genuine reasons to be happy. If I stopped this medication, the new medication might not be as effective, and if the seizures resumed, I had a 70 percent chance that my simple partials would evolve into grand mal. If the pain in my feet returned, I would become restricted once again in my mobility, unable to walk more than a block to a restaurant without excruciating pain, let alone hike or ski. Outdoor activities made me genuinely happy. I was concerned that the withdrawal of the upswing medication might possibly cause a downswing that would dump me into prolonged depression. Instead of crying for fake joy, I would cry at stop signs. So, in comparison to the risks and benefits, what was wrong with being too happy? Whatever the medication had done to my brain, I had become protective of my new sympathetic nervous system friend.

Time solved some of the concerns. The side effects of the medication settled, the happy-go-lucky surges decreased in frequency. I am no longer waking up with cheeriness and a song in my heart; I need coffee. I do get stressed at airports. I can indeed stop laughing. I still get the tickle in my heart, but my brain is a bit more discriminatory.

It happens when my little dog makes repeated attempts to lead me, a clueless human, to play fetch with a toy that is bigger than he is.

Because the ticklish responses had become less frequent, I started analyzing them; for example, how long they lasted in comparison to how truly heartwarming the stimulus had been (i.e., my cute dog versus a cute dog in a dog food commercial). And that's how I made an odd discovery: I always felt the visceral reaction—the tickle spasm—before I was mentally aware of the emotion. The delay was only a fraction of a second. But having experienced it so often, I knew that this was the sequence: heart tickle, oh how cute. The tickle was like having someone tap me on the shoulder to call my attention to my dog's wistful expression. The body's reaction was preconscious, and it led me to wonder if the same held true in fearful situations. Would my heart race before I was consciously aware that an earthquake was happening? I've asked others about these sensations, and no one recognizes what I'm talking about. Perhaps I'm the only one whose emotions and vagus nerve are ever so slightly out of sync. Or maybe you need to experience the spasm and accompanying emotion a thousand times to discern the very fine gap. Whatever the case, I am actually pleased that a medication meant to tamp down neural activity also tampered with my moods. It led to my investigation of the cause, and thus my discovery of the connection between emotions and the vagus nerve.

My ongoing interest in mind-body reactions made me aware of yet another neurological process that is significant to me as a writer: in heightened situations, the vagus nerve releases a hormone, norepinephrine, into the part of the brain known as the amygdala, where the strongest emotional memories and their original reactions are stored. The more fearful the experience the greater the surge of norepinephrine into the amygdala, and that increases the amygdala's ability to store vivid, more strongly felt, lasting memories. They are called *visceral* reactions for a reason: the viscera react subconsciously when memory of the traumatic moment rises, often unexpectedly. For assault victims, the popped balloon instantly brings back the moment they were shot. This is not where you'll find happy memories of birthday parties or trips to the zoo—unless the birthday cake exploded and the lion escaped the cage and ate your ear. In the amygdala reside the horror stories of our lives: the worst experiences we've had. This is memory lane for people with post-traumatic stress disorder.

I recall a time in Italy when Lou and I were in the backseat of a rental car, and two friends were in the front. The husband was driving eighty miles an hour on the autostrada, a speed that is slow by the standards of natives, who drive treacherously fast on freeways. About a mile from our turnoff, we heard a mysterious beep in the rhythm of a heartbeat. It soon grew to the speed of a racing heart. "What's that sound?" I asked, and it stopped. A few moments later, it started again, a slow then faster series of beeps that soon turned into a continuous blare for a second before a car slammed into us, sending us caroming down the autostrada. Lou and I gripped each other's hand, but we were absolutely silent as the car spun, then hit a barrier and spun in the other direction. By then I was certain we would die. We made no protest to fate, no plea to God. I just hoped we would not suffer. Just when it seemed we were going to flip over, the car hit another barrier, tilted, then it righted itself and slid to a stop. The car was crushed every which way, the windows knocked out, the wheels twisted under. But we were uninjured, unlike the passengers in the other car. Actually, I did receive a scratch on my right elbow, and although it did not bleed, it turned into a scar, which I still have today, a reminder of the miracle. The wreckage closed the autostrada for three and a half hours. Later that evening, we made it to a friend's outdoor dinner party. I thought I had recovered, but my body shook and my voice quivered as I described our close call. Over the next week, the moment I awoke, I would half jokingly ask Lou, "Are we dead?" Our window overlooked a vista of hills and columnar trees, the landscape backdrop of Renaissance paintings. Maybe we're dead and don't know it, I mused. We're ghosts on holiday, like George and Marion in the 1950s TV show *Topper*, gadabouts who died in an avalanche while skiing in Switzerland. Instead of ski slopes in Gstaad, our afterlife was in a four-hundred-year-old hunting lodge in the hills above Lucca. We returned home, and the memory of that auto accident soon traversed into becoming part of our stock of close-call anecdotes, told with just a few humorous embellishments—

"As the car spun, I was thinking I won't have to finish writing that novel after all." If we could laugh about it, we had clearly recovered. A few months after the accident, I was in Melbourne, being driven in a hired limousine to an event. As the driver backed up to turn around, I heard a beeping sound and in an instant, I yelped and flattened myself onto the seat. My heart was still racing when I sat up a few seconds later, laughing with embarrassment. The beeping sound was part of a car warning system, not yet common in the United States, which lets the driver know how close objects are, be it a parked car or one tailgating in the high-speed lane of the Italian freeway. After that, my amygdala took the beep out of circulation as a fear-inducing stimulus, which was good, since the next car we bought was equipped with the same warning system.

I have gone through my share of terrifying moments—being held up at gunpoint, being trapped by a mudslide, nearly drowning, cartwheeling down a glacier, watching the World Trade Center's second tower collapse while I stood on the street—events that have provided a ready supply of true-life tales for dinner conversation and sober thought. I have also gone through horrific emotional traumas, like the time we accompanied a police detective into a former roommate's apartment, where I saw blood on the bed, the rope that had been used to strangle him, and a strong odor of fear. We had to identify items that may have been stolen and then look at a morgue photo to identify him. For several years, even after I thought I had psychologically recovered, I lost my voice the day before the anniversary of his death, which happened to be my birthday. My subconscious was still speechless with horror.

And then there are the experiences that were a secret to myself. They may not have been as dramatic as murder, but they may have been dangerous in others ways—to my psyche perhaps. Everyone has them, big and little frights, emotional pain long buried. Invariably I am surprised when they rise up, often when writing fiction.

One was shocking: my mother on the verge of killing me. How could I have forgotten *that*? It wasn't my conscious choice to forget. My subconscious shoved those memories to the back of the vault, having decided on my behalf that it was best for the sake of my well-being. The protective subconscious soothes: *there, there, it's over, no use dwelling on it.* How does it decide what it should hide, what it should protect me from? Maybe it was necessary to forget when I was younger, but surely age and hindsight have removed the danger. Who wants to go back into the haunted house to see chopped-off heads and the ghosts who own them? I do. I want to find those moments that my subconscious has hidden. I am more than curious— and it's not because I'm a fiction writer who seeks a good story to write about. What's in there is what made me a fiction writer, someone who has an insatiable need to know the reasons why things happened. In the amygdala are vast stores of disappointments and devastations, pain and wreckage. There are those moments when I was lost in a store or on the streets, and the imagined reason was not simply that I had gone off in the wrong direction. I was unloved and had been abandoned. The bad stuff gave me the emotional reactions I have today—my quirks of personality, my volatility and secretiveness, my sense of shame and indignation, my fears and obsessions, and my expansiveness or constriction of hope. Those memories made my imagination an at-the-ready survival mechanism. I want to know what those experiences were.

Mind you, my intention is not related to self-psychoanalysis, or to solving in some Sherlock Holmesian way a crime committed against my soul that will enable me to press reset. I don't want to change myself and be less afraid or more open or more forgiving, or what have you. I like that I am unhappy about certain things, that I have fears others think are unnecessary, or that I privately think about death every day. None of that is unbearable. Those are my idiosyncrasies, my individuality. They are what make me who I am. But I also want to know what the amygdala kept, because therein lies thousands of stories of how I became me. How do I return to my origins?

Just today I realized the answer, and as Dorothy says in *The Wiz-*

ard of Oz, it was there all along. The fictional mind can take me to what it knows and bring that knowledge to the surface and onto the page. Obviously, I can't prove how the fictional mind works with conscious and subconscious memory, but I have a hypothesis, and it is based on my intuitions of how it works for me. It has to do with the way the fictional mind allows imagination to bring back free-floating emotions as clues. I am not referring to the kind of fictional imagination that has to do with making up details, as if choosing a paint color from a color wheel. This is the fictional mind that lets go and allows free-form imagination to take over. That freed imagination floats and it conjures up what seems random and not that meaningful, like the odometer that appeared with my seizures. Its modus operandi is to allow "whatever comes to mind." Instead of sticking to what really happened, it improvises. It requires that I let go of logic, assumptions, rationale, and conscious memory. I am guided by intuitions, and as I put together the story, the origins of those intuitions return, and not just as a distant memory of *what* happened, but as if I am going through the moments and the heart-pounding suspense *as it happens.*

It might begin this way. I first choose a setting, which will serve the fictional world. I can change it later, if I wish. So for the sake of expediency, let's say it's a birthday party and that it takes place in a tract house where I lived when I was eight. Family friends have come over, both kids and their parents, and everyone has gathered at the kitchen table where a homemade cake sits, already studded with eight candles that her father will soon light. The table also holds wrapped gifts. (Here, my rational writer's mind does a quick assessment: eight is a good age for a birthday party. A kid that age wants to appear more grown-up. But it also matters what she gets as the main gift from her parents. Will it be what she wants, what she has hinted to for weeks, say, a doll? If she gets it, it will be proof of love. Or will it be what her parents have hinted would be good for her to have—a pair of school shoes?)

As the writer, I consider the options for what the present might be: (A) what she wants; (B) what her parents want; (C) what her parents want, but what they also give her as a second gift, which is what

*Oakland, July 1955: I am the big grinning girl on the right,
one week older than the girl second from the left.*

she wants; (D) what she wants, but upon receiving it she realizes she
does not want it and must conceal that fact. And so on and so forth.
As the writer, I would reject those options. They come from the conscious writer toying with plots, fairly standard ones. Now it is the
time to let go and write whatever comes to mind, even if it makes no
sense. This is where I find surprising intuition. From here, I impro-
vise for this in-the-moment exercise:

Eight candles stud a white cake with a girl's name written in
curly letters. The candles are different sizes and colors, fat pink ones,
sticklike blue ones, ones with swirls—the motley leftovers from previous birthday parties. Her younger brother points to the yellow one
and says he likes that one. Three neighbor girls call out their favor-
ites. Before her father lights the last candle, the red one that looks like
a candy cane, he says she should ask herself what God would want
her to wish. She nods but she already has a secret wish: to be more
popular than another girl in school who everyone likes but who has
been mean to her. If her father asks, she will say she wished that her
cousins in China could one day come to America; that's what they
pray every day. Her father moves the match to the eighth candle,
and she gets ready to inhale. *Bang!* A big explosion rocks the house

and white light flashes in the room. Lightning? Someone outside is screaming. Other voices are shouting. It must be a car accident, says her father. One of the kids yells that Cuba just dropped the bomb, and he runs out. Everyone follows. Only the girl remains at the table in front of a cake whose seven candles are melting into the frosting. She doesn't care what happened outside. She's mad. She wants to make her wish. But if she blows out just seven candles, she might die. She slides out the yellow candle to light the candy cane one, then yelps when hot wax burns her thumb. She runs to the sink and runs cold water on her thumb until it stops hurting. As she walks back to the table, she sees a puddle of yellow wax on the linoleum floor and a wavy halo of flames. She stomps on it, as if it were a poisonous snake, squishing it dead. She sees a skim of wax on her toe and a yellow waxy pancake on the floor. She laughs. She peels off the one on the linoleum. Her heart thumps hard. There is a black spot the size of a pencil head. The edges are brown. She tries to rub it clean, but it only makes the burned middle look deeper and blacker. She covers it with frosting, then wipes that away. It looks even darker. She doesn't want to see the hole anymore. It doesn't matter that it's her birthday. Her mother will be mad and that will be the end of the birthday party, the cake, the presents, and her wish. Her brothers will go outside, and the neighbor girls will go home. She starts to cry. She can't help it. Her lower lip is quivering, bowed out like a cup to catch tears. She lets out loud sobs. This is the loneliest, most miserable she has ever been. Just then she sees a white lady standing at the back of the room, a stranger. Had she always been there? Is she a friend of her parents? Did she see what happened to the floor? An ominous feeling turns her stomach. The white lady looks sort of familiar, but she does not know why. Above her is a crack in the ceiling that has been growing over the last week. Maybe the lady came out of the crack. The lady holds up a little music box and motions her to come over and see what she brought her. She winds the music box to prepare for the music to come out. The girl stares and whispers, "No," but she cannot will her feet to run away. She knows this lady, but she can't remember why, only that it's for a bad reason. Her arms are weak. She wants to tell the woman to go away. But she is only eight and cannot talk to grown-ups like that. The woman looks impatient, and the girl now thinks that God sent her because she was disobedient to Him. She was going to make a selfish wish and let her cousins starve. The lady is an angry angel. The angel will punish her even more than her mother. She is helpless to change that.

Nothing of what I've just written is taken from my life, except for what I imagine as the setting: a table in a kitchen. I have no idea what will happen next. But somewhere in my deepest memory, I'm sure there is an emotional match to what I've just imagined. It feels so familiar. I can follow these clues by simply being conscious now of the feeling in my body, the lopsided weight of a fast-beating heart, the boneless limbs. Even if I never consciously recall the true event, I am already glad to have found the heart of it, what was necessary at some point in my life to survive by making sense of what is before me. Those are the genuine emotions. The fictional mind wandered and found them. The writer can put them into a story that never happened, and yet did in the deepest of ways.

CHAPTER FIVE

THE FEELING OF WHAT IT FELT LIKE WHEN IT HAPPENED

A few years after I started writing fiction, I participated in a workshop called "Finding the Story." It was led by the late great Gill Dennis and was part of the screenwriters program affiliated with the Squaw Valley Community of Writers, where I attended my first writers workshop. There were about ten of us in the room, strangers to each other. The star participant was the director of an Oscar-nominated indie film. A couple of people had had low-level jobs in the film industry and the rest of us were fiction writers with one or two published stories to our credit. I fell into the latter category. I had recently published my first story in a little magazine.

The workshop took place in the dining room of a ski house perched on a bluff overlooking a ski run. In the winter, you could slap on your skis in the patio and get right on a slope that took you to a chairlift. I appreciated the location because I was a skier, albeit a mediocre one, and this was my favorite ski terrain. But now it was a warm afternoon in August. The windows were open, and we could see the tram taking summer visitors to the upper mountain. It was an idyllic day, but danger was now in the room. Gill said we were going to do an exercise. "I want you to think of a moment when you thought you were going to die," he said. "Write that down."

Our location in Squaw probably had something to do with my choice. I recalled a time when Lou encouraged me to go down a ski run that he said I could manage, no problem. When I got to the run, I was horrified. It was steep, icy, and full of moguls. How could he possibly have thought I could ski into an abyss? It was too late to backtrack up the hill. Lou skied to the bottom and waited for me. I stood at the top, unable to move. For fifteen minutes, he yelled for me to come down. Finally, I stiffly started. On my second turn, I slipped and went tumbling on my back. My slick ski outfit on ice made it impossible to stop and I was screaming for my mother all the way down, certain I would fall off a ledge or smash into a tree. At the bottom, I was hysterical and when I finally came to my senses, I cursed Lou. Then I puzzled over the fact that I had called for my mother, as I might have when I was a child. That must be a sign that I thought I was going to die.

When we put down our pens, Gill said in a hypnotizing voice, "Whatever you've written, I want you to put that aside. You probably remembered something in which you thought you were doing to die for about ten seconds. But then it was over." True enough. Gill went on: "I want you to think harder. A time when you really thought you were going to die."

I thought hard and came up with something that happened when I was nineteen. I had caught a ride with a housemate who was headed to the community college I attended. I had missed the previous class, one in English literature, so it was important that I be there that day. It was the first rainy day of the fall season, and as we passed over a bridge, the car slipped sideways, my stomach lurched, and the car went on a mindless course, hydroplaning across the center of the road, aiming us into two lanes of oncoming traffic. I closed my eyes, certain I was going to die. The car had no seat belts. Just before we would have collided head-on with a truck, our car slid to the right, fishtailing across three lanes and headed for a light pole. A moment later, I had a terrific headache, and medics were helping me out. I must have been knocked out when I flew headfirst and smashed the windshield. When they took me toward an ambulance, I refused to get in. I had no money to pay for that. I also told them I had to get to my English class. They insisted I go to a hospital. By coincidence, I was taken to the hospital where my mother worked. Her worried face hovered over mine. An X-ray determined that my brain was fine, but my nose was slightly askew, and the right side of my face was swollen. Diagnosis: black eye. I then hitched a ride to class. End of story.

Again Gill said, "I want you to put that aside and think really hard—a time when you really thought you were going to die." I remembered a few other incidents, but none worse than my first two. There was an encounter with six black bears on a backpack trip, but that was more humorous than scary. What else? All at once, an overwhelming surge of emotion came up and I was in tears. Gill gestured for me to speak. I sobbed as I released a memory that was as unstoppable as vomit.

My mother is holding a Chinese cleaver, the one she uses to slice raw beef. She's coming at me and I'm backing away. We're in the bedroom we share. She locks the door with the skeleton key in the keyhole, and throws the key to the side. She keeps coming toward me and I keep backing away from the cleaver until I'm flat against the wall. I won't show her I'm scared. I'm stronger than she is. I can make myself not feel a thing.

But her eyes are really strange, different this time—shiny, wide open, and it's as if she can't see me. That's when I know she's crazy, really crazy. She's so close to my face. I can feel the heat of her breath and the spit from her words. I can't look at her anymore. So I look out the window on the left side, at the snow on the mountains and Lake Geneva. It's so beautiful, and it's such a waste, all that beauty. I'm so lonely.

And then my mother says in a strange low quaking voice, "I can't take it." She isn't shouting. It is like a growl, which is worse. She says, "I can't watch you destroy your life with that man. No more

waiting. It's time we be with Peter and Daddy. I kill you first, then
John, then me. We all go to heaven together."

She invoked their names, Daddy and Peter, and she'd threatened
before to kill herself to be with them. Now she wants to take us all.
She might actually mean to do what she says this time. And then I'm
instantly angry. It never stops—her suicide threats, now her threats
to kill me. She can't take it anymore and I can't either. I'm shouting,
"Go ahead. Do it. Do it right now." And I realize too late I might
actually die. I just egged her on and she won't be able to back down.
She's breathing harder, pumping up her chest. She's actually going
to do it. It's in her eyes. I'm going to die. It's the end and I'm lonely
and so sad. It's going to hurt. But I don't care anymore. I just want
everything to be over. I close my eyes. And then I hear a disembodied
voice come out of me—not my voice—and it's wailing, "I want to
live! I want to live!" And I'm so goddamned mad that this voice
betrayed me.

When it was over, I was self-conscious that I had done this emotional striptease in front of a bunch of strangers. They didn't know
anything about me—that I was sixteen when this happened, that my
father and older brother had died the year before, that my mother
had gone crazy and taken us to Europe to escape a curse, that we
lived in Switzerland in a Bavarian chalet with gorgeous views of a
lake ringed by mountains, that she had been shouting at me for days
over my boyfriend, a German Army deserter, unemployed hippie,
who did drugs and was suicidal. They didn't know that my mother
had threatened suicide for as long as I could remember, but that this
was the only time she had threatened to kill me.

I recalled my feeling that the disembodied voice had a will of its
own and went against mine. Did that mean I had had a psychotic
break? Why did it say "I want to live" and not "I don't want to die"?
Perhaps my psyche deposited it in forbidden memories, knowing the
experience had taken me to the edge? I considered other frightening
questions: Would she have done it? She had always been *overly* protective. Would she have *killed* me to *protect* me? It was possible. Did

my mother put the cleaver down and gasp in horror at what she had almost done? Did she unlock the door right away and let me out?

And then I considered that maybe the episode had never happened. If it had, I wouldn't have forgotten it—not for twenty years. I related this episode to my brother, but he had no memory that anything like that had ever happened. If he had been in the other room, he said, he might have thought it was like all the arguments my mother and I had had. I eventually called my mother and came right out and asked if she had ever tried to kill me with a cleaver when we were in Switzerland. She immediately confirmed it, and without any remorse in her voice. She said she had lost everything, Peter and Daddy, and she was losing me as well. She could not take it anymore. I asked her why she stopped. She said she didn't remember.

M y mother had had suicidal thoughts ever since she saw her mother die of an opium overdose. She was nine and said she wanted to fly off with her mother. For some reason, she believed she had something to do with her own mother's death. It occurs to me now that she might have stood up to her mother, as I had to her, or that she had refused to show sympathy for her mother, who was a widow, which was what I had done to my widowed mother as well. Or perhaps my nine-year-old mother had shown fondness for one of the other concubines, which might have infuriated her mother, especially if the concubine had insulted her. Whatever the case, while my mother blamed her mother's second husband for her suicide, she also blamed herself. She was always looking for answers to why things happened, and by looking for guilt, she found it.

Lijun, my mother's youngest daughter from her first marriage, said that our mother tried to kill herself to escape her husband, a man named Wang. Lijun also hated Wang for his cruelty and disavowed him as her father. She was rescued by our uncle and raised within his family. Jindo, the middle half sister, remembered our mother's threats, as well as a few attempts, one that required hospitalization. She was only seven when our mother left China without her. She has never expressed deep anger at our mother for leaving her and her two sisters in China. She understood why she had to leave, she says. She still loved her and dreamed she would come back. She kept our mother's fur coat, even after she washed it and all the fur fell off. But how could she not have been angry and deeply wounded? During the Cultural Revolution, when Jindo was seventeen, she was sent to work in the rice fields and remained there for the next nineteen years. She slept on a plank in a communal shed, through which water flowed in torrents during heavy rains. She used to picture our mother living in a mansion. While that was hardly the case, my mother's hard life could not compare to Jindo's. Our mother later visited her daughters in China several times. But Jindo did not get to know our mother well until she immigrated to the United States. While visiting her in California, she experienced firsthand how easily provoked our mother was and how sharply she criticized people, their habits, their stinginess, their lack of cleanliness, and especially their cooking. She found that our mother could not let go of any wrongs, especially those committed by her first husband. She would recite a litany of his evil misdeeds and would repeat variations of them for hours at a time, intermittently asking us listeners, "Can you imagine?" or "Who can take this?" or "You see why I hate him?" One time, our mother learned that Jindo had used two hundred dollars she had given to her as a gift to pay for her father's expenses when he came to the United States. To our mother, this was an act of betrayal. She asked Jindo many times, "Did you love him?" And Jindo would say, "Of course not." After our mother died, Jindo said she knew she should not say anything that might have let our mother know that she had been fond of her father. He was a bad man, she acknowledged, and he did nothing to stop his second wife, the stepmother, from physically abusing his children. "But my father was my father," she said to me in apologetic tones, "just as my mother was my mother." She added that even though she now knew our mother had been a difficult person, she still would have wanted to grow up with her by her side.

My mother was my mother. There were many times in childhood when I wished that were not so. But when I was grown, she was inextricably part of the way I thought and observed, and to wish she were not my mother would be like wishing I were a different person. So much of who I am comes from her genetic traits, as well as from the nightmares inculcated by her vivid warnings, and from my own rebellions against her. I cannot imagine who she would have been nor who I would have been had she had a sunny disposition and not a stormy one with periodic tsunamis. Part of my psyche had been shaped by those slow or fast windups that would lead to her shattering announcement: "I might as well kill myself! Then you be happy." My father, brothers, and I could never pass off her words as empty threats. She had shown us she would do what she had threatened, especially if she suspected we didn't believe her. We were her hostages and each other's witness in endless emotional battles. Sometimes she declared she would kill herself right before our eyes. Other times, she was quiet and sad, and would say that it would be better for her to die now than to let us suffer. When I was six and declared I no longer wanted to play the piano, she went silent, and after many minutes had gone by, she said in a quivering voice, "Why you should listen to me? Soon, maybe tomorrow, next day, I dead anyway." I became hysterical. I was at an age when getting lost in a department store was traumatic. I begged her not to die and she soothed me, saying she would stay if I truly wanted a mother to guide me through life. Perhaps her mother had said something similar—that she might as well die if no one wanted her advice. Perhaps she didn't listen to her mother on a few occasions; no nine-year-old child is perfectly behaved. Her mother had had a history of suicide threats and had made at least two serious attempts. According to one report, when my grandmother was twenty-four, she threatened to swallow gold—a common form of death by toxicity among more well-to-do women— because her parents did not want her to marry a poor scholar, the man who became our grandfather. I wonder what emotional tightropes my grandmother made my mother walk. What gave my mother her nature—a pattern of incredible resilience, which could, in an instant, become a furious impulse to hurtle herself into oblivion.

*1960: After my father's successful delivery of his sermon
as a guest minister.*

Growing up, I never thought of my mother as depressed. I believed people suffering from depression were sad, unable to get out of bed, and looking sick and listless. My mother always got up out of bed. She had an excess of energy. I cannot recall her ever having a cold or the flu. The main problem, as I saw it growing up, is that she was negative in her thinking. She saw falsity in people who were nice. She saw slights in how people treated her. She could not tolerate having others disagree with her. If someone in the room received more attention, she took that as rejection. She saw tardiness as lack of respect, a loss of love, and imminent abandonment. Other times, she saw humor in the same. She was witty and could imitate people's false insincerity with all the perfect nuances, complete with simpering smile. But when a bad thought crept into her mind, it remained there, festering. She could not get rid of it until she expelled it in an explosive threat.

The threats were a constant in our lives. They may have occurred every day during a bad stretch, or every week, or twice a month, or not at all during a relatively peaceful time. Had I chronicled every outbreak, I doubt I would have found a reliable pattern. It was, in fact, the sheer unpredictability of her threats that made us alternately vigilant and then blindsided. I would look for small changes in my mother's moods and presume too soon that nothing was going to set her off.

Tonight I watched a home movie of a dinner party made by friends. My parents appear in two scenes. The first is from 1963, when I was eleven. My little brother, John, stands in the doorway, mute and spellbound in front of the movie camera. My mother arrives next and has on a red dress and cream-colored swing coat. Her bouffant hairstyle has a lovely sheen of white hair. She gives out a dazzling smile and encourages my little brother to smile and go inside. My father arrives next and gives a look of surprise at those already present, and grins as he adds a gift to a pile. My mother is beautiful. My father is handsome. They are happy. The second scene is a year or two later. My brother and I are off somewhere playing with the other kids. My parents are at the same house with about ten or twelve friends, all Chinese, crammed around a dining room table. They are drinking from Chinese soup bowls. The others are ten or fifteen years younger than my parents. The women are well coiffed and wearing party clothes. My mother is wearing a white sweater, the one she wore with her nurse's uniform. Has she come directly from work? Or did she put it on as a statement? Her hairstyle is misshapen, the result of a bad perm. My mother, who had once prided herself on her Shanghai movie star looks, is now middle-aged, and while still beautiful, she has become frumpy. Everyone looks up at the movie camera and smiles, laughs, waves or calls out a humorous remark. When the camera reaches my mother, she obliges with a smile for a millisecond and then returns to looking down at her soup with a morose expression and slight frown. When the camera returns her way, I am guessing that the friend behind the camera said, "Hey, Daisy, give us a beautiful smile," because she glowers, stiffening her mouth and shakes her head. Frame-by-frame her expression is dark, angry. My father is still smiling, but he seems tentative, not at all his gregarious self. Something happened. My father might have said something at home and she arrived in a foul mood. Or he might have said something to another woman, complimenting her food or

Tianjin, 1945: The start of the affair.

hostess skills. I suspected that a fight broke out as soon as we were in the car driving home. And then I watched a third clip. It is 1970, about two years after my brother and father died. I was away at college. My mother is standing on a lawn among other celebrants. On first glance, she seems happy. She is smiling most of the time. But then I noticed that people are in clusters talking to each other next to her, behind her, or in front of her, but no one is talking to her. No one has asked her to join in. Without my father, she is lost in a party like this. When the signal is given for everyone to stand for a group photo, she goes to the far end, and as she continues to smile, the man next to her leans across her to talk to someone else, as if she were not there. Later, her sense of rejection would turn into anger and hopelessness. I wondered how she expressed that when she was alone. I had tears in recognizing for the first time how isolated she was, how fragile. I saw it clearly but was too late to protect her.

Growing up, I searched for signs of danger in her face. The bunched-up chin, stiff-lipped smile, and deadly stare. Her quiet demeanor and pretense in not wanting anything to eat, in not wanting to join in on anything. Her sudden turnaround in mood—from argumentative to overly agreeable. Once she got going, there were few stopping points on the way to the cliff. Sometimes she came back to her senses when my little brother, John, became hysterical. But that was when he was a sweet and helpless little boy. When he was older, he simply went quiet in front of her. He once called me in tears after he and I had endured another high-stakes episode: "I'm forty-two years old and she still makes me feel like a kid who's scared she's going to do it."

Her last attempt came shortly after she had been diagnosed with Alzheimer's disease. We were in a restaurant and she was getting worked up over her delusion that her daughter Lijun had stolen from her the starring role in a movie. At the time, a British television company had been planning to make a documentary of my mother's life, so there was partial basis for the movie star delusion. We had canceled the production when we learned my mother had Alzheimer's disease. But now we had to play along with the delusion. We assured her there was no way that anyone else could star in it because the movie was all about her. I foolishly added that Lijun was not the kind of person to do such a thing anyway. "No one believes *me*," she said. "You all rather believe Lijun." In that crowded restaurant, she said the dreaded words, "You never have to listen to me again. I kill myself right now." She shot up out of her chair and ran out the door, toward busy Van Ness Avenue and its six lanes of traffic. She had already stepped off the curb and into one of the lanes when my husband grabbed her and carried her over his shoulder as she kicked and pounded her fists on his back. We put her in the car and took her to the hospital. When a doctor came and talked to her, she became meek. Doctors always made her obedient.

For the first time she was put on antidepressants, and the effect was noticeable. She talked to a psychiatrist about the tragedies in her life. She would ask him, Why did this happen? She told him the stories I had heard most of my life. "Depress because cannot forget," she said.

When my first book was pub-lished, my mother was de-lighted that my stories contained bits of her life, especially the sad events of her mother's death. She, more than anyone, knew how much of those stories were fictional. But she could also see that she was in those stories—in the mothers' ways of thinking, in their insistence that the past was important, in how they were strong enough to change fate. Because the stories were fic-tional, however, she asked that the next book be her "true story." I had

Shanghai, 1934: Daisy, age eighteen.
"Beauty ruined my life."

already started another novel but was flailing in getting it to come to life. Why not base the next novel more on her life? What better gift could she give me but her truth? What better gift could I give her than to be her witness and sympathetic companion to the past? She began by reciting the same stories she had told me countless times. So I drew her back to an earlier point in life, when she was still happy. What did her baby son do that made her think he was so smart? Where did she go with her mother? To be useful to me, she would call me often to tell something she had just recalled. She would talk for an hour or even longer. A few hours after hanging up, she would call again, saying, "One more thing." My fiction had become the conduit for her woes. She was overly generous in sharing all the details of her life, in giving her opinion about people she once knew—what they had said, what she had said, what they did in return—and then she would ask what I thought of this woman she had just talked about. Was she fake? Was the woman being sincere? There were many times when my brain was oversaturated listening to her anger, her grief and fears. But how could I tell her I did not have time to listen when she was telling me how lonely she felt when her mother died? How could I tell her I had to go back to work when she was weeping at the other end of the line?

One day I invited her to the house for a full day of storytelling. I promised myself I would listen without judgment, with absolute patience. I set up a video recorder. When my mother saw the recorder, she became shy. She worried she would say something the wrong way. But soon after she began talking about her first husband, "that bad man," she seemed to lose awareness the camcorder was even there. She spoke fluidly, openly, and with strong emotion—her clenched fists beating her chest as tears fell. At one point, she came out of her spell and said, "Maybe you don't want to record next part. I talk about sex things." I told her she could say anything she wanted. She told me about the early years of marriage: about this girlfriend and that, this lie and that. She told me how she got out of having sex with him. She pretended to have diarrhea. I laughed at her cleverness. She moved about the room and laid out the scene she was seeing in her memory. She pointed to the doorway and said that the bad man was there with a gun. She crouched on the floor, pointing to where others cowered as her husband waved his gun wildly and threatened to shoot them. She heard the gun click, and then he laughed at everyone for being scared. It was a joke. "What kind of joke is that?" my mother said to me. "He just wants to see you jump and kowtow. But you have to take it serious." The next day, when he got mad at a pig that was slowing traffic, he jumped out of the car and shot the pig. The farmer ran to the pig and was crying over the loss of his valuable property, and then "that bad man" threatened to shoot the farmer, too. "One day he told me he divorcing me. I was so happy." She mimicked signing a document. "He sign the paper then put a gun to my head and told me I had to sign, too. I said I don't need a gun. I happy to be divorce from you." So she signed the document quickly and handed it to him, and as soon as she did, he pushed her onto the bed, told her she was now a whore, and raped her. While telling her stories her voice trembled. She shouted. She cried. She was there reliving her past, the worst moments of her life, the ones she could not forget, with all the fury and fear she had stored in her memory and her body.

I know that there must be many traumatic episodes in my

life that my subconscious has put away. Some I have pushed away deliberately—like the awful-tasting first kiss, or mean things I may have done as a kid, and any of a number of humiliations. I am actually quite good at avoiding unpleasant thoughts. But what about the memories and truly horrific experiences—those that might be similar to my mother holding a cleaver to my throat? Might more turn up if coaxed by the hypnotic voice of a workshop leader, or by even my own willingness to use a pickax to go beneath what is safe? Many painful or poignant memories returned when I started writing fiction. It takes effort to shed self-consciousness, more so than it does to avoid unpleasant thoughts, and effort in itself is anathematic to what I seek. But once the fiction-writing mind is freed, there are no censors, no prohibitions. It is curious and open to anything. It is nonjudgmental and thus nothing it imagines is wrong. It is not bound to logic or facts. It is quick to follow any clues, but it can also be easily diverted to another direction, especially if it detects a secret or a contradiction. But its most important trait is this: it seeks a story, a narrative that reveals what happened and why it happened. That is the divining rod. It seeks shards and not whole pieces, what was fractured. It combines those relics with imagination and stumbles across the pattern, and some essential part of the pattern lies in the memory of a true experience. It can lead me to the origins of what now causes the knot in the stomach and my limbs to turn cold. Even when I change the facts of what happened to fit a story, its nucleus is the original experience. The story resonates as true. It is the feeling of what it felt like when it happened.

I've been thinking about something that occurred when I was nine or ten. I sense the memory in only the sketchiest outlines. It took place in a car with my family. There was tension that led to something worse than expected. When I think about this vague memory, I notice unpleasant sensations—a tightness in the jaw and throat. I swallow. My limbs go a little weak. It's like a warning from my subconscious to not go there. And I have not for all those many years. But now, having thought about the nature of memory and physical sensations, I wonder if I can retrieve the original experience by following visceral discomfort—the tightness, the squirminess. I sense that the worse I feel, the closer I will be to the source. It's like that game of "hotter and colder." If the tension lessens, I am moving away from the cause. The fiction writing state of mind can be guided by what my body is feeling. Would that turn up the ghost of an actual memory? How would I know?

It's time to go into the haunted house. I make one concession: it is both the safety and freedom of experiencing this in third person. My heart is already racing.

The girl and her brothers are sitting on the backseat of the car, coming back from church. Her mother and father are in the front. It's hot out and all the windows are rolled down, but that doesn't help. The breeze blowing on her face feels like heat from the top of the toaster. It is the kind of hot that makes everything hot—she found that out earlier when she went to the car and grabbed the handle. It nearly fried her hand off. Her father had to use the Sunday church program like an oven mitt to open each door. And he had to pull really hard on the front door where her mother sits, and after she gets in, he has to lean in and push hard until it makes another cracking sound and closes. There was something stuck in the joint, something that broke off a while back, and no one could figure out what, except that the door would make stretching, scraping noises, until it went bang, as if someone had hit it with a hammer, and then it would finally open or close. When the girl got in the car, she sat down right away and burned the back of her legs. Her little brother couldn't stop laughing. He is six, but everyone still treats him like a baby. Her legs stick to the plastic seats. They are soft from the heat. She wonders if the road is burning the tires. Maybe they won't melt because the tires are rolling and no part of it touches the hot road for that long. But what if the car is not moving—will the tires fry and pop? Her father puts on the blinker, and once they are on the highway, he steps all the way down on the gas and the engine grinds and sounds like it will explode. Her heart jumps, even though she knows the car always sounds like that before it settles into that speed. Her father moves

*into the fast lane. He puts his bent arm on the window rail and
uses his right hand to steer. He is whistling the hymn that they sang
in church that morning, "I Walk in the Garden Alone," which her
mother plays at home sometimes in the style of a waltz, which is also
how her father likes it. But now she hears her mother say in a hard
voice, "Slow," and her father stops whistling and slows down and
puts both hands on the steering wheel.*

*She can see only the back of her mother's head, but when her
mother turns to look out the window, the girl can see some of her
mother's face. She is frowning and her mouth is a straight line. Is
something happening? Her throat grows tight. Maybe her mother
is frowning because the sun is hitting her eyes. She hopes that's the
reason. But then she notices that, even though it is Sunday, her
mother's hair is messy, and it's not just because the window is open.
The hair at the back of her head is flat where she slept on it, and
the girl can see the pink part of her mother's scalp peeking through
the cowlick. Her mother did not do anything this morning to make
her hair look nice. For church, her mother would always roll up her
hair in curlers the night before, and in the morning, she would tease
up her hair and make it smooth all around. She would put on one
of her best dresses, then draw in the curves of her eyebrows with a
pencil and make her lips bigger with lipstick, and then she would
smack her lips and look in the mirror, turning her head this way and
that to see if all the shapes of her face were right. After she sprinkled
perfume in her palm and patted her neck, she would pose and ask
everyone, "What you think?" The girl and her brothers would
answer in unison: "Pretty!" Their father would put his finger to
his cheek to pretend he was trying to decide, and then he would say
what he always says: "The most beautiful girl in the world," and she
would smile back and give him their secret happy look.*

*The girl now thinks that her mother's messy hair means that
whatever is happening now actually started last night. She is also
wearing a limp brown dress that is not fresh like the new ones. So
that's a sign, too. The girl didn't notice any of the signs because
of what her little brother did this morning as they were getting*

ready for church. He had taken her favorite handkerchief with the goggle-eyed owl, and when she got it back, she saw that the owl was missing one of the plastic bubble eyes. She yelled at him and he yelled back, and then her big brother yelled at both of them to yell somewhere else. Then their father yelled from the front door that it was time to go to church. The girl was still mad about the missing owl eye, and that was why she hadn't noticed anything else, like her mother's messy hair and ugly brown dress. She also did not notice anything at church, because she was looking at the hymnal and counting how many times the word death *appeared. She always looked for signs that her mother was going to explode, so she could get ready for it, but this time she forgot.*

Her mother is looking away from her father. Her mouth is a tight straight line across, and her lips are sucked in. That's what her mother does when she's in pain from having cut her finger or hit her leg against a low table. The girl's little brother is sitting next to her in the middle. He swings his legs and his left foot taps the back of their father's seat. Then his right foot taps the back of their mother's seat. He's going to make things worse, the girl thinks, so she gives him a stern face and mouths, No. He frowns back before kicking harder on the back of their father's seat. "Stop that," their father says, and her brother looks down at his lap, chastened. The girl smirks at him.

And then she hears her mother talking to herself in a loud voice: "Why he tell his son stop when he can't stop himself?" She sounds strange, as if she were asking how rain is made. The girl looks over at her older brother and he shakes his head. His eyebrows are squeezed together and when he sighs, his chest rises high and stays there a long time before he lets the air out. He leans his head out the window, as if he is trying to blow off dirt on his face, and the wind pushes his short hair in one direction then another, making his hair look like velvet nap. The girl leans her head out the window, too. Her ponytails whip her face. She keeps her mouth and eyes closed tight. Her mother once told her that an ugly bug or a piece of garbage could fly into her mouth and give her a disease. Or a bee could pierce her eye and go all the way into her brain. She can feel her eyelids fluttering, as if the wind is trying to peel them open.

They drive past the curve in the highway where the bread factory is. She loves the smell of baked bread. But all she can smell now is the grease her father squeezed in the joints of the front door where her mother is sitting. Her father turns to her mother and says something that gets lost because a big truck is slowly going by. After a few seconds, her mother answers: "What you care I think?" Her father frowns. He looks tired. No one moves, not even her little brother. She knows that whatever happens next will determine what happens before lunch, then after lunch, then before dinner and after dinner—who knows for how long this time. The girl looks at her big brother and he shrugs in a way that means he doesn't know and he's nervous, too. Her little brother's eyes are big and his top teeth are biting his bottom lip. He always does that when he's scared. He keeps turning his head to look at her. He starts to whisper to her but she shakes her head and turns her face to the window so he can't ask her anything. She feels him tugging on her sleeve, and she wants to shout that he's going to wreck everything if he doesn't stop.

Her mother turns to her father to say something, and right away, she knows it's bad. Her voice is broken, squeaky then jagged as words scrape through her throat. "That what you want?"

It's happening. The girl makes her hands into fists, which is what she always does to stay strong and keep from crying. But this time her hands feel weak and floppy. She can't squeeze them hard.

"You want to go, then go," the girl hears her mother say. "Or I go first." The way she said "go" is so harsh it sounds like "ko," like coughing. Her mother turns toward her father, and the girl can see a fine spray of spit as her mother speaks. "No one wants me here. So I just ko."

The girl's legs feel like worms are crawling inside them. She wants to shake them. She wants to run. Her throat hurts. Something sharp is stuck down there and she needs to yell to get it out. She wants to yell at her mother, Go. No one's stopping you. Right away, her mother screeches like a scared bird, as if she heard what the girl

was thinking. Her father reaches for her mother's hand, but she
snatches it back, as if he was trying to steal it. He tells her she's
tired, and they can talk more at home. But she won't look at him.
She is mumbling to herself and breathes stronger and stronger like a
monster. The girl's stomach tightens and she says to herself, Hurry,
please hurry, and she looks out the window for signs that they're
close to where they turn off to go home. But she sees only fields of dry
yellow grass.

Suddenly her mother goes quiet. It's getting worse, and just as
she thinks that, her mother grunts something that sounds like "mm-
hum," like she's agreeing with herself, and it happens: "Maybe I kill
myself right now. Then everybody happy."

The girl looks at her weak fists and tells herself: Don't forget this
day. Remember what she did to us. Don't cry. If you do, she'll win.
Her body feels far away, and then it feels big and heavy. She can't
move it. It is just her mind that is working, and she sees everything,
even though she does not want to anymore. She can't take it
anymore, the way her mother goes up and down, which makes them
all go up and down, without anyone knowing what will happen. She
hates her mother. She wishes she were dead. And just as she thinks
this, she hears the car door creak. It's cracked open and her mother
is pushing against it with her shoulder. Her father yells, "Hey!" and
grabs for her mother. The car swerves, cars honk, and she and her
brothers scream and fall every which way. When she sits back up,
she sees her mother is still shoving the door with both hands. But
the door stays stuck. The girl remembers that the door is broken.
Nothing bad will happen. But then she hears a scraping noise and
the hammer bang, and the girl leans forward and can see the door is
now stuck wide open. The road below is a dark river running fast.
Her stomach feels like it turned upside down. When she screams, it
comes out in a whisper because she doesn't have enough air to shout.
Her father is driving with his left and reaching for her mother with
his right. The car swerves one way and then the other. Her little
brother shrieks, "I'm scared!" Her older brother is calling, "Mom!
Mom! Please! Mom." The girl is dizzy. Her chest is so tight she can

*hardly breathe. Her hands are so weak she can't even hold on to
the backseat of the car. All she can do is look at her mother and the
moving road. Her mother's hair is blowing like a crazy lady's. She
puts her right leg out the car door. The girl gets an awful feeling in
her chest that she knows what is about to happen. But instead of her
mother falling out, the road grabs her mother's right shoe and it's
gone in an instant, which surprises her mother so much she pulls
her leg back in. The girl thinks that maybe the worst is over. Two
seconds later, her mother leans her whole body out, and again the
girl knows what will happen—that the road will take her mother as
fast as it took her shoe. It'll tear her to pieces. Then the car swerves
again and she feels the tires slip and go off the road, and her body
grows tighter and smaller as she waits for the crashing sounds that
mean they are dead. But the car keeps moving, now more slowly, and
soon she hears the sound of crunching gravel, until they stop. When
she sits up, she sees her mother is still in the car. Her father's hand is
gripping her mother's wrist. She's screaming and beating his hand.
But her father's hand is like metal. Every muscle on his face stands
out, pulled hard. Finally, her mother gives up. She leans back and
says in a howling kind of voice, "I want to die." The car door is still
stuck open, like the broken wing of a stupid bird. The girl is so angry
she says to herself: I hate her. I hate this car. I hate the car door. I
hate everything and everybody.*

*Her father loosens his grip and shuts off the engine. The car is
quiet. Everyone is quiet. The trucks rumble by, and the cars passing
them sound like wind gusts, but it still feels quiet, so quiet the girl
can hear what sounds like a singing insect in her ear. Her mother
sits up. She pushes back her hair, as if she's just waking up from
a dream. Then she jumps out the door. Her big brother shouts,
"Mom!" Her little brother screams. And the girl can't think or move
her mouth. She is watching her mother running for the highway.
She's going to throw herself in front of the cars. She tried that before.
But this time, she's stumbling with only one shoe on. Her father is
already out his side of the car and grabs her and takes her back to*

the gravel. Her mother tries to yank away from him, so he lifts and carries her off like a bride and sets her down when they reach the shady part of the overpass, set back from the turnoff. The girl can see her mother flinging her arms up and down, like she's trying to fly up. Her little brother is still crying, burbling drool as he chants, "I'm scared, I'm scared." The girl puts her hand on his arm and he falls into her lap and cries into her skirt. She pats his head a few times with her tingling hand. Her big brother is staring ahead. He doesn't blink. He doesn't move. His lips are moving, like he's praying. And then the girl feels her cheeks. She's crying and doesn't know when it started. She wasn't strong enough. Her stomach hurts and she needs to lie down, but she can't because her little brother is lying in her lap and he's a baby.

She watches her father hug her mother. Her mother's arms are limp, like hers. Only her mother is there in the cool shade and she is still here in the car, where it's getting hotter by the second. And now she's angry at her father. What about us? He should worry about us, not her. She caused this. The girl's throat hurts so much. She needs water. How long will they have to wait? When they come back, where will he put her in the car? Up front? What if the door won't close? What's going to happen when they get home? Will they have cereal for dinner like the last time? How long before her mother comes out of the bedroom? How long before she talks again in a normal voice?

But now she doesn't want to know anything anymore. She's dizzy and her nose is clogged from crying and she can hardly breathe. She leans her head back against the soft plastic seat. She smells the cars going by, the oil in the door, the dry grass. The tires are going to melt and she doesn't care anymore. She just wants everything to be over. She just wants to stop shaking.

I just wanted to stop shaking, and I could not for more than an hour after writing this.

One of my close friends, a psychiatrist who knew my mother well, said that I had remarkable resilience as a child, and that it was a wonder that I didn't suffer from a disabling psychiatric disorder as an adult. While I don't have suicidal tendencies, my childhood experiences did leave their mark on me. I am intolerant of emotional manipulation. I bolt from people who dangle threats and uncertainty as power, and there is no forgiveness for those who try. The body does not like what it once felt.

And yet much of my writing, I realize, is about uncertainty—the heartbreaking moments when something is not clear, when the situation is changing, when a truth turns into a half-truth and then a lie. My childhood with its topsy-turvy emotions has, in fact, been a reason to write. I can lay it squarely on the page and see what it was. I can understand it and see the patterns. My characters are witness to what I went through. In each story, we are untangling a knot in a huge matted mess. The work of undoing them one at a time is the most gratifying part of writing, but the mess will always be there.

A Mere Mortal at Age Twenty-Five

[From the journal]

SAN FRANCISCO, 1977. *I recall a scene in a D. H. Lawrence novel—I don't remember which book—but it was about a young man traveling in a train and seeing glimpses of people in landscape as the train went whizzing by. The young man wondered how he could be capturing only a fraction of many people's existences, people whose lives have cast as intricate a web around others as his own. Yet the transitory glimpse was as much as those people would ever imprint in his memory, in his existence. I have a God-like feeling, a feeling of omnipotence that makes me think that all that goes on is a perception of moments I can then embellish on. I see a woman with brightly colored clothes talking to a man in a restaurant and immediately I have sorted out this woman's life history. It's a curious thought to imagine that others who have seen me would imagine the same thing, and would never realize the terrors I've had, the ecstasies I've enjoyed, the feelings I've embraced. It scares me that perhaps even I would never know those things about myself as I look back and try to remember what I saw, what I felt. With a flick of whimsy, I can blot out a bad memory, recall an experience and make more of it than was actually there, and then never know what was.*

A Mere Mortal at Age Twenty-Six

[From the journal]

SAN FRANCISCO, 1978. *The me that was six years old is the same me that is now twenty-six. There has been no break in times. It's sneaked on by, and before I realize it, those six-year-old's thoughts are now a twenty-six-year-old's thoughts. I've always had this game: as I walk along, passing some inconsequential moment in my life I think, "You'll remember this moment when you are old because right now you feel lonely and the only one who can share this moment is the you when you were eighteen." Eighteen for some reason seemed like the age of becoming.*

Today I wonder what inconsequential experience will be deemed worthy of recall. Of course, there are those experiences which one can't possibly forget, such as feelings of grief, hatred, of love, all extremes on a continuum of feelings.

How to Change Fate: Step 1

[From the journal]

To change fate, you do not choose small steps. It is not about your will. It is allowing what comes to you. It is like seeing a ship turn in the Eastern Sea, slowly but surely, against the natural stream. And when it arrives, you step aboard and go to where it will take you. And somehow you know its course.

III

RETRIEVING THE PAST

THE UNFURLING OF LEAVES

On a spring day along a sidewalk in Shanghai, I stopped to watch a man rolling his hands over tea leaves in a dry wok warmed by the sun. He did this with a touch so light it reminded me of magicians who coax spoons to bend. He was brushing the flattened tea leaves—those choice top two or three leaves recently plucked from the bush—to roll them into cylinders as fine as needles. I had learned at a tea-tasting class that connoisseurs prize the unbroken needles, made possible only by hand rolling, as opposed to the mindless ease of machine rolling. The best of teas required hard labor to become both aesthetically and aromatically pleasing. The best of teas did not need the perfume of flowers, unlike teas with inferior qualities.

When I told a friend later that week about the tea roller, he remarked that the best teas were composed not only of the rarest tea leaves but also of the pleasing scent of the person who rolled them. This information did not immediately cause me to admire such rarity but to wonder about sanitation. The scent of hands—wouldn't that be sweat? So what exactly did sweat impart? A quick consultation on this very question led to the short answer: acidic moisture, the oil of sebum, and alkaline minerals, including the salty sodium that my dogs like to lick. Perhaps the hand-scented tea was also influenced by what its laborer had eaten that day, say, an abundance of garlic or stinky tofu, an aroma that leaves me gagging.

Further mind rambling led me to consider that the scent was also influenced by its maker's chi, the balance of elements, heat and cold. And maybe the scent was affected by virtue, spirit, and the peccadilloes of personality. Some people more than others emit the pheromones of sexual attraction. And, as evidenced by dogs and their superior noses, an odor can contain all sorts of information: age, gender, aggression, submissiveness, fear, illness, and so forth. Human scents must contain the same, even if they are imperceptible to our noses. Or are they? In some parts of our brains do we subconsciously register those subtleties? Can it register the scent of a person with literary appreciation?

Whatever the qualities that imbue sweat, that must be what the tea roller gives to his tea leaves. My scent, I surmise, is similarly evolved, for I do not dab any ready-made concoction at my wrists or the back of ears—nothing to mask my "inferior qualities." Rather, I am a daily infusion of many unpredictable elements: the dousing of shampoo and conditioner provided by my hotel for the night, Chinese porridge with pickles, too much morning coffee, the bleak mood after reading the international news, the joy of hugging an old uncle wearing a camphor-preserved sweater, the aroma of perfect needles of a rare tea unfurling in my cup, the blast of taxi fumes as I leave the teahouse, the cloud of smoke in which I stand on a busy sidewalk in China, watching a tea roller patiently caressing his leaves, while the ash of his cigarette threatens to fall into the medley.

Interlude

THE AUNTIE OF THE WOMAN
WHO LOST HER MIND

September 1990. I do not ask my uncle and aunt where they stand on the "June Fourth Incident" from last year, what Americans call the "Massacre in Tiananmen Square." We are family, not a forum. They are nervous that I, an American writer, may do something that will cause trouble for the family. They told my mother that. They've been in trouble before, and not for reasons they had control over. During the Cultural Revolution, they were branded counterrevolutionaries. My aunt had half her head shaved bald and was branded a ghost cow. My uncle was also punished for having a sister, my mother, who left China for the United States. But their patriotism to the Communist Party never faltered.

Two years ago when they were staying with my mother in California, they expressed a desire to return to Beijing sooner so they could attend an important meeting. My mother argued that it would be hard to change their airplane tickets. She told them to skip the meeting and stay. My uncle insisted that the meeting was important. So my mother asked: "Who is more important? The Communist Party or family?"

"The Communist Party," they immediately replied. My mother was furious. Shanghainese tempers flared, shouts erupted, airline tickets were changed, and soon my aunt and uncle were headed back to China to attend a plenary session of the Central Committee of the Communist Party of China, an important meeting indeed. Even if the meeting had been less important, I can understand why they would choose party over sister. They had often readied themselves to die for their idealism when they were young revolutionaries in the 1930s. They knew the martyrs who became the models of loyalty to the party. For devotion to the Communist Party, they, two students who did not know each other, married as ordered. Comrades one day, man and wife the next. For the safety of their comrades in hiding, they gave their crying baby over to the care of a peasant family.

My aunt and uncle say nothing about the reasons for the June Fourth Incident, nor do I. While I don't think the situation is black and white, we would likely have different opinions on what the complexities are. So instead they tell me about their terror as bullets ripped through the building. They demonstrate how they had lain flat on the floor as the bullets hit. Two neighbors who looked out the window were killed, my uncle says. It does not make sense to me that the troops directed their guns at this well-known residential building for retired high-ranking members of the Communist Party. But I don't say that, either. That would bring up the question of which side was to blame and who was out of control. The only question they ask me each morning is whether I would like millet, rice, or red bean porridge. Over breakfast, my uncle plays what I call Party Hits of the 1950s, beginning with the Communist anthem, "Internationale."

Today our driver, Xiao Chuan, "Little Spring," is taking us in a Toyota sedan owned by my uncle's work unit. The back windows are tinted and covered with pleated white curtains, which makes us feel like false foreign dignitaries. We are headed to an apartment building near Beijing University where students and professors live. I ask my mother to remind me who we are seeing.

"She is the auntie of Du Zhuan, the daughter of the second concubine," my mother says. "You know the one, lost her mind but still cried to see me the last time we came."

"We're going to see someone who's lost her mind?"

"How can you be so stupid?" my mother says. "That was

Du Zhuan—she already died. This is Du Zhuan's auntie. Her mind is still sharp. Over ninety years old and she still keeps everything very clean. No dirt, no dust. Not like most Chinese people today. You can call her *Aiyi*." For me, this is a convenient word. Every woman older than I am is *aiyi*, "auntie." That is also how you address maids.

At the entrance to the apartment compound, Little Spring stops the car next to the guardhouse. The security guard is talking to someone who is obviously his buddy. They are smoking cigarettes, guffawing over jokes, deliberately ignoring us, it seems. Let the privileged ones wait. See who is in charge now. After a few minutes, the security guard turns to us, his smile gone. "State your business," he demands. Little Spring gives the name of the woman we are going to visit, as well as her building, floor, and apartment number. The guard peers in the car window, staring at us, one by one, as if he can discern our lies and real intentions.

The guard grunts and tosses his head, indicating we have permission to pass. As we mount the two dark flights of stairs, my mother tells me that Aiyi will be surprised to see us.

"You didn't call to say we're coming?"

"How can we call? She has no telephone. Doesn't matter. She never goes out. How can she? Too many stairs. Her feet are too small for walking."

Just as my mother said, Aiyi is home and surprised to tears to see us. The hallway is so dark that at first I can make out only the outlines of a woman who is no more than four-and-a-half-feet tall, several inches shorter than my mother. She leads us with a wobbly gait into a long, narrow sitting room, streaming with sunlight and lined with tall bookcases. Now I can see her clearly: an oval face that is nearly free of wrinkles after ninety years of seeing births and deaths, wars and revolutions. Her hair is salt-and-pepper, neatly pulled into a bun. She is wearing a white blouse, gray trousers, and black

slippers, the unofficial uniform of old ladies in China. My
mother tells me in Chinese to look at Aiyi's feet. Aiyi sees
me staring and smiles with clear pride. They are exception-
ally tiny and I immediately know why. They were broken
and bound when she was a little girl. Although her feet are
no longer bound, the deformity is permanent. Her arches
are two swollen clumps that taper down to squished-in toes.
Maybe she's proud that she is among the few women still
living whose feet were bound. Or maybe she wants me to admire how tiny her feet still are. As painful as they look, they
are a marvel to behold, a condensed history of the suffering
of Chinese women.

The room we are in is actually Aiyi's bedroom and her
son's study. Her son is a professor, who is often away from
home. This time he has a fellowship in Germany. "Look at
these books," Aiyi says to me in Chinese, pointing to a row in
one of the glass-lined bookcases. Inside are English-language
volumes on business management. I take one out and pretend to admire its contents. I can't imagine someone learning English just to enable them to read these books.

"See how clean?" my mother says to me, pointing to
Aiyi's neatly made bed. The bedding is turned out in the traditional Chinese fashion: a top sheet pulled tight over the
twin mattress, a silk batting quilt folded at the bottom of
the footboard. Aiyi makes the obligatory apologies—that
her eyes are getting so bad she can't see all the dirt hiding in
the corners. She pats the bed for my mother to sit down next
to her. Side by side, my seventy-four-year-old mother and
Aiyi look like young schoolgirls, their feet dangling above
the floor. Suddenly, I remember—I've forgotten to give Aiyi
our token gift. It is something hard to come by in Chinese
stores, five pounds of foil-wrapped toffee candy. As I give it
to her, my mother says, "It's nothing," in her usual offhand
fashion. And this time, it is true. The toffee is one of the ge-
neric gifts we purchased at the Price Club, not knowing who

we might run into at the last minute. I wish it were reams of silk, a cashmere sweater, a new pair of tiny shoes. Aiyi is already rummaging through her drawers, looking for her own version of "nothing," which turns out to be a half pound of white ginseng root, which is worth far more than cheap candy.

"For your health," says Aiyi to my mother. "I am already too old to worry about mine." "What are you saying?" my mother says in return. "Look how good your health is." And then they launch into a lengthy gossip session about the maladies or demise of the various concubines and children of the Du patriarch who made my grandmother his fourth wife. There were seven wives altogether by the end of Du's life. Every now and then, I ask for both a translation and explanation. I understand part of the conversation, but I don't know the names of all Du's wives and their children. My mother gives an update on her half brother in California, citing the successes of his children. They talk about Du's younger son and his claim on the patriarch's entire estate and family home in Shanghai, which my mother's half brother also owns. "That son told us to go to the store with him. He put orange juice, milk, and cigarettes on the counter and told us to pay. He didn't ask. He ordered us. Can you believe it?" My mother complains about the difficulty in getting her own house back. She filed a claim, but the problem was the tenants—ten families. She would have to pay them to leave. "Why should I pay? It's my house. And they ruined it. They put cardboard up for walls. They tore down the doors to make a hallway into a room. They never clean the kitchen. The spiderwebs have fifty years of grease on them and hang down to your nose like oily yarn. How can people live like that? Why?" The gossip continues for two hours and covers the secrets and ties of a convoluted family with a complicated history of loyalty and resentment.

"Anyway, she never liked her mother-in-law."

"Anyway, I never trusted her."

"Anyway, she was never the favorite."

"Anyway, someone had to tell her the truth."

"Can you believe it? She is that greedy."

"Can you believe it? She was that stupid."

"Can you believe it? She was that quick to get another man."

"Can you believe it? She gave that bad man my money."

"Now I'll tell you something no one can talk about."

"Now I'll tell you something about what I said would happen."

"Now I'll tell you something about the lies she keeps telling."

"Now I'll tell you why I can no longer keep my mouth closed."

"Guess who I saw."

"Oh, this is too sad to hear."

It is the same type of gossip I heard repeatedly as I was growing up. Back then, I was bored by chitchat about the old days—about people who lost their morals, lost their fortunes, went crazy, or died. But now I am fascinated. They are the people she talked about for so many years, people she grappled with, fought, found comfort with, or confided in. They influenced who she became and what was important to her, and by extension, those same people influenced me. They are the characters I am putting in my novel.

Guess who I saw, I hear my mother say once again. And I continue to listen to the gist of things that will later require a fuller story: the gist of misery, the gist of betrayal, the gist of suicidal rage, the gist of survival, the gist of trickery, the gist of enduring friendship and its proof. I imagine Aiyi telling the next visitors who climb those two flights of stairs: *You remember Du Ching, the one who married Wang Zhou? She was here with her American daughter. Her health is still strong. Her daughter is very tall. Look at this big bag of American candy they gave me. It is the best kind, they said. But you take it. I'm too old to eat candy. It would pull out the only teeth I have left.*

May 2017. I just learned that Du Zhuan, the one who lost her mind and cried to see my mother, was the Du patriarch's eldest daughter, also known as Tu Chuan. She was supposed to marry Wang Zhou, the pilot, in an arranged marriage. But Wang Zhou favored my mother for her beauty and married her instead. I thought Du Zhuan might have been grateful to my mother for having married a man who revealed himself to be a cruel man. He left in his wake the destroyed dignity of many women and young girls. Instead, I discovered that Du Zhuan never stopped loving him. She traveled far and wide to be with him. Yet she and my mother liked each other well enough over their lifetimes to seek each other out. In fact, Du Zhuan let my mother use her college diploma to get a student visa to the United States. Now it is too late to ask them why.

CHAPTER SIX

UNSTOPPABLE

There is a particular word in Chinese my mother used to describe my personality: *li hai*. Depending on context and how forcefully it is said, it can mean "fierce" or "formidable" in doing what is right, or it can mean "unrelenting," "persistent," or "unstoppable" in doing what is wrong. As a kid, I was often called *li hai*. One time it concerned a Halloween costume. I wanted to wear my mother's red charmeuse wedding skirt, which was embroidered with hundreds of tiny flowers. She thought I should wear her white starched nurse's cap, a clever detail, she thought, that would provide the verisimilitude of a tulip-gathering Dutch girl. I said everyone would think I was a nurse because I did not have wooden Dutch shoes. She said I would get the wedding skirt dirty. I cried and said everyone would laugh at me. She told me I was *li hai* for arguing about this. I cried even more to prove how *li hai* I really was, and she shouted that my crying meant I would have no costume, no trick or treat. That year, I marched around the schoolyard in the costume parade wearing the cap of a Dutch girl—a hat that had been made out of a white napkin. At night, I went trick-or-treating in the Chinese wedding skirt, and with my mother by my side to make sure I did not drag it on the ground. So that was a time when we were both *li hai*.

If my mother added the words *na me* and said, *"na me li hai,"* with a frown and tone of incredulity, she meant I had such an unbelievably strong disposition that I would probably prefer she were dead than to have to obey what she had asked me to do. She often said *"na me li hai"* when I was unremorseful after being accused of doing wrong—like yelling at my little brother. But why should *I* apologize when it was *his* fault for provoking me?

When I was eighteen, my mother said I was acting too *li hai* toward my boyfriend's mother, who had tried several times to coerce me to break up with her son. The woman escalated her disapproval by threatening to have me arrested for violating the Mann Act, which prohibited the transport of minors over international borders—in this case, Canada—for immoral purposes, such as sex. I reminded the woman that I was eighteen and her son was nineteen. The not-so-subtle subtext had to do with race, which she conveyed as "the unpopularity of the Vietnam War." I told my boyfriend to stand up for me. *Them or me, you choose.* We broke up every Thanksgiving and Christmas. My mother said my demands would only make things worse. He's too young to know how to break off with them, she said. She advised I be patient and let the woman know me better over time. And then, without telling me what she was going to do, she drove over to meet my boyfriend's parents at their home and tried gentle persuasion: "They're in love," she explained. "They're young. Who knows if it will last? For now, we should let them be." My boyfriend's mother responded that she was only thinking of her son's future as a lawyer—his colleagues might not be as understanding as she and her husband were about my race. My mother shouted, "You prejudice against us? I even more prejudice against you!" My heart was so full when she told me that. So in that situation, my mother and I were both *li hai*, but I thought her approach had been better than mine.

She, too, was *li hai* when it came to love. A few weeks ago, a cousin told me that when my mother and father fell in love, his family strongly disapproved. He was the eldest son, the most eligible. Why would he choose a woman who was already married and had a powerful husband so vengeful that he had her put in jail? My father stood up for my mother by breaking off relations with family members who would not accept her, including his favorite sister. That happened around 1946. I had never known until last month what a great sacrifice he had made for her. I then remembered a time when my mother and I were in the same city where the favorite sister lived. Over fifty years had passed since the breakup and my father had long since died, but still, my mother declined the sister's overture to visit. *Na me li hai.*

When I was older, my mother would say I was *li hai* as an expression of gratitude whenever I had authoritatively taken charge after she felt she had been treated as if she were stupid, like that terrible woman who neglected to tell her that she was supposed to fill out a certain form before coming in for her appointment, a form they never gave her. One year, right after I quit my job to strike out on my own, she said in a gentle voice that I was so *li hai,* and she meant that in a good but worried sense—that I was right to leave a job where I had been demeaned but that I would have to be especially strong to make a living as a freelance business writer. Fortunately, as a parting shot, the former employer said, "Writing is your worst skill. You'll be lucky if you make a *dime.*" His ten-cent farewell proved to be exactly the amount of encouragement I needed to trigger the *li hai* response for quick success. When I had made enough money a few years later to buy my mother a condo, she again asserted I was *li hai,* and that's why I had become a success. When I later became a fiction writer, she repeated the compliment many times.

Over the years, I came to know all the nuances of that word through my mother's character and her moods. It described her integrity and resolve, her stubbornness and persistence, as well as her determination in solving any problem on behalf of our family. It also described her fury when it was unstoppable and dangerous.

My mother was Shanghainese, and there is something about the word *li hai* that applies to many Shanghainese friends and family members I know—or, actually, to many I know who live in a big city crowded with people who have more ambition than opportunities. You need to push harder to get ahead. The line is long. You have to cultivate the right connections, or at least know people who know people. In China, it's called *guanxi*, and it is liberally applied. A nephew in China once approached me for help. He needed to prove he was proficient in English to obtain a student visa to Canada. He hardly spoke more than a few memorized sentences, so he asked me to tell the immigration officials that he could speak English. "You're famous," he said. I advised that he study instead. When he did not get a visa, his angry mother came to me and insisted I find a way. You should use your *guanxi*, she said. For some people, "finding a way" is synonymous with *li hai*. She was exasperated that I was so lacking I had given up before even trying.

While gross generalizations are always dangerous, I do think there is something about the nature of Shanghai that influences the behavior of its denizens. Shanghai has accommodated strands of foreign influence, but what dominates is still quintessentially Chinese. It gives more than just a respectful nod to Chinese history and tradition, aesthetics and approach. Status is hugely important and I hear it mentioned in many ways—what is the latest, the rarest, the most expensive, the highest paid, the most profitable, the largest in size, the smallest in size, the most prestigious, the most luxurious, the most high-tech, the most famous, or the most original, be it art, fashion, food, hotels, cars, film, technology, Internet businesses, or mass transportation. These same things may be important to people in other countries as well, but the demand and competition in Shanghai feels much more intense. There is willingness to spend unfathomable amounts of money for status and to beat the West at its own game. Shanghai has had a volatile love affair with the West.

During the first half of the last century, foreign trade boomed, and the city gave rise to arguably the highest echelons of wealth, status, and decadence, as well as the most miserable gutters of poverty. Its spheres of influence created many new ways to delineate social standing beyond the old ones that placed respect for scholars ahead of merchants, and old money before new. There were new ways to develop and use *guanxi,* the best being those provided by the wealthy, the warlords, the political poo-bahs, the go-betweens with the Westerners, and the gangsters. They could arrange for scandals to disappear. The wealthy man who adopted my mother, for example, paid journalists to stop reporting news of my mother's love affair and her imprisonment. That kind of influence over the media still goes on today, so I learned at a dinner with two Shanghai-born friends who knew someone whose father quashed a story involving a movie star and a family friend.

When the Communist Party took control in 1949, wealthy landlords were paraded in the streets, as were those who had relatives who had left China. My family in China was among those who suffered. My half sisters were sent to the countryside to work in rice fields. One remained there for nineteen years because she could not get a residence permit to return to Shanghai. When China warily opened its doors a crack in the 1970s, change slowly occurred. By the 1990s, the pace quickened then exploded. Pent-up ambitions ran wild. Every time I returned to Shanghai, I saw dramatic change. The first time I went to Shanghai, I visited the mansion that had belonged to the wealthy man my grandmother married. The place had fallen into disrepair. The front gate was gone, my mother noted. Two large wings were missing. The next time I visited, the lower floor of the mansion had been turned into a cheap electronics shop. Another year, it was an Internet café, and later a Zen-style spa. Eventually it was put on the market for an astronomical figure.

No matter what changes have transpired, the city remains Shanghainese, and as an American who has never lived in Shanghai, I can't explain exactly what that is, but it comes across as pride comprised of many things. Some of it is the Shanghainese dialect, which is largely incomprehensible to those who speak only Mandarin or Cantonese. The dialect gives its speakers an immediate identity that sets them apart. A friend once took me to an exclusive restaurant in Shanghai, where she spoke to the waitress in Mandarin. I asked why she had not used Shanghainese. "She's not Shanghainese," she said. I asked how she knew. "Shanghainese girls are too proud to work as waitresses," she said. I also sense pride in people whose family history is linked with Shanghai's dramatic one. My mother's father reportedly participated in the secret meetings of young revolutionaries working to overthrow the Qing dynasty.

Shanghai-style wealth and prestige are not subtle. Disdain is openly expressed. Once, at a dinner party for patrons of the arts, I was enjoying a lively conversation with a young Shanghainese man sitting next to me. I knew by his last name and a few details he casually dropped that he descended from a prominent family with vast wealth. He evidently thought my family was of similar stature—otherwise why would I have been invited? He asked what my grandparents' business was. I explained that my grandmother was the widow of a poor scholar and later married a wealthy man as his fourth wife. He abruptly stopped talking to me, turned away. He never looked at me again the rest of the evening. I was shocked, and while I have never been the submissive type, in this room of wealthy patrons, I could do nothing to jeopardize the organization's dependence on their patrons' support. A moment later I realized that the man's insult was an unintended gift to a fiction writer: the punch in the gut that enabled me to viscerally feel what my mother and grandmother had endured, what I had tried to capture in stories. My pain was temporary. Theirs was an unalterable part of life.

As a fiction writer, I love inconsistencies, gaps in information, contradictions, false leads, and changing details. That is often where truth is clumsily hidden and can be teased out. I examine each variation and always with the question, "Why would it have happened this way?" The stories about my grandmother contained exactly those elements.

An early version of her first and second marriages, as told by my mother, went like this. When she was twenty-four, she fell in love with a poor scholar. Her parents, who doted on her, tried to prevent the marriage because the man was unemployed. My grandmother told her parents that if she was not allowed to marry him she would "swallow gold"—the romantic way that heroines in novels poisoned themselves. I don't know whether she would have really swallowed gold versus rat poison, but her parents were scared enough to relent, and she married the scholar around 1914 and became his wife, the first wife, my mother emphasized. My grandfather remained unemployed until 1919, when he was appointed to a civil servant's job in another province. He borrowed money to return home in a mule-drawn carriage. But soon after he arrived, he took ill and died a week later, leaving behind his wife, a three-year-old son, and two-year-old daughter, my mother. My widowed grandmother went to live in her older brother's house. He was a cheapskate who gave them only a roof over their head and food to eat. For money, my grandmother pawned her clothes. One day, a rich man named Du spotted her walking around a lake. He instantly fell in love with her. Although she should have remained a widow, she remarried and became Du's wife. It was a shameful thing to do back then, my mother said, but at least she became the first wife and not one of his concubines. As the first wife, she was given the best room. When she and her husband smoked opium together, her daughter—my mother—would pretend to be their maid and pass the pipe back and forth, which made everyone laugh because she was only eight years old. Less than a year later, her mother gave birth to the man's first son, and around the Chinese New Year, she accidentally took too much opium and died, leaving my mother an orphan.

Then came the variations, some of which I deduced and which my mother later admitted were true. The rich man saw her walking around the lake and told his second wife to invite her to their home on the island. Everyone enjoyed the evening, and since there was no boat that returned to Shanghai at such a late hour, my grandmother stayed the night, sharing a bed with the second wife. In the middle of the night, the second wife got up and the rich man took her place. He held a knife to her throat and said he would kill her if she did not submit, and then he raped her. The next day, everyone knew what had happened. Even worse, she became pregnant. When she apologized to her brother, he kicked her for having caused the whole family to lose face. She should have let the man kill her. With nowhere to go, she married Du—not as his first wife, but as a concubine. A fourth wife, I wrote in a story. After she gave birth to a son, she killed herself to escape her shame. My mother told me that she was at her mother's bedside when she died. She cried that she wanted to fly to heaven with her. A pattern of suicidal thought was thus set—that of a dead mother who would comfort her daughter when she joined her in death. My mother said that Du felt so guilty he promised the ghost of my grandmother that he would raise her daughter like one of his own, and he kept his word. She had the same privileges as his other daughters, including an education and nice clothes. She received a generous dowry and lavish wedding. Yet she always sensed that others in the house did not treat her like a true family member. She was not the daughter of the patriarch by blood. Instead, she was lucky to be there.

The details about the visit to the island contained another twist, told to me by another relative. When the second wife got out of the bed and the rich man took her place, he held the knife to his own throat—not to my grandmother's—and declared that if she did not marry him, he would kill himself. I wondered why there were two versions, both concerning a knife. It did not make sense anyway that the rich man would have killed her and risked jail and his family reputation for a woman he hardly knew. He was the owner of shipping companies, textile mills, and utility companies. He was much admired, a philanthropist who had built the schools, hospitals, roads, and much more on the island. He had three wives and could easily have had his choice of more. The knife, I guessed, was a red herring. I wondered if she and Du had actually been lovers, and when she became pregnant, he concocted the story about a knife. Others in the family may have pretended to go along with the story, but few would have believed it. They knew what kind of man the patriarch was. Perhaps the other concubines continued to gossip about it, and that is what my mother overheard when growing up in the mansion.

There was another puzzling detail mentioned in two versions of the story. Once my grandmother was ensconced in the mansion, she became the favorite and was given the best room. She was the one who shared his opium pipe. Yet she did not want to remain in that house. My mother remembered riding in a carriage with her mother, who complained that life on the island was so boring she could no longer bear it. That's why she made a bargain with her husband: if she gave birth to a son, he would give her a house in Shanghai where she could live apart from his other wives and their entourage of children. Since her husband lived in Shanghai as well, he would have plenty of opportunity to see his son. He agreed to the deal. But after the son was born, her husband reneged. She was so angry she ate raw opium around New Year's Day. One version places the day on the eve of the new year, when debts must be settled. Another version emphasized that the opium was buried in sticky rice cakes and their glue made it impossible to extricate the poison. My mother said it was an accident. She only meant to scare Du into honoring his promise.

The permutations continued to arrive. My grandfather, the scholar, it turned out, was already married when he met my grandmother. That meant my grandmother was his second wife, a concubine. While it may have been shameful for a wife to remarry, it was less so for a concubine. A report came from an elderly relative who lived in the mansion as a child. She heard stories from her elders that my grandmother ruled the household with her temper. She was indeed the favorite of the patriarch and if you did not agree with her opinions, she said, you would be sorry later. She was not quiet after all.

My mother cried whenever she talked about her mother. "They treated her like some kind of prostitute," she once said. "My mother was a good woman, high-class. She had no choice."

I said I understood. And she replied: "How can you understand? You did not live in China then. You do not know what it's like to have no position in life. I was her daughter. We had no face. We belonged to nobody. This is a shame I can never push off my back." She raged about the lack of respect people showed her mother and later her—as if they lacked morals and feelings. Her chest would heave like bellows, filling with despair, expelling it as fury. She was right. I didn't understand until recently, when I was treated like a pariah.

A few months after *The Joy Luck Club* was published, a relative complained to my mother that she should not be telling me all these useless stories. "She can't change the past," he said. My mother told him: "It *can* be changed. I tell her so she can tell everyone, tell the whole world, so they know what my mother suffered. That's how it can be changed." My mother gave me permission to tell the truth. She wanted the secrets exposed so that the power of shame could be replaced with outrage. By then, she believed I understood far more than she had previously thought. I had captured her loneliness as an orphan. I had even described the rooms and furniture exactly as they were, and the conversations as if I had been there to hear them. How did I know these things? You told me, I said. She insisted she had not told me everything. She wondered aloud if her mother had come to my office to help me write. "You can tell me," she said gently. "It's okay." I was touched that she thought that I would have hidden visits from her mother. I said that was not the case. But the truth is, there had been many times when I wondered if my grandmother was in the room. The writing changed. The stories came out effortlessly. I could see the scene clearly. My imagination was fuller. I understood more.

If there is indeed a universal consciousness, it makes sense that mine would conjoin with it when the doors of imagination are flung wide open and all possibilities are allowed. It makes sense I would seek companionship to help me sort through confusing ideas, thoughts, and beliefs, mine and others'. My characters are already like companions in that way, although I am always aware that they are fictional ones I created. Yet I have periodically felt I have with me a spiritual companion who drops hints and guides me toward revelations, ones I never would have stumbled upon. At times, I am alarmed to read sentences I do not recall writing, or, even more disturbing, when I read thoughts penned in my journal that I don't remember thinking. The thoughts are not contrary to what I believe. It's just that I don't remember thinking about those things at that particular time or in quite that way—which often seems to be more insightful than I could ever be. This isn't the flip side of my personality or a fragmented psyche. Whatever it is, I don't need to analyze it any further. I simply welcome this benevolent companion when I write, be it my grandmother, the universal consciousness, or a deeper layer of my subconscious unleashed by imagination.

About seven years ago, I went to the Asian Art Museum in San Francisco with my family to see an exhibit on the art and culture of Shanghai. Some of the tour showed the city's changing landscape and architecture. These were changes my family had seen. My siblings and I had inherited three Shikumen houses that sat side by side on a narrow lane in the former French Concession, until they were demolished to make way for a subway station. The mansion on Chongming Island still stands, but it is now a government building occupied by clerks instead of concubines.

About a third of the way into the museum tour, we came upon a pen-and-ink illustration of women leaning over a balcony to view the city. The docent explained that they were first-class courtesans, women who were quite influential in introducing popular Western culture to Shanghai's elite, the officials and businessmen who were their clientele. Another illustration showed lively courtesans entertaining men in a room furnished with a billiards table, cuspidor, Victorian chairs, and heavy drapery with tiebacks. The docent said that the courtesans were the only class of women who enjoyed great freedom in going out and about the city unescorted. They rode through the park in horse-drawn open carriages to show off their latest fashions. Schoolgirls were so excited to see these icons of pop culture they fainted. The courtesans stayed out late at parties and arose from bed in the early afternoon. They ordered food to be delivered from their favorite restaurants. They decorated their rooms with the latest Western furnishings. And they were also fodder for the tabloids, which reported public fights between courtesans, as well as warnings to men about courtesans who were known to accept lavish courtship gifts before choosing a younger, more handsome suitor. To be successful, these young courtesans, many in their teens, had to distinguish themselves in style, talent, and cunning to earn as much as they could. They clearly met the multifold meaning of *li hai*, especially in dealing with the much darker side behind this facade of glamour.

As a fiction writer, I immediately envisioned possibilities for adding a character to the novel I was already writing, one that concerned a young woman whose family had become outcasts in a small village after an accidental fire. It was a bildungsroman in the tradition of *Oliver Twist*. Just as Oliver unwittingly winds up in the underworld with Fagin the thief, my character might meet up with an aging courtesan in the world of flowers. At the museum gift shop, I found a research-laden book on courtesans, titled *Shanghai Love*, written by a scholar of fin de siècle courtesan culture in Shanghai. I later found several other academic books on the same subject. Over the next week, I read about the early beginnings of courtesan culture, one quite specific to Shanghai. The early courtesans embraced the arts and were talented musicians respectfully called Maestro. Their profession evolved into small salons that provided musical entertainment where men brought gifts to the musicians they admired. These salons became courtesan houses, where a lengthy courtship of weeks to months could lead to sex, which then required further gifts of appreciation. I was astonished to learn that it was the women who decided who would receive their sexual favors. Their ability to choose anything in life was in striking contrast to women who were expected to submit to arranged marriages and the dictates of husbands, mothers-in-law, first wives, and the social order.

In turn-of-the-century Shanghai, the courtesan houses operated in many ways like a men's club, where a customer could meet up with his friends and spend the night eating, gambling, and listening to entertainment in the company of friendly, beautiful women who feigned reticence as a prelude to seduction. If a man could not afford to visit the luxurious first-class houses, he might go to a second-class house, where the furnishings were of lesser quality but where the courtesans were more accommodating after a brief period of courtship. At the lower rungs, a man could find quick pleasure in opium flower houses, where sex followed a few intoxicating pipefuls. At the far end of the sex trade one could find the chopping sheds where young kidnapped girls lay drugged on the ground and were forced to take on twenty to thirty men a day until they died of exhaustion, disease, or suicide. The sex trade was so rampant in Shanghai that by the early 1900s, one out of every hundred women worked as a prostitute, at least part time. Those were the demographics of misfortune in a big city to where girls kidnapped from the countryside were brought, to where abused concubines fled, and to where newly impoverished widows and daughters went to survive in anonymity. Some were women whose husbands had squandered the family fortune through their addictions to opium or gambling, or who had fallen prey to any number of get-rich-quick schemes in Shanghai. I read about cases of schoolteachers who had lost their jobs and resorted to doing business in rented rooms. What else could they do? Suicide was an option. One out of every four concubines took it. I don't know the figures for courtesans.

Surprisingly, there were almost no written records of sex techniques, only allusions to courtesans who were popular because of their special tricks of the trade. The wives of rich men paid courtesans to teach them those techniques to encourage their husbands to stay home rather than spend their time in courtesan houses. Rumor has it that Wallis Simpson, Duchess of Windsor, received tutelage in the "Shanghai Squeeze." I had some idea of the activities men might have paid for—they can be found in the pornographic scenes of classic literary novels, most notoriously, *The Flower in the Golden Vase*, whose literary greatness was excised to provide a faster-paced narrative romp.

During the brief period of a courtesan's career, usually between the ages of fifteen and twenty-four, the smarter ones built up their savings, paid their debts to the madams, and started their own brothels. Some courtesans married clients and became concubines. For most, a grimmer future awaited—a slide into a lower-class house, a cheap brothel, or even a gutter, which was the fate of one of Shanghai's most popular courtesans during the early part of the twentieth century. I read heartbreaking letters of courtesans who had been charmed by men who promised love and marriage, but absconded with their savings.

I have always had distaste for the stereotypical descriptions of Old Shanghai as "Sin City" or a "City of Pleasures." It conveyed the notion that the pleasures were a mutual exchange between lusting men and licentious women. On the surface, if you looked only at the numbers of brothels, it would seem that Shanghai deserved the sobriquet. But its sex trade, like the worldwide one that exists today, was supplied by women and girls who had been kidnapped, sold, enslaved, and abused to keep them from running away. In Shanghai, prostitution was illegal in the Old Chinese City. But in the International Settlement, where foreigners lived and conducted business, brothels were allowed to exist. That was where the first-class houses were found. The common reality beneath the surface of "Sin City" was tragedy and an early death for most women trapped in the sex trade. I looked at many photographs of young courtesans, most of them girls with vacant eyes, which made them appear either emotionless or hardened to abuse.

One day, while leafing through the pages of *Shanghai Love,* I came across a photo taken in 1911, titled *The Ten Beauties of Shanghai.* They were courtesans who had won a popularity contest based on the votes of their clients. Five of the courtesans wore identical clothes: a cap with a tight headband of intricate embroidery that came to a V in the middle of their forehead. Their hair was tucked under the headband, which pulled their eyes slightly upward into the much-admired almond-eyed "phoenix" shape. They appeared to be wearing winter garb: a form-fitting, padded silk jacket with a tall fur-lined collar that went up to their earlobes, sleeves that ended just below the elbows, with a white lining that extended to the wrists. Their matching trousers were also snug. The style of clothes looked vaguely familiar, and then I realized why. In my favorite photo of my grandmother, she is wearing similar clothes. It was, in fact, the photo sitting at the other end of my desk.

As I compared the two photos, I saw that her clothes were identical in nearly every detail. I guessed that this was a popular fashion of the time. Perhaps many young women wore the same style. But as I read further, I learned that these clothes were specific to courtesans. They had their photos taken in Western photo studios, which were distinguished by a backdrop of landscapes or mansions, and the presence of flowers, whether in pots or vases, painted onto the backdrop, or held in the courtesan's hands. They were the obvious symbol of a courtesan's profession in the Flower World, one where beauty, from bud to bloom to fallen petals, was fleeting. While reading, I felt a strange mix of both fear and excitement. I had stumbled into a forbidden place. It seemed impossible that this had been part of my grandmother's life. To even consider that felt blasphemous to her memory. It went against family history, which cast her as old-fashioned, traditional, and quiet, a woman of few words, a woman who was widowed early, and who would have remained a chaste widow had she not been raped and forced to become a concubine. I examined her photo. There was no doubt that she had gone to a Western studio. The photo contains all the signature elements—a painted backdrop of mountains, the balustrade and stone steps of a mansion, a vase of flowers on the table, and five pots of flowers at her feet. Another woman is seated at the table, and her clothes are identical in style but of a more lustrous silk. She is not wearing a cap with headband. Instead, her hair is pulled back tightly, save for two curved locks in front of her ears.

I brought out an old photo album. Some of the photos were the size of postage stamps. I took out a magnifying glass and saw with new eyes. In one, my grandmother appears to be only thirteen or fourteen. Her hairstyle would be considered radical even by today's standards—parted asymmetrically with the two sides hanging like curtains that reveal only part of her face. Her pose is daring: one arm akimbo, hand on hip, the other resting on a fake rustic fence. She is staring directly at the camera but does not have the deadened gaze of

LEFT: *Shanghai, circa 1910: My grandmother* (right) *and an unknown woman* (left). RIGHT: *Shanghai, circa 1912: My grandmother.*

a courtesan. In fact, she looks confident, amused, even mischievous. She has a meaty chin, a plump lower lip, and an uneven upper lip. Her hands are large. I have the same hands. The ensemble in that photo is identical to what two other courtesans wore in the ten beauties photo of 1911—a skirt and a dark-colored jacket made of what appears to be heavy brocade with a high fur-lined collar, short sleeves and white lining. There is another woman in this photo, different from the first photo. She is wearing an identical dress and is seated on a stone bench, leaning back on the rustic fence at an awkward angle. She looks quite a bit older, but perhaps that is the effect of her hairstyle—a turn-of-the-century Western bouffant, what would have been quite modern back then. Her hands are large, like my grandmother's, and her chin is also large. They must be related. I recall my mother saying her mother's stepsister was fond of her. Or was it a cousin?

I found a third photograph. The backdrop suggests a Victorian parlor with trompe l'oeil parted curtains. She is posed next to a Victorian chair, her elbow on the tall armrest, her other hand on her hip. She appears to be older. Her eyebrows are thick, as if she has darkened them. Her expression suggests insolence or defiance. There is no smirk or hint of mischief. Her hair is similar to that in the last photo, parted in the middle so that her two locks form a curtain that obscure the sides of her face. She wears a light-colored ensemble— what would have been suitable for warm weather—a jacket and pants with a high collar, shortened sleeves, and white lining. Her footwear is odd: Persian-style slippers with her heels slipped out of them. She is standing on tiptoes to give her the additional height needed to balance her elbow on the armrest.

I found yet another photo taken when she was older and more traditionally dressed in a low-collared jacket, loose sleeves, and a plain skirt. She is beautiful but not glamorous. Her fringe of hair covers her eyebrows, and the rest of her hair is pulled back into a bun. Her white-stockinged legs are crossed at the knees. Was it inappropriate for a woman in the 1920s to sit like that?

There is a younger woman, sitting in a hunched posture on a ledge with her feet dangling above the ground, which suggests she is short. Her clothes are plain, which made me think at first that she was a maid. But then I recalled my mother telling me about a cousin or half sister who had a hunched back. The backdrop looks torn, the upholstered chair is shabby, the flowers look fake, and the hay-strewn floor suggests better days have long departed. Why did she choose such a dilapidated studio?

The last photo I found was taken when she was thirty-six. Part of a column can be seen on the right side of the backdrop. Leaves peek out of the trees—leaves and no flowers. As with the photos of her youth, one arm rests on a tall white stand and her dangling hand clasps the other. Her face looks fuller. Her bangs have a triangular wedge cut out at the center. She is wearing plain black shoes that show her deformed feet; they were crushed and bound until she was twelve. Her jacket is loose fitting and the sleeves are wide. It is the clothing of a traditional woman. By then, she had become the fourth wife to the wealthy man. As evident by her hands resting over her belly, she appears to be six or seven months pregnant. She was thirty-six years old, and it is the last known photo taken of her. I noticed

Chongming Island, 1925: Last photograph of my grandmother.

one more thing and enlarged the photo so I could see what is on her wedding finger: the imperial jade ring that my mother gave me when I married. I still have it, just the setting. That rare piece of jade mysteriously fell out the first time all my siblings were gathered under one roof.

For days I studied the photos and reread the research on courtesans. Wearing a courtesan's costume did not mean she had been a courtesan any more than my wearing a nurse's cap meant I had been a Dutch girl. I reminded myself that there were also many photographs of me dressed in a dominatrix's outfit—a short strappy leather dress, fishnet stockings, studded necklace, wrist cuffs, ankle cuffs, fingerless gloves, and wide belt, along with high-heeled thigh-high boots, a patent leather police cap and a cat-o'-nine-tails in one hand and a fake glowing cigarette in the other. That was the costume I had worn annually for over twenty years of performances with an all-author literary garage band whose poor musicianship and humorous antics helped raise money for kids' literacy programs. Perhaps I had inherited a fondness for costumes from her. Maybe she, too, had worn the daring costume as a joke. We both wanted our costumes to look authentic, down to the last studded detail. But why had she worn hers?

The very act of questioning who my grandmother was was dangerous. If she were alive, would she have taken my questions as an insult? I have to guard against willingness to pry open a locked box simply because its secret contents are intriguing to me as a fiction writer; I may be prone to mistaking inconsequential junk as fictional treasure that intrigues me as a fiction writer. I am a woman living in the twenty-first century. I cannot view the world of courtesans through a sociological viewpoint. I have to see her as she would have wished to be seen in 1911. I have to consider how she would have wanted to be remembered. But then I think: How would I want to be remembered? Would I want to be entombed in memory as having the traits of a stranger? Perhaps my grandmother wanted to eject the passive old-fashioned woman who replaced her. Maybe she wanted me to stumble upon the photo of the ten beauties.

The story of my grandmother is like a torn map glued together with so many bits and pieces that there is now more glue than map. The pieces haven't led to verifiable truth. I have imagined what the truth might have been, based on my own emotional and moral character. Others have done the same. We see what we want to believe. We are all unreliable narrators when it comes to speaking for the dead.

Yesterday, in Beijing, Lou and I took a walk. It was a rare spring day, sunny and absolutely clear of smog. To avoid the lines of people trying to get through the main gates of the Imperial Palace Museum, we took a detour through the grounds by the Hall of Ancestry Worship. The large courtyards and corridors were nearly deserted. We saw only photographers here and there with their clients, young wedding couples. The photographers directed them to look straight at the camera, then to the left, upward, as if seeing a bright future together. They were told to gaze lovingly into each other's eyes. The brides were all dressed in bright red wedding dresses of a similar style—sleeveless bodices, large flouncy skirts, layers of mesh, filmy veils stitched with seed pearls, and ten-foot-long trains of red satin, which the new husbands dutifully carried as they followed behind their brides, moving from one location to another. Had they all gone to the same store with a fire sale on red wedding dresses? And then I realized something obvious: the wedding photographers provided those dresses as part of a package deal. You could probably get the wedding dresses in white as well. Fresh flowers were extra.

I had another thought: Could it be that the photographers at Western photo studios provided the fancy courtesan clothes, down to the last detail? I then remembered that teenage admirers of courtesans fainted at the sight of their idols. In the 1920s, girls from wealthy families surreptitiously had clothes made to imitate the fashions of their favorite courtesans. They walked to school wearing those outfits, and their teachers admonished them and sent them home. What would girls earlier in the century have dared to do? I imagined it— the exact moment my grandmother decided to wear the costume.

She is at the cloth shop that her cousin's parents own. She is fourteen and her cousin is older, nineteen. She has always treated my grandmother like a sister. They even look alike; they have the same plump chin, uneven upper lip, and large hands. It's a cold winter day and they are bored. But then they hear a commotion on the street and run out. Two courtesans riding by in separate carriages are having a shouting match, exchanging shocking insults. My grandmother and her cousin are mesmerized. They hear other girls nearby praising the beautiful clothes the courtesans are wearing. One girl says that the photo studios two streets over have the same clothes, which you can wear to get a picture taken. The other girls say they wouldn't dare. My grandmother and her cousin look at each other and a second later they are walking to the street with the photo studios. They choose one that offers the complete package for the cheapest price. They pick out the costumes each will wear and giggle while putting on the illicit getup, every last detail. They decide the mansion backdrop is not as shabby looking as the others and take their places by a fake fence. The photographer tells them how to pose. Put your hand on your hip, rest your elbow there, stand straight, don't move, don't laugh. The next day they pick up two copies, one apiece. They laugh at how authentic they look, and then they agree they should do it every year.

I want to believe that is the reason the photos exist. She was not old-fashioned. She was a daring girl. I want to believe I am like her, that the past is connected to the present, a continuous evolution of who we become, which can even manifest as a penchant for outrageous costumes. My mother saw her mother in me, and no wonder. We are alike in so many ways. We have strong opinions. We can't tolerate insults. And look at what we did for love. We did not give up because of disapproval. We became more determined. After Lou and I married, I remained angry at his parents for their continued slights. I was angry at Lou for not standing up for me.

One day my mother told me once again to not be so *li hai*. "Be good to your mother-in-law," she said. "Not for her sake but for your husband. Don't make him choose. Don't make him one day regret what he did for you when she is gone." I instantly knew she was right. In time, my mother-in-law did come to love me, and my husband regretted only a little that I arranged one year for her to spend a solid week with us on a cruise ship to Alaska. As exasperating as she often was, he remained devoted to her, and I told him during the most trying moments how much I admired him for being not just a good son but also a good person. When his mother died at age 101, my husband had no regrets for how he had treated her, nor did I.

And now, just this moment, I realize why my mother told me to let go. She could not forget my father's sorrow over what she had forced him to do—to never again see his favorite sister.

Time and Distance: Age Twenty-Four

1976. *My own death seems so remote—like a faraway foreign place—separated from the here by distance of time. Being forty now seems more tangible. Life signs like freeway signs occasionally pop up, I'm getting there and I want to get there faster. Without the stops and turns and detours. I want to be forty and have all those forty years behind me. Forty is secure. At forty, you are a full-fledged being. Not awkward, not groping, not waiting. It's an arrival point. There's so much that I don't know. So much I am not sure about. When will I overcome this feeling that I've been foolish for twenty-four years?*

I don't have too many lines engrained upon my face. I look rather pixieish. Sometimes I wish that as I get older my eyes would become more lined and take on more character. It just looks like I haven't suffered enough in my life.

Time and Distance: Age Fifty

2002. *I have a sense of my life as a percentage of what has been used and what is likely left. And I get impatient now when I waste time trying to find lost things, or doing mundane chores, and so when I dwell on the unpleasant, when I give my mind to it. So I will kill those moments—banish them—and try to find the moments that can be relived. That's the role of imagination. It is like reassembling what has happened. Yet it's still inaccurate.*

Time and Distance: Age Sixty

2012. *Every day, I think about the fact that I will one day die. Every day I think about the possibility I will lose my brain. Every day I think about deadlines & that I am late & that I might not ever be able to finish because I am no longer able to write. It's gone. And it is this last daily thought that makes my heart race and my limbs to grow weak. That one is the most immediate and it is the most possible, and it is the one that would most likely cause constant misery, as awful as any paralyzing disease. Because if I died I would not have the anxiety of thinking I will die. And if I had dementia, I would not realize it, or I would cease to care. But if I cannot write, I would have no further knowledge of myself. I would fail to find the clues. My pastimes would be a placeholder—one after the other—with no coherent story, just a bookmark in hundreds of books, partly read, partly written.*

IV

UNKNOWN ENDINGS

CHAPTER SEVEN

THE DARKEST MOMENT
OF MY LIFE

I recently went caving on Easter Island. Caving is a caver's term for going into a cave, and true cavers require special equipment because the caves they go into can be a little tricky to get into and out of. I was with people who had that kind of equipment—helmets and headlamps, guano-proof jumpsuits, knee pads, elbow guards, and gloves. I had on regular clothes and nitrile gloves, the kind that nurses use to give you a flu shot. Caving is fun for cavers who have no fear of becoming stuck in a hole or being buried alive. I had a little bit of fear, but I went along because the sun was blazing hot and it was like being baked in a toaster oven. There was no shade other than what was under the van. I figured I would be a lot cooler in a cave, and that's because I read somewhere that on average caves run about fifty-five degrees year-round. This cave was not average. It felt like I was in a sauna. When you factor in dragging yourself forward using your fingertips, you're soon hotter than you were outside and this might make you feel you are running out of cave oxygen. The cavers in jumpsuits were really sweating. The next time someone tells you that a cave maintains an even temperature of fifty-five degrees, tell them I said that is a big fat lie.

The caves that cavers go into are not like those you see in movies—you know the ones, they're hidden behind fake bushes and open into a cavernous great room, with stalactites that resemble chandeliers, a stove made of rocks, a small pool for bathing children under a skylight, and sleeping chambers on other levels. That is a Hollywood set. I read that a caver's dream cave has an "advanced" rating, meaning, the passages might twist and turn or lead downward into something similar to a drainpipe, and that your weight and gravity might push you downward into a U-bend that requires Houdini-like flexibility. You wouldn't be able to back up vertically because you're constricted like a rabbit being swallowed by a giant anaconda. You know those stories about curious kittens that go into a drainpipe and wind up with just their piteously freaked faces sticking out? The kitten always gets rescued by passersby who cut open the pipe with an electric chain saw they happen to have in the trunk of the car. On Easter Island, no one will open a cave from the outside with a chain saw. For one thing, Easter Island is a World Heritage Site. You can't even pick up a rock and take it home. A friend tried.

This is the reason you should always have a caving expert with you when caving—or even two experts, one leading you and one following you, so that you can be either pulled forward or pulled backward, as the better case may be. Our caving expert was named Seth. There were five other people, including myself. Someone who had already come out of the caves earlier in the day let me borrow his helmet with headlamp. When we entered the cave, I was fooled by how spacious it was. It was like the Hollywood set, but without stalactites, because this cave was not limestone. Seth explained that the caves were lava tubes that formed when a volcano erupted and the lava, running down from volcano to ocean, slowed every now and then and developed crusts that eventually became tubes. When more lava flowed it squeezed through the tubes, which is similar to how bowels work, an unfortunate metaphor. The result is a cave that squeezed in and out, with some sections resembling a spelunking version of diverticulitis. This is important to remember because when you are moving ahead in a dark cave and looking down at water flowing and wondering if it will get deeper, you can easily bash your forehead when the ceiling suddenly drops a foot without any warning whatsoever. Never go fearlessly forward into the dark. I went from walking erect, to shuffling forward hunched over, then waddling in a crouched position, and then crawling on my stomach. It was like going backward on some evolutionary scale, *Homo erectus* to worm.

When you are in a cave, you cannot help but think who lived in this place thousands of years ago. They had to move around inside the cave in all these postures. I would guess that a hunched position was the most used. Maybe the survival of the fittest meant genetic selection of the shortest or those with early osteoporosis. But that can't be true. As a race, the Rapa Nui are particularly beautiful and have excellent posture. When I was crawling in a viscous substance, I tried to imagine it was brownie mix and not another kind of oozy substance befitting lava caves being called "the bowels of the Earth."

Finally, after what seemed like miles of cave crawling, we reached a dead end with a waist-deep pool. The caving expert was not alarmed. Having consulted maps ahead of time, he had expected this. He suggested we take turns getting into the pool to cool off. We did not have to worry about creatures in the water since this was not an environment that would sustain life, not even plants. But then I got to thinking that it was possible that some species of bacteria could live in such a place. Bacteria always defy expectations. After all, the earliest strains came out of thermal vents and then became the start of life on Earth. Before we *Homo sapiens* were Neanderthals, we were bacteria. These are the kinds of things I think about when I am in a strange place. I imagine things.

The cave expert suggested we turn off our headlamps. In a few seconds we were plunged into a lightless state. I had never considered what pitch-black meant, but this was it. This was a deeper darker black than what you would experience going into a darkroom. There was no electric hum, no pulse of the human race. When anyone spoke it felt like the words departed the lips and immediately fell unconscious to the floor, overcome by the heaviness of silence. I felt disoriented. Although my feet were firmly on the floor of the cave, the space we occupied had become formless. My body—not just my eyes—was aware of the total lack of light. I sensed that the body has receptors for light. For one thing, the melanin in our skin cells recognizes UV light. People who are tortured and kept underground in solitary confinement without light often become insane. The body and not just the eyes need light. I was in that lightless part of the cave for only a minute before I realized this was the darkest moment of my life. As far as the body was concerned, there was nothing there. Only the mind could compensate for lack of stimuli.

I recalled an essay I wrote when I was fourteen called "The Value of Nothing." The teacher told us to use the next hour in class to write an essay on "anything." I could not think of anything. I thought of nothing, and that was how I decided to write about nothing. I found that two-page essay recently and had to read it twice to try to make sense of my adolescent existential views. A lot of it read like a motivational speech, as you can see in this partial extract:

> One seldom realizes the true value of nothing, although we are consistently stumbling upon this obstacle. . . . Actually, we shouldn't find anything of value in nothing since there is no actual physical existence of nothing. It is a psychological state that requires only the thought of the person to make it present. . . .
>
> There are many moods of nothing. Usually one is absolutely mortified in finding they have nothing to do. But in a completely different, optimistic view, they should show a sense of accomplishment for this is one of the few occasions one knows what he's really doing. The absence of something leads us to think we have nothing and we develop a sense of insecurity and want.
>
> Something always comes out of nothing. When we say we have nothing to do, we are simply not applying ourselves to get out of that reprehensible state. Upon closer examination,

one can usually find nearly everything man has created came out of the effect of knowing we had nothing. From nothing we have created materialism. There is want for an item and once we have it, we consume it.

Of course, throughout the ages nothing will continue to follow us. Its end will come with the end of the world. From then, we will know we will always have everything. But, as for the present, as mortal needs and whims for perfection plague us, why not make the most of it?

The fourteen-year-old mind that thought about that was with me now in that cave. I thought the cave would be the perfect atmosphere for me as writer—no stimuli, no distractions, nothing to capture the attention of the eye. Imagination would be everything. I could simulate a state of darkness by wearing a blindfold before the start of writing each day. I could capture the state of nothingness. It would be like dreaming. Darkness and dreaming were good, expansive, without boundaries. I bet there is a seminar on inner awareness that has capitalized on this idea. Perhaps they even go into caves to experience the freedom of nothingness. "Out of darkness comes enlightenment," that sort of thing.

I don't know how long my fellow spelunkers and I were in total darkness. Time runs differently in the pitch-black. The diurnal body rhythm starts switching to a nocturnal one, and some alteration of the brain begins. Deep darkness condenses time and I suspect that an hour of this could be the equivalent of an entire night. Seth instructed us to turn on our lights and when we did, we saw a cockroach. We should have known better. Like bacteria, cockroaches can live in any conditions.

All too soon it was time to return to our starting point: the outdoor oven. What had seemed like a mile going in was now much shorter. Fear of the unknown elongates time. We did not know what we were getting into. Now we knew what we were getting out of.

The caving experience left me thinking about other moments people typically refer to as "dark"—those involving tragedy. Why do we refer to them as dark? Is being in darkness really such a negative experience? If not, is there another metaphor that is closer to how I feel when I am overcome with despair? Is it a sensation that I am lost or falling? What I feel most acutely is a vacuum, of being sucked out alive. I do not picture darkness where my mind is free to imagine all kinds of things. I picture only the one who I have just lost. I picture my mother. I picture my dog. I picture my friend Bill.

Darkness is no longer the word I would use for despair, not since going into that cave. I now think that the metaphor of pitch-blackness is a good one for starting afresh, for thinking before writing. In darkness, the old forms and assumptions vanish. Time is suspended. Noise is blocked. In darkness, I have only imagination.

Nipping Dog

[From the journal]

SAN FRANCISCO, 1977. *It's troublesome to think about the whys and wherefores of all that I do in life. Sometimes I feel like a worried little dog nipping at the heels of sheep to keep them within the pen when the sheep keep roaming day and night.*

CHAPTER EIGHT

THE FATHER I DID NOT KNOW

On New Year's Day, 1962, my father wrote his first entry in his new pocket diary: "This has got to be a good year." My father, the minister, prayed to God for a boost in blessings. He wrote that he got a fresh start for the New Year by cleaning the hardwood floors with a floor polisher he had bought my mother for Christmas. Despite prayer and polisher, by the end of that same day, bad luck was already settling into the floorboards. The next morning, he was too weak to go to work. By the third day, I was found delirious in my bedroom with a 105-degree fever. And then we were both hospitalized for pneumonia, an experience I actually loved—the hospital part, that is. After being pumped full of penicillin, I felt pretty good by the second day, and the rest of my weeklong stay was like a vacation in a fine hotel with constant room service, breakfast in bed, unlimited TV, and visits with my father. We shared a serious illness. We were both special together.

No one yelled at me, even when I accidentally depressed the call button. Every morning there was toast and little tins of strawberry jam and margarine. The nurses loved me and I cried when I had to go home. I took with me the tiny tins and wore my hospital ID bracelet until it fell apart.

That memory of our having pneumonia together counts as one of the best of our special moments together. I had a whole week with him. He was not busy going off at night to counsel someone, or concentrating on writing his sermon. I kept the margarine tins and broken hospital bracelet until I went to college and had to throw out most of what I had collected in childhood. Those were among the last I let go.

Despite a rough start that year, my father continued to express optimism in his annual diaries. He seldom made note of the birthdays of his children. He must have figured he did not need to be reminded of what he knew perfectly well. The tiny space for daily entries was dark with pencil marks that itemized the exact amounts spent for piano lessons, fixing cavities, a dent in the car, a weekly tithe to the church, a weekly check to the babysitter ($20) and the rare new dress for my mother ($4.15). It also included notes of fights with my mother. "Did not sleep until 3 a.m." Most of his entries concerned sermons he was scheduled to deliver as a guest minister, or the prayers he had selected to deliver as the assistant pastor. "Delivered sermon Come and See. Attendance was low, but sermon went over well." He confessed to doubts that his service to God was good enough. He reported encouragement he had received from mentors, and ended with a pledge, double underlined, to do more. He noted the names of people he was scheduled to visit to provide consolation or counsel. He wrote about a fight between two boys, who both refused to go to church if the other was there. Without explaining what he did, he noted in another entry that the problem had been solved. In reading his diaries, I saw that he lived in distinct worlds, the church and home, and he was much more preoccupied and happier with the former than the latter.

I found my father's diary for 1967. It measures only two and a half by four inches, so his handwriting is cramped and his entries are sometimes cryptic. From February until June, he made copious notes of my brother's symptoms of illness, his subsequent diagnosis, the surgery, the coma, the visits by friends, another surgery, my brother's hand squeezing theirs, and the hopes they placed in one more new treatment. On June 6, he wrote that he could not hold a bowl while having lunch with church friends. "Left arm feels numb." On June 8, his left pinkie finger no longer worked, leaving missing letters as he typed his sermon. On June 10, he wrote words in Chinese as well as English, including "attack," and "Dr. Zhivago." The attacks were likely seizures, and they worsened over the next five days until he was finally admitted to the hospital. His doctor initially diagnosed him with the flu. In reality, he had a tumor in his brain the size of a grapefruit. As with all hardships, he took this as yet another test of faith. He almost seemed glad he had been called upon to endure it and show how great his faith was. He would pass the test and save his son. While he was recovering from surgery, no one dared tell him that Peter had died. By my mother's request, I had taken over writing the progress reports on Peter and what occurred to both of them following my father's surgery.

If music had been scored for the themes of his diaries, it would begin with a sweet hymn for two bars before being drowned out by Mussorgsky's "Night on Bald Mountain." Those two songs, set to repeat.

I 've had readers ask me in public why I have not included fathers in my stories. I've answered that fictional characters must be dimensional, complex, and morally ambiguous—in other words, flawed, rather than idealized. I pointed out that I have actually included father figures in my novels, and it was not coincidental that they died an early death; my father passed away when I was not quite sixteen. After his death, my memories of him became an idealized view of him—the two of us standing in the mirror of the past, face forward, seeing him in a one-dimensional state of perfection fixed in grief. My stock of memories has been enough for me to believe he was kind to others, compassionate and giving to strangers, honest in his dealings with everyone, and inspirational as an American Baptist minister.

Fresno, 1954: Me, age two, with my father.

He was also handsome, a raconteur, a stylish dancer, a good singer, smart in versatile ways, charming and gracious in exactly the right ways, which always made people glad to see him. I remember thinking on many occasions that I was proud that he was my father. If I had had a choice, I would have picked him. He was special, the best in a roomful of fathers. One other thing, he was not a hypocrite. I have often publicly cited that. His beliefs and his actions were consistent, and that was very important to me when I was a teenager and prone to idealism and rapid disillusionment.

Today, the day after the 2016 presidential election, I am disillusioned—devastated and angry. My party lost, and the unthinkable has happened. America has changed overnight. It has already shown that it will be governed under an openly racist agenda, one that sees immigrants as the cause of economic woes, crime, and terrorism. A significant percentage of the public are expressing their antipathy to anyone who does not look like he or she is white, heterosexual, and conservative. There is a new mainstream America. Some of my friends have already experienced these attacks. I have received racist insults on social media, which typically include some variation of the words "Commie," "go back to China," and "you're not an American"—the latter meaning being quite different from someone being told their ideas are un-American. I was so distraught by the open hatred that I wanted to know who among my friends and family had supported directly or indirectly that party's antiimmigrant position. I could no longer respect those people. I was thankful that everyone in my family—brother, sisters, cousins, nieces, and nephews—had supported my candidate. Many of them had been immigrants before getting their U.S. citizenship. Had my mother been alive, I have no doubt that she would have voted as I did. We would have agreed on most, if not all, of the most sensitive issues.

Immediately after thinking this, however, I was startled to realize that I did not know how my father would have voted. He had been an evangelical Christian, whose faith redoubled in crisis. He might have voted for the party viewed as the evangelical choice. And merely in thinking that, I was treading on my memory of him as perfect.

I can think of nothing else now: How would he have voted? I fear the answer I might find. I am afraid of forever seeing him differently, but I cannot avoid looking. My grief over this election forces me to examine all that I believed about him and have never questioned.

My earliest memories of my father took place in Fresno, where we lived for the first two and a half years of my life. Fresno is notorious for its hot summers, which vies with my father's birthplace, Wuhan, one of the Four Furnace cities of China, where hardy locals eat chilies to stay relatively cool. My father joked that when the devil was placed in a pot of oil in hell, someone asked if he was now suffering for his sins. The devil replied, "Not at all. It is like a comfortable bath compared to Wuhan." My father might have told that same joke, substituting Fresno for Wuhan, while suggesting to his parishioners that they should aim to go to heaven rather than finding out that the devil was not telling the truth. He had a ready joke for any situation and a Bible passage for every doubt. I was told that when it was evident he would die, a member of the church asked if he had made his peace with God. My father said, "Why no! We've never quarreled."

I am remembering one of those typically hot days when I must have been a little over the age of two. As a toddler, my memory would have been naturally imprecise, and my adult mind has likely filled in the blanks for cohesion. I do know that my memories from a very young age have much to do with emotional sensations tied to spatial perception, the nearness to and distance from my mother and father, the feeling of being in an open space compared to a smaller one with dark corners. I remember making an effort to not cry when my parents left me in the arms of others. I remember crying when a piece of fruit fell on my head and my parents laughed. I remember being in an enclosed space—a large station wagon—packed with older children, who were much larger than I was. They were dressed in swimsuits and were very excited. My father, the church minister, was driving down a road lined with tall trees. When we stopped, all the other kids ran off in different directions to reach the public swimming pool. My father walked me to the pool and had me step in a little bit at a time, and then he put his hand under my belly so I could float and flap my arms, as if I were swimming. We must have been in the shallow end of the pool, because he could stand and walk around. Later, we got out of the pool and went to the water slide. He helped me climb the steps and seated me, then told me to wait. This whole sense of where I was felt very different once he was no longer right there behind me. I saw him at the bottom of the slide. I'm sure the distance was very short. But in my memory, my father looked very small and the slide was long and steep. He said to come down and he would catch me. Even though I was uncertain, I trusted he would do as promised. He had always done so whenever he threw me in the air or balanced me standing on the bottoms of his feet. All the kids loved for him to do that. They, too, trusted him. So I let go, but instead of catching me, he allowed me to plunge into the pool. Stinging water went up my nose. He was laughing as he lifted me up. He probably asked if it was fun. I might have nodded to please him. But I was now afraid of the slide and the bottomless water. After that, he took me to the wading pool, which was likely six inches deep, and I sat there and slapped the water to watch a penny on the bottom change shape.

I noticed that my wet swimming suit was turning dry and the ruffles stood out again.

I recall another time when I was three and a half. We lived in an apartment in Oakland. I was standing at the top of the stairs, and my father was downstairs in the living room, sitting in an armchair by the window. I wanted to reach him, and in the next moment, I was tumbling down the stairs. When I finally stopped, I was crying, still scared. I had a child's indignation that this was not supposed to have happened. My mother and father came to me, and my father scooped me up and placed me against his chest and sat down in the armchair, patting my back. When I finally felt a little better, I opened my eyes and saw blood on his shoulder and I screamed louder than ever. It was probably just a bloody nose, but in my child's memory, half his shirt was already drenched with my blood. As he hugged me closer and patted my back, I remember an odd mix of feelings—caught between comfort and terror as I lay pressed against him.

We lived in another house when I was four and a half, a ramshackle place, big enough for our family, as well as my uncle, aunt, and four cousins, who had just emigrated from China. I recall a night when my father was bathing me as I crouched in the white pedestal sink. I had to stand so he could rinse me off. When he finished, he walked away, probably to get a towel. My back was to him, and he might have taken only two steps, but it seemed like he had gone out of the room. So I turned to see, and immediately slipped on the curved sink, and fell backward onto the cold tiled floor. As a child, I felt like I was alone for quite a while before I was discovered. In reality, it must have only been seconds. I don't think I was injured, but I cried mightily, mostly from residual fear and some other mix of a child's emotions—shock and anger that my father had made this happen by leaving me.

My memories are more vivid by age five. I had started kindergarten and the school was only a block away from our apartment. It was enclosed by a tall chain-link fence. Most of the playground was asphalt, but at one end, there was a sandbox, monkey bars, swings, a spiral slide, and a stand of shady trees where we girls used twigs to define areas of a make-believe house. One afternoon, my father took me there, just the two of us. It probably was a Saturday or Sunday, because the playground was empty of children. I wanted to go down the tall curly slide. That was the most popular feature of the playground and was usually controlled by older boys, so I had not yet had a chance to try it. My father stood behind me and helped me climb the steep steps. Once I was at the top, I sat down and held on to the side rails as he climbed down. As with the swimming pool slide, without him behind me, I felt instantly vulnerable. He called to me from the bottom, but because of the twists and turns of the slide, I could not see him. I was higher than I had ever been in my life and to let go I would have to believe my body would be able to take those three loops down and deliver me to my father's arms. I was afraid. My father continued to call for me. That particular moment of paralysis replays whenever I am standing in my skis during a snowstorm, unable to see the slope in front of me. As in childhood, I can be overwhelmed by uncertainty, and I find my inability to go forward to be maddening. It's as if I were two people—one who is adventurous and wants to leap forward and experience the thrill, and the other the same little girl who refuses to budge because she does not trust that her father will be there. But I did eventually let go, and as I headed for that curve, I was suddenly yanked back and pulled over the rails of the slide. The hem of my skirt had snagged onto a sharp metal edge and I was now dangling off the side of the slide. I was screaming and a long time seemed to pass before my father understood what the problem was and came to rescue me. That memory includes an element that could not possibly be true, except as part of my high emotions in being rescued from a dangerous situation: along with my father helping to bring me down, there were firefighters and a long ladder.

Just now, in recalling these memories, I am struck by the similarities—memories about the downward sensation of falling and a feeling that my father was supposed to protect me. Did this say something about how I saw my father? Actually, I have other memories of falling that had nothing to do with my father: sliding down a curved banister with my cousins and landing on my tail-bone; riding down a hill on a small bike without brakes and hitting my forehead on the sidewalk when I tried to stop; flying with a centrifugal force off a push merry-go-round that older boys had made go faster in response to my protests; landing hard on my end of a teeter-totter when the other kid suddenly jumped off when I was at its highest point. There are probably many more incidents I might be able to recall if I thought long enough, matching scabs to causes. My overall sense is that I had somehow cast my father in the role of hero and I had expected him to protect me from bodily harm when we did exciting and often scary things together. My mother, on the other hand, prevented me from doing anything risky. She held tight on to my hand, told me what I should not do, and scolded me if I did not obey. She filled my mind with visions of every way I could be squashed, dismembered, burned alive under a hot water faucet, or electrified by lightning or lamps.

I have no photos of any of those falling incidents. They are recalled only from a child's gut memories, and in a way I trust that they are true, more so than the recollections I have that are associated with photos. With the latter, I am guessing I have created a patchwork story that matches the photo. But even if both those kinds of memories are not strictly factual, they do contain the emotional *sense* of what was true at the time.

Because my father was an amateur photographer, I have hundreds of photos that he took with his Rollei. He developed some of them in improvised darkrooms and I was allowed to watch as he bathed the photographic paper in a smelly solution. He made many copies of the photos he liked. His earliest photos of my mother were taken in Tianjin, where she and my father lived after she ran away from her husband in Shanghai. One photo shows her waking up in bed, looking blissful. It's obvious that she has already combed her long hair and arranged it to spread across the pillow. In another, she is stretching out her arms as demonstration that she will soon get out of bed. Next, she is sitting on the edge of the bed, legs crossed, and reaching down to put on a silk slipper, while looking up at the camera. Then she is standing in her pajamas in front of a mirror, running her fingers through her long, neatly combed hair. He took many photos of her outdoors as well—by a lake, sitting on stairs, standing with her back flat against the wall of a building, and always looking radiantly in love. In some she is wearing Western clothing, and in others, it is a hybrid of East meets West—a Western cardigan over a plain checked Chinese dress. In that photo, her shoes are oxfords and ankle socks, which was unusual. My mother was quite proud of her size four feet, as was my father, who sometimes took photos of only her feet. In most of the photos, she is beaming at the camera, but in a few, she has been posed sitting in a certain position, while gazing off into the distance with a thoughtful expression.

He put me in specific poses as well. I remember being told during many photo sessions to cross my feet at the ankles, or to clasp my hands in my lap, or to point up to the sky, or to sit cross-legged with my shoes peeking out from my dress. I think he was inspired by the poses of calendar pinup girls. In one, taken when I was four, I had to thrust out my chest and bend my arms back to hold on to the top rail of a chain-link fence. I am wearing a pink-striped, puffy-sleeved chiffon dress and patent leather shoes, so it must have been a Sunday after church. My hair is tied in two ponytails and strands of hair have escaped from a multitude of barrettes. I recall that the pose was uncomfortable. My twisted arms ached. But in the photo, I show none of that discomfort. I am smiling, holding up the fence with sheer bravery and a desire to please my father. He probably said many nice words of encouragement: "What a pretty smile. Good girl." That same day, he also posed me in a birch tree. I remember my uncertainty in being hoisted up into the V of the tree and then trying to remain there without showing I was scared. It was not a comfortable place to sit. The photo is highly posed—one arm resting on one limb, the other lightly touching the other limb. My feet are crossed at the ankles. And there again is the signature look—gazing off into the distance. My lips are tightly sealed, so I might have been afraid and trying hard not to show it. On that same afternoon, he took photos of my little brother sitting in the crook of the same tree. In one he has the concerned frown of an eighteen-month-old. In another he looks like he is shrieking. I suspect that my little brother's photo had been taken first and I wanted to show that I was not a crybaby like him. I was a skilled competitor for love. These days, I am more cautious than I am brave. My mother's warnings stuck. However, there are times when I am emboldened by another person's fear. When others remark on the steepness of a ski slope, my hesitation vanishes and I launch my skis downward and take off. I take perverse delight in wrapping snakes around my neck to see others run off screaming. No bravery on my part is required, since I like snakes and the ones I hold are harmless. Actually, one was venomous, but I did not know that until several years after the photo was taken.

My father was competitive, and he wanted us to be competitive as well. You needed ambition to become the best. I remember now an afternoon in the same park when I was six. We happened to walk by a grove where a Hula-Hoop contest was about to begin. Most kids knew how to use one. Gas stations gave them away for free with a fill-up. My father encouraged me to enter the contest and signed me up to compete with the six-year-olds. I was handed a Hula-Hoop and proceeded to shimmy along with the other kids. It was clear fairly soon that compared to those kids, I was an Olympiad. As I walked forward and backward, I wiggled my hips at different speeds so that the hoop eased up from my waist, over my arms and then to my neck. One by one, the other children lost control of their Hula-Hoops or tired and let their hoops wobble to the ground. I kept going. I shimmied the hoop down to my knees, then even lower to my ankles and easily brought it back up to my waist before taking it up to my neck again. I performed these gyrations with seemingly no effort, and in the end I won a giant Hershey's bar, the child's equivalent of a million dollars. In a strange way, I felt I had cheated because my father and I both knew almost from the start that those kids had had no chance of winning.

I think my father wanted me to not only be better than other kids, but excessively so. When I received a "Needs to Improve" rating in penmanship in the second grade, my father bought a book on calligraphy. He taught me to make letters that were shaded on one side of the letter. It required me to apply pressure on the pencil with each down stroke. Sure enough, my penmanship received an "excellent" rating on the next report card. In the sixth grade, when I had to choose a science project, my father reminded me that I was interested in planets and rockets. All the kids knew about NASA's Saturn project. My father suggested I might do something with solar cells, which were being tested for use on satellites. My father knew this because he made transformers for the electrical systems of satellites. For my science project that year, he coached me every step of the way—starting with my writing a letter to the famous Dr. Wernher von Braun of NASA to beg for a few solar cells. Dr. Von Braun did not write back, but someone else at NASA did—a three-page letter explaining how solar cells worked and how they were being tested for use on satellites and rockets. I eventually received nine solar cells from a company that supplied them to NASA. My father gathered the other parts I needed: a capacitor, resistor, circuit board, wire, switch, and a buzzer. He let me use the soldering iron to assemble the parts to the board. I wrote a detailed paper on solar cells and their use for satellites in space and for door buzzers on Earth. My teacher said I had done an excellent job, but I knew that without my father's help I would have been writing about the growth rates of tomato plants in milk cartoons. While I was glad that my father had spent so much time helping me, in a way, he had lowered my confidence. The brilliance of coming up with a solar-powered buzzer was his. He assembled the circuit board. He explained what an electrical circuit was, and even after he did, I still was not sure I understood what all the pieces were for. Through his efforts I had been thrust into the stratosphere of sixth grade science, and instead of feeling my project was the best, I knew it was a sham. Then again, it's likely most of the kids had help from their fathers, and the only honest project was the tomato plants.

At times my father was my secret compatriot. We were the mutual victims of my mother's anger. I recall a day when we brought home a watermelon. This took place in our home in Hayward, the first home my parents owned. I was seven or eight. The watermelon slipped onto the kitchen floor and cracked open. I can't remember how it happened, but I must have been to blame because my mother was furious with me. Only the rind had touched the floor, but my mother said it was too dirty to eat. She told me take the whole watermelon to the garbage can and throw it away. Because of what I had done, none of us would have watermelon. My father said he would carry one half and I should take the other. I followed him out the kitchen door to the garbage can by the garage. I was upset, of course, and I might have also been crying. My father set the broken watermelon on top of the can and signaled that I should remain quiet, and then he gestured for me to scoop out watermelon with my hands and to eat as fast as I could. So then I knew he did not blame me. We were like thieves, greedily stuffing ourselves with purloined goods. By doing what was forbidden, we had made a pact.

He was also my compatriot on my ninth birthday. It was Sunday, and for some reason, my mother did not go to church with us. But when we returned home, we saw that she had turned the living room furniture upside down—big heavy chairs and the coffee table lay on their sides. Objects had been thrown onto the floor, including my birthday cake. I thought she had done this simply because it was my birthday. I began to cry and my father led me outside, put me in the car, and took me to lunch. I cried but tried hard to stop, because I knew he wanted to make me feel happy. He took me to the ice-skating rink, and I wobbled around a few laps. I knew I should be glad to have my father to myself, but when I asked him why my mother wrecked everything, he was evasive, which made me think I was the reason. At the end of our afternoon, he took me to the top of a grassy hill. We walked to the summit and saw the valley below. He posed me leaning against a fence. He did not need to tell me to look off into the distance. I had turned my face away because I was still crying and my eyes were swollen. I have no memory of what happened when we returned home, whether my mother had calmed down enough to make dinner and another cake. She never would have apologized for what she had done, but if she had made me a cake, I would have known that she was sorry.

I have memories of my father and me reading aloud the Word Power multiple-choice quiz in *Reader's Digest*. It was the monthly time we spent together, just the two of us in the living room, learning words as equals. He loved words and so did I. He wrote down new multisyllabic ones he liked and so did I.

There was a terrible memory, the day he found me crying in the laundry room. I was holding my cat Fufu who had returned home mewing softly after being hit by a car or mauled by a dog. I was trying to put her intestines back into her torn body. My father came back with a towel and wrapped her up and placed her in my lap when we got in the car. She purred the whole way to the vet and I sobbed. My father was with me when the vet said it was hopeless and that I had to say good-bye to my cat right there. Only my father and I had seen both my cat's and my agony. Only he knew what it meant when I told people that my cat had died.

I do not recall my father spending much time with me after that. He was always working. He had his full-time job as an electrical engineer. He still did volunteer work for the church and delivered sermons as a guest minister at First Baptist churches up and down Northern California. He continued to think of the ministry as his calling and engineering as his occupation. He was working toward a master's degree in engineering at Santa Clara University. And like many engineers in the future Silicon Valley, he started a business. His niche was a small doughnut-shaped transformer the size of a Life Saver candy. They were the smallest transformers for the high-voltage needs of electrical systems, such as those on satellites. He believed that this product would be the breakthrough that would make us rich. My mother, older brother, and I were recruited as unpaid employees. We took turns using a noisy, clunking machine, holding the transformer in place with our fingers and turning it as the threading machine moved up and down, winding copper wire around the transformer. It was like sewing a giant buttonhole. I was always nervous that I was winding the transformers the wrong way or with too many or too few loops of wire, which would then damage a satellite and make it fall to Earth. Fifty years later, I think the real damage may have been our daily and direct contact making and testing transformers that emitted strong electromagnetic wave frequencies. That may have been the reason why my brother and father developed malignant brain tumors in the same year and my mother a benign one, also around the same time. It makes more sense that this was the reason over random bad luck, and it also makes me think a similar fate awaits me.

None of us saw my father much anymore, except at dinnertime. As soon as he was done eating, he left to study. One day I went looking for him for some reason I no longer recall. I found him working on his engineering homework, which was spread out over a small bathroom vanity that served as his desk. He handed me a sheet of yellow graph paper covered with precisely written Greek symbols and numbers. "What do you think?" he said. I don't remember what I answered, but I was happy that he had asked for my opinion.

His constant work also left no time to take vacations. When visitors came, my father took them on a tour of Santa Clara University. To my mind, our lives were boring and monotonous. I occupied myself by reading and drawing in my room with the door closed. I signed up for many church activities—youth choir, BYF, a trip to the mountains, outdoor games in a park. I spent as much time as I could at the homes of my friends.

In 1966, my father wrote the usual mimeographed Christmas letter.

> *This year, we decided not to take a journey-worn vacation, but to spend the money for relaxation at home. We bought a RCA 120-watt stereo system with 15" woofers to bring the house down. It is absolutely sensational to vicariously sit in the middle of a hundred-piece Philharmonic orchestra that sets your heartbeat in resonance with the bass drum. Even the Beatle [sic] music sounds wonderful.*

He added he would not do the usual bragging about his kids being a chip off the old block. The tone was joking. But then he did mention that we had become extroverts and were now class officers. His next few sentences wounded me.

> *When it comes to domestic responsibility, their IQs drop to a*
> *negative value. Clothing and hairdos become a perennial fuss. It was*
> *a relief to see Amy push away the dark clouds in front so we could see*
> *the stars, but when the long, long silky black hair dipped in the thick*
> *dinner soup, Alas!*

How could he make fun of us to others? He always ended his letters with dialogue between my mother and him, which he might have modeled after a George Burns and Gracie Allen routine— George always gave the straight line and the naive but wise Gracie delivered the inadvertently wise or hilarious punch line. In my father's version, he had the punch line.

> *Across the candlelit table, John was admiring the "salt and pepper"*
> *on her head—"Daisy, you are always young and fair to me." She*
> *looked at the "soy sauce" on his head—"How come nothing seems*
> *to worry you too much?" John pointed his finger up, "I listen to the*
> *Boss, upstairs."*

Two months later, he wrote a different kind of letter to friends and members of the church with the following prologue:

> *Peter is now arguing with the other Peter about crashing the Pearly*
> *Gate without a validated ticket.*

The rest of the letter is written in the style of Biblical verse, paraphrasing Mark: 9:14–29.

> *And Jesus said, "According to your faith be it done to your boy."*
> *Then he said to the dying boy, "By the power of God, I make you*
> *well." And the boy cried with a loud voice and was convulsing*
> *terribly, foaming in the mouth, then was lying there like a corpse: so*

that most of the famous neural [sic] surgeons invited for consultation
said, "He is dead." But Jesus took him by the hand and lifted him up,
and he arose picking up his admission to the University of California
in Santa Cruz and went surfing for the Lord.

    This is our faith in God, our hope in His mercy, and our love for
Peter. Pray for Peter and pray for us.

    "That's the way!" Daisy's famous last word.

    "That's the only way!" John adds.

Santa Clara, California, 1967: Mementos of my brother's
death at age sixteen.

Everyone thought it was a wonderfully written letter. And now,
upon reading it fifty years later, I remember why I did not believe
what he had written. It was disingenuous. He had written, in effect, a
sermon in the voice of a minister. His modified Bible passages had reduced our chaotic, murky, and fearful life into Christian testimony,
which he spread via hundreds of mimeographed pages to churches.
My father was acting out the story of Abraham. God asked him to

prove his faith by killing his son. The Lord was testing us and we were going to pass the test and Peter would come out of his coma and ask my mother for potstickers. My mother had already promised to make them. People who visited us at the hospital to console us went away inspired by my father's faith. They made a prayer circle and I was the silent weak link. I knew my brother was going to die. I watched my mother and father exhorting him to open his eyes. They interpreted every muscle to be a message of love. I wanted to shout for them to stop. My little brother and I became shadows in the house. They yelled at me for not being more helpful. All the days at the hospital passed by with little variation. For a while, my brother's head was swathed in white bandages. Then he was bareheaded with crooked train-track stitches over his scalp.

I kept a diary that year, but what I wrote was so trivial it is clearly pathologic. There are no entries about my brother. Instead I methodically recorded the names of the top one hundred songs on the radio. I noted what certain boys had said to me. It was 1967, the Summer of Love. I wanted love. I wanted to be an ordinary teenager. I wanted psychedelic adventures. I did not want to hope I would not die.

And now I remember something else from that time. A few weeks before Peter died, some high school friends and I decided to see the newly released film *Doctor Zhivago*. My father had noted the name of the film in his diary. I was excited because I had a crush on one of the boys who would be there. To him, I was just a nice kid. But if he even looked my way or said hello that would have counted as a success. When we arrived at the theater complex, I was horrified to see my parents and little brother standing near the entrance. They were smiling and came toward me, thinking I would be surprised and delighted. I am guessing now that I accused them of spying on me, or that they had come to deliberately embarrass me, words to that effect. Whatever I said festered in my father all night. When I returned home, he was standing by the front door. He yelled at me and accused me of having no love and concern. We should all want to be together as a family as much as possible. His tone of voice suggested that he hated me. Something was ending. All that we had been to each other had never been true. We had never been compatriots. I must have shown an implacable face because my mother and father shouted that I had no feelings. My expression must not have changed, which so enraged him, he lifted his arm to strike me, but instead of landing a blow, his arm involuntarily flopped heavily onto my shoulder and slid off. My mother cried out. My father tried to lift his arm again. He could not. They both thought he had suffered a stroke and I thought I had caused this to happen and was immediately sickened with guilt. They left me by the door, forgotten, as my mother rushed to get her purse and the car keys to take my father to the emergency room.

I t has been a week now since the election, a week since I went into the garage and found more boxes of my father's papers and documents: the essays and thesis he wrote for his theology degree, his typed and handwritten sermons, his Bibles, more little black diaries, address books, and mimeographed Christmas letters, his last letter scrawled to a friend, photos of him with a shaved head and radiation-tanned face, photos of him in a casket, and several lengthy typed eulogies, remembrances in church bulletins, and notes of sympathy. I took them to my office and have been searching through these piles, searching to understand my father.

As a class assignment when he started at Berkeley Baptist Divinity School, my father wrote a sermonette:

> I was born in a well-to-do modern Christian family in China. I received a good education, got a good job right after graduation from college, worked my way to the title of radio engineer in five years. In 1944, I was successful in passing a competitive government examination for a scholarship to come to the United States to study radio engineering. I was to go to study at MIT, then I transferred all my records to Harvard, intending to study business administration, but finally I found myself studying at BBS, preparing for the great task in life.

Obviously he had not yet found his charismatic voice as a minister. He had provided facts that contained little about his feelings of either his past life or his new one as a devoted Christian. He offered no explanation why he switched his plan to study from engineering at MIT to business at Harvard to theology at divinity school. He did not tell the story, as he would in later years, that he had been like Saul the Pharisee. On the way to Damascus, Saul was startled by a flash and fell off his horse. He and his men heard Jesus's voice asking Saul why he had persecuted him to death. He told him to go to the city and receive instructions. Saul stood up and realized he was blind. His men led him to Damascus. After three days, he heard a voice saying Jesus was before him, and instantly his eyesight was restored, and he could see Christ. Saul was immediately transformed into the Apostle Paul and penned a letter to the Corinthians about the nature of love. My father often used the metaphor of being blind to the presence of Christ in our lives. But he did not mention what persuaded him to make the ministry his life's work. He had been blinded by love.

Long after he died, my mother told me about the terrible guilt he felt for having fallen in love with her. He bore responsibility for breaking up her family and for causing his own parents and sibling turmoil. When he came to the United States in 1947, he must have said nothing about my mother, the married woman he loved. Two years later, when the minister of the church he attended announced that my father's bride was coming from China, a few girls cried out in shock and one fled the church hall in tears. One family friend recalled that everyone pictured his bride would be a tall woman who looked like a movie star. She was not even five feet and weighed only eighty pounds. I think the young women who gasped were his photo subjects and those who sat next to him at picnics. He took many photos of one young woman dressed in a wide-sleeved embroidered Chinese jacket and pants, who he posed next to columns and reflecting pools. In some photos, she stared with a dreamy expression at some unknown horizon.

No one knew that my father's bride was still married and had other children. When he wrote that sermonette assignment, it was only a few months before my mother would arrive. I wonder if he had ever been tempted to tell her that he had changed his mind. I do not doubt that he loved her and that she had been his "first true love," as he described her in one letter. But his love for her had broken one of the Ten Commandments: "They shall not commit adultery." By marrying her, he would be reminded daily of that sin. He must have been tormented by the fact that she left behind her three daughters to be with him. Keeping her past a secret was the same as telling a lie, the sin of omission. To counter his sins, he wanted his faith to be unshakeable. I think that was why he adhered to the other commandments so strictly. Remember the Sabbath and keep it holy.

I don't recall him issuing hell and brimstone warnings at home, but he was strict on certain matters that most Christian families might not have been. For example, we could not say "gee," "gosh," "golly," or "darn," because those were blasphemous derivatives of "Jesus," "God," and "damn," a violation of the commandment: Thou shalt not take the name of the Lord in vain. For some reason, "doggone-it" was exempt. He considered drinking alcohol to be a sin, although that was not the belief of most Christians we knew. They drank wine at Christmas celebrations. But we had no alcohol in our house, ever. On one occasion, he came home from the store and saw he had accidentally bought a six-pack of ale, not ginger ale. Instead of returning to the store to exchange the ale, he called us over to the kitchen and had us watch as he opened each can and poured the contents down the drain. I thought it was a terrible waste of two dollars, especially on a hot afternoon. Meanwhile, my mother simply went along with whatever my father wanted to model as good behavior. No alcohol. Fine.

Throughout my childhood, we prayed before every meal— without fail. Most of the time, my father would say the prayer, but sometimes he nodded to one of us to say it. Our prayer was not like the inspired, oratorical prayers he gave in public. It was a faithful recitation of the same words, delivered in one breath: *BlessohlordthisfoodweareabouttoreceiveandmakeusevermindfuloftheneedsofothersinJesusChristamen.*

When my father was hospitalized, our mother stopped praying

at home. The first few times we sat down to a prayerless dinner, my little brother and I would look at each other. And then we would shrug and start eating. Something had changed, and it felt dangerous.

I came across several binders with typed sermons. The citations for prayers were typed in red. I marveled that there were few typographical errors. If only I wrote so assuredly. In looking through my father's sermons, I found one from 1963, around the same year we did the science project on solar cells. He titled it "In God We Trust." It was his response to that week's headline: "Reaction Mostly Mild on Outlawing the Lord's Prayer in School." His reaction was not mild. "Like many others," he said in his sermon, "I was deeply disturbed and incensed over the action of the Supreme Court concerning prayer in our public schools. It seemed not only the reversal of our historic tradition but also to undermine the very foundation of our American democracy." He talked about his hope that this would actually serve as a revitalization of both religion and democracy.

On this issue, we definitely would have had disagreement. I imagine myself at twenty, arguing about the Lord's Prayer in school. I would have cited the First Amendment: "Congress shall make no law respecting an establishment of religion," and he would have cited the second part: "or prohibiting the free exercise thereof." We had King Solomon's dilemma. Did Solomon propose we cleave our country in two? That is certainly what happened with the 2016 election, I would have pointed out. Surely he did not think that Jews and atheists should be forced to say the Lord's Prayer. He might have said it would not harm them and might even be good for them. I would have exploded with a sharp retort. In that

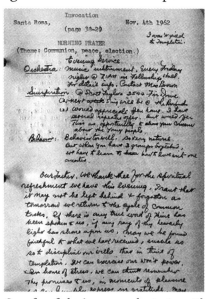

One of my father's sermons, beginning with a prayer.

same sermon, he explained that even in a pluralistic society, we must follow the historic American position: "In God We Trust." I would have pointed out that the first time "In God We Trust" was used it was on a penny in 1864, not when the United States was established. It took a while for those words to be added to a nickel, and much longer before they were added to a dollar bill. Trusting in God when it came to money matters did not make it a historic American position, I would have said. And the reason it supplanted E Pluribus Unum was because of McCarthyism fears. It was a Commie Pinko litmus test. If a man coughed in trying to get out the words "In God We Trust," he was un-American. It was adopted in 1956, only seven years before he gave his sermon, which was a rather brief amount of time to describe it as a "historic American position." The words "under God," were not added to the Pledge of Allegiance until 1954. Since I was born in 1952, I would have sarcastically asked if I was more historic than the Pledge of Allegiance. We would have argued about prayer and God in the classroom ad nauseum. Had he still been alive today, as a way to stay on speaking terms, I probably would have suggested that schools should give students a two-minute period of silence at the start of the day. They had the option of praying to whichever God they believed in, or they could meditate on peace, daydream, think about life goals, or listen to music through headphones. No establishment of religion, and no prohibition either.

How much would we have argued? Would a gulf of inharmonious beliefs have separated us?

I read his letters, his sermons, and his diaries, trying to find the father I loved and had believed was perfect. I was confronted with evidence that I had heavily edited my memories. Nearly all his writings were religious sentiments, scripture-like thoughts, all but the letters he sent to the Department of Justice when his and my mother's student visas had expired. In a letter to a close family friend who had received electroconvulsive therapy, he wrote about faith and mercy, but he did not inquire how she was feeling or where she might want to go when she was released from the hospital. He offered no help. It was simply the prayer. So little of his writing seemed spontaneous or—dare I say it?—personal and genuine. His diaries were passages from the Bible, a list of expenses, phone numbers, and appointment reminders to meet parishioners. He made one entry of my birth, and another entry years later that it was my birthday. But on subsequent birthdays, his calendar showed he had scheduled meetings on those evenings. If these papers had been the sum of what I knew about him, I would have concluded that he was sincere but lacked intimacy.

But then I read some of the eulogies given at my father's funeral. They included fond exaggerations, and also some misinterpretations, all of them harmless and kind. But he was there—the prankster, the charmer who always had a humorous aside, the father I had chosen to remember. When he was in the hospital, one person said, he took time to go to the children's wards to spend time with those who were crying. He went to strangers who looked out of place and made them feel welcome. The sermons he typed would not have included any of his spontaneous actions, remarks, and personal stories. They contained none of his humor. And yet, as many recalled, there was never a time when he did not leave them laughing.

When I finished reading those eulogies, I found nothing had been said about his relationship with his two younger children, John and me. He was admired for his devotion to my older brother, his dying son, and his steadfast love and gratitude for his wife. As an adult, I can understand why he and my mother chose to be with my older brother as much as possible, leaving little time for his healthy children. I would have been similarly consumed. I can also understand why he had to provide testimony of his faith to others—it was to make himself worthy enough to petition God to save his son. He had broken the Ten Commandments out of love for my mother. He neglected his other children out of desperation to undo what his adultery had wrought.

My father's last letter, written four months before he died, went to one of his closest friends, another minister. By then my father's damaged right brain made him unable to see the full width of the page. He wrote only on the right half of the page, which became increasingly narrow, as if to represent how diminished he was becoming. His once-beautiful handwriting was now uneven and spider-like. His ability to say things gracefully was gone. He lacked the beautiful words, which had enabled him to hide his feelings of terror. After his greeting, he expressed frustration over the complications of his care and his concern for his exhausted wife, whom he described as "my first true love." The second paragraph was heartbreaking:

> *On top of everything, we have "teenager" problems. Amy suddenly became unreasonably rebellious. Early in the morning, she'll read the newspaper for two hours never lift her small finger to help her mother. . . .*

His thoughts meandered into other areas, fears that he had always been a bad Christian:

> *For the last eighteen years of my ministry I was a hypocritical Pharisee, which Jesus hates. I could preach fervently about the love of God, but I seldom practiced what I preached. . . . I am so ashamed of myself I wished that I were dead to run away from guilty conscience.*

He then returned to his thoughts about me:

> *Amy's indeferent [sic] attitude probably is a result of my own negligence to provide her an act of sacrificial love of Jesus Christ.*

Still later, he added in the margin more thoughts on this:

> *Actually, this is an exposure of my failure to show her the love of God. Love never fails. Now it is not love that fails. It was me that failed.*

I felt terrible that this was among his last memories of me: a selfish, uncaring girl. What he had said was only partially true: I was rebellious. But that's because I was fifteen. And it is true that I *seemed* to be indifferent. But I was not. I could not bear what was happening and I had to withdraw. He should have understood that no fifteen-year-old should have to see death approaching every day. If he failed me, it was because he saw me through the eyes of a minister who had had no time to make an appointment to see me. He had forgotten how to be a father. I did not want him to show me the sacrificial love of Jesus Christ or the beliefs he found in scripture. I wanted his love, the one that had once protected me and scooped me up after I had fallen. I wanted the secret compatriot who comforted me when my mother went into a rage over a watermelon that had rolled off a table and broke. I wanted the father who believed I was smart enough to launch a solar-cell-powered rocket to the moon. That was the father I had already been losing even before he and my brother fell ill. I had been losing him to his ambitions as a minister, a student, and an inventor. When he died, I lost him in all ways possible. I lost the future of him seeing me change into a considerate and helpful daughter. I lost the chance to see his relief that I had chosen a kind man for my husband. I lost the chance for him to encourage me whenever I started a new job or a new novel, just as he had when I stood at the top of the slide, terrified, while he patiently called for me at the other end.

Those were my losses and they make me realize that he did show me enough love to want to exult in more of it with others. Among men, he was a great man. Among fathers, he was a great father. But I also realize this painful truth: he loved God far more than he loved me. He would have admitted that was true. He would have explained that we should all love God more because God's love for us was greater than what a mother and father could give. Having read his diaries and his sermons, I think his love of God was based more on fear of God. To fear God is to love God—that was what many evangelicals believe. He feared he had not loved God enough and that was why God was giving him trial after trial. He felt he had let God down. He asked for forgiveness. He renewed his faith after each crisis. When more crises came, he had to do more for God. He had

to be ambitious for God. But it was still not enough. God was taking his son. God took his son. God was taking him. I remember that
he asked aloud when he was ill, "God, why have you forsaken me?"
Others heard only the joke that he did not need to make peace with
God since they had never quarreled. They did not hear his doubts
and why he was afraid of God's wrath.

I would have told him fear of God wasn't love. It was also not
love that compelled an evangelical relative to tell my father he should
ask God to forgive him one more time for his sin in marrying my
mother. Fear was one of the last emotions my father felt while he was
still cognizant. How could I embrace a religion based on the notion
that eternal torment awaits those who have not become converts?
What about babies who die of malaria before they ever have a chance
to be saved? I posed the question to a Christian relative who believes
in boiling vats for the unsaved. "Unfortunately, the opening in the
door to heaven is very narrow," she said. Was my father also narrow-
minded about the exclusivity of heaven?

As my brother lay dying, my father's self-imposed desire to
please God and inspire his flock blinkered him. He did not understand I was flailing with fear and coping through numbness. I had
lost my brother and I had lost hope that God or doctors would save
my father. I was scared that I would soon have a bald head marred
with stitches, and would mew incoherently while being spoon-fed.
He was too busy appeasing his God to notice his daughter, except
when he was angry that I was doing nothing to help my mother. He
was too scared of God.

His fear did not turn me away from God. It made me reject the
notion that God must be constantly pleased and feared. If my father
were alive, I would try to talk to him in his framework of Christian-
ity. I would tell him that I can't worship a God who is synonymous
with prohibition and the threat of punishment. Fear, I think, is the
worst element of religions of all kinds. It is used to justify more fear,
as well as hatred, lack of compassion, intolerance, and war. My God
is not a deity I have to worship in any particular way. My God is
always there, I would tell him, wherever I am. It is a consciousness

greater than mine but also includes mine. It is the full knowledge
that love, joy, and peace are the same thing and it is in all of us. We
don't have to be better than someone else to have it. I would tell him
that I have experienced the fullness of it when I was able to lose fear,
preconceptions, and worries, and turn off the cogwheel that churns
out endless thoughts that are not important. I have had to let go and
be open to the mystery of love and how huge it can be. Love, peace,
and joy are somewhere in Christian doctrine as well. Just get rid of
the fear, I would say to him. Jesus died because of hatred. Did Jesus
really want people put in hell for not believing he sacrificed himself
for them? Isn't heaven really a metaphor about sharing the wonders
of love that unite us? I would ask if he truly favored the idea of an
exclusive pearly-gated community. Was his future in heaven more
important than the future of Earth and of the coming generations
who would live on it? Imagine more; obey less. That is what I would
tell my father if he were alive and still considering he might vote for
a candidate who promoted fear.

But now I realize I am giving my father short shrift. My father was
flawed, and he admitted it. But in all my memories and in everything
I read in his sermons, I never found any evidence of hatred or lack of
sympathy. He would not have abided by any position that required it.
Had he lived, he would have also experienced all the changes in the
United States for several more decades—the hundreds of ethnicities
who had come to live here, the plight of refugees, the new epidem-
ics, ethnic cleansing, and terrorism. We might have talked about the
Vietnam War and the peace marches, as well as the assassination of
Dr. Martin Luther King Jr., an American Baptist minister. He would
have been among those who mourned Dr. King's death and committed himself to fight racism. He would have been deeply moved by
the peaceful civil rights march. He would have praised those who
advocated for faith and kindness. I know he would have written a
sermon about immigrants, and as part of it, he would have told the
story of his and my mother's fears of being deported back to what
had become Communist China. He would have used humor to con-
vey his sentiments about a more-inclusive world: something about

the Tower of Babel and discordant voices, something about our need for an interpreter of all the languages so that we could hear what we had in common. He would have joked that he had a nephew for hire, an excellent simultaneous interpreter, and a Christian, to boot, who would probably give them a discount. He would have joked that when Jesus delivered the Sermon on the Mount, Chinese food was delivered and it was enough to feed the multitudes and put them in a peace-loving mood, because everyone loves Chinese food. I can easily imagine him saying all that.

We would have found common ground in most places. Like my mother, he would have met our friends who are Muslim, gay, lesbian, and transgender. Like my mother, he might have complimented some of our gay friends for having better relationships than many heterosexual couples they knew. He would have performed their wedding ceremonies. He would have written a revision to that sermon, "In God We Trust," to express his sadness that trust was a diminishing resource and suspicion of others was rising. I imagine we would have agreed on many concerns having to do with those who were impoverished and ill. He would have known that I have an incurable disease, and what might have happened to me if I had not had the means to get medical care.

I would thank him for giving me a foundation for thinking about meaning and compassion. His need to find meaning and to provide compassion led to the ministry. My need for meaning and to show compassion led to my writing stories.

There is only one issue that leaves me uncertain whether he would have voted as I did: a woman's right to chose. For many evangelical Christians, that was the single most compelling reason why they voted for a man who did not believe a woman should make her own decisions. For those people, none of the other concerns mattered, not even health care for those who would die without it. Would he have considered voting with a collective conscience that saw the multiple dangers of a drastically different order? Would he have voted based on the importance of the big picture, knowing he could continue to fight with others on specific concerns? I know of many Christians who voted for my candidate with that kind of conscience, my father's friends, for example.

And now I realize that I do know how he would have voted, and the reason that it would have been impossible for him to have voted any other way. My mother. I know what she felt about a woman's right to choose. She told me when I was twenty-eight. We were sitting in my car, about to go into a restaurant. As rain pelted the windshield, I told her I was upset because I had just learned I was pregnant and that this occurred sometime during a two-week vacation when I had been consuming alcohol—a bloody Mary in the morning, a margarita at night. At the time, I worked in the field of developmental disabilities, and babies were just then being diagnosed with a newly recognized congenital condition, "fetal alcohol syndrome." It was not yet clear how much alcohol might be damaging nor during which trimester it was consumed. What's more, neither Lou nor I had the financial means to raise a child. He was still in law school, and we depended on my meager income to survive. Because of my profession, I knew full well what attention and extra time would be required to raise a child with a disability. I knew what I would have to fight for. I confessed to my mother we were not even sure we wanted to have children. Lou's parents often hinted about their desire for grandchildren. We could not tell them that we felt no need to pass along our custom DNA. Lou and I had already agreed that if we changed our minds, we would adopt a child with special needs. But now I was six weeks pregnant, and I was forced to consider what to do.

My mother had remained completely silent as I spoke, and when I finished, she said in a calm voice: "If you want a baby, even if you are poor, nothing can stop you from caring for this baby. You will find a way." And then she said in a forceful tone, "But if you do not want a baby, no one—not your husband, not your mother-in-law, no one—can tell you that you must have this baby."

When she was married to "that bad man," she said, he tortured her and would not give her a divorce. He would not use birth control. He used her like a sex machine. He kept her pregnant every year. She had four children, and three abortions. "Only you can decide," she said to me. As it turned out, I did not have to decide. A few days later, I had a miscarriage. Having been caught between two choices, I felt a mixture of relief and sadness. But most of all, I felt grateful for what my mother had said. It was not just about my right to choose whether to have an abortion or a baby. It was about everything in life. I don't remember how old I was when she first told me that I was not equal to a man—that I was better.

She had also said that I had to be stronger than a man to make a man believe I was better. She told me many times, over many years, that I should never let anyone look down on me, and that I should never look down on anyone, either. I should refuse to let someone tell me who I was and who I could be. When she was married to "that bad man," she had had no choice but to "just take it." But I had a choice. I should not be afraid to stand up for my own mind. Although she thought my husband was a good man, she made him buy me a 24k gold bracelet. Gold was the currency of refugees. She informed my husband, with good humor, that his wife now had the means to leave him if he ever mistreated her. The bracelet was worth about $200, so I would not have gotten far, but we knew what she meant.

If my father had disagreed with a woman's right to choose, he would have had to endure my mother's arguments throughout the years: "So are you saying I was wrong and that bad man was right? Are you saying everything was my fault and I made you commit adultery? Are you saying you are better than me and you should decide my fate?"

His fear of God would have been overshadowed by his fear of my mother's anger. But he would not have voted entirely out of fear of either her or retribution from God. The fact is, he had always stood up for her—against her abusive husband, against his disapproving family, and against the selfishness of their daughter for not lifting a finger to help lighten her mother's burden. He would have acknowledged his responsibility in their affair and that their love and passion were mutual. They had pledged to be together through better or worse. There would have been no argument. They would have voted for better.

Reliable Witness

[From the journal]

AUSTIN, TEXAS, NOVEMBER 2008. *I realize over and over again that my journal writing is like a witness to the moments I've lived. When I read what I've noted, thought about, the words come as a surprise, something I would have forgotten, and often don't even re-member thinking. So to read them, I recapture them. Being present is the necessity of recording consciousness. I think of each moment as gone, and they are like little deaths, millions of little deaths be-fore physical death. Writing is the witness to myself about myself. Whatever others say of me or how they interpret me is a simula-crum of their own devising.*

I imagine an enterprising graduate student in Asian studies who has a premise, a theory, and uses the archive selectively to prove her/his point. I have never read an analysis of my work or me that reads as accurate. It's because they start off on the wrong path, have created the map and thereby see only those points and conclusions. There is no symbolic immortality to be had in giving one's archives to a library. It's perpetual misinterpretation. Who I was will have been missing since before I stepped off Earth's floor.

V

READING AND WRITING

Interlude

I AM THE AUTHOR
OF THIS NOVEL

I am the author of this novel, which is told by a first-person narrator, who is not me, as one particular reviewer suggested is the case. For one thing, I am not half-Alsatian, half-Cherokee. My mother is from Lichtenstein, my father from China. And I have not been married four times, only twice. I have sons not daughters, cats not dogs, a house on the seaside not the lakeside. And I do not smoke or take Ecstasy.

But in a deeper sense, the *story* itself *is* me, because its circular narrative drive, historical themes, and mythical imagery embody my patterns of thought and *my obsessions with the past*. But I am *not* the first-person narrator. I am the author who determined the *voice* of the narrator, which, by extension, is the voice of the entire narrative. By voice, I am not talking about voice quality—melodious, hoarse, foreign-accented, and so forth. Voice has more to do with a character's subconscious running over her conscious self, and her *observations* as that happens. The narrator unfolds the story naturally and seamlessly—however, to make that appear so, I have to use contrivance in an artful way, which is more difficult than the result would suggest. The voice also has to do with how much she *recognizes* herself as the story progresses. It is a cliché to have a narrator be completely oblivious to what the plot will turn on.

So, by voice, I mean more the *mind* of the character and her *identity*, how she perceives herself in the world she inhabits, and not what kind of job she has or how much money she makes or whether she is beautiful—although, in the case of this story, physical attributes do form a subtle narrative motif, especially when beauty around her is destroyed by an earthquake—the "Big One" everybody knew was coming but denied—which simultaneously marred her face, left it askew, because of plastic surgery with a shaky knife. It takes only a jiggle. The main point is: her mind is not *my* mind, and her identity is not *my* identity—except in that larger and deeper sense of *understanding* the difference between internal versus external identity—experienced especially among women of a certain era who subverted their identity to receive admiration in exchange for being cooperative and who then found themselves stuck in a Jell-O mold they had to wiggle their way out of. Similarly, our narrator is forced to struggle out of sticky situations due to her unexamined thoughts, beliefs, emotions, morality, and psyche as they relate to unorthodox sexual preferences. Where she is perhaps like me at a conceptual level is her confusion between intentions and rationale, which are issues I have wrestled over, and which I've embedded into my last two novels—that is, the self-governance and judgment of one's own morality when it comes to strong sexual desires for characters who have no morality or critical thinking.

As the author of seven novels, two off-Broadway plays, and six children's books, I have found that all stories have some degree of moral and political subtext—however, I don't take as my mantle Orwell's mission for why he writes, or, rather, wrote. If I wrote stories about the economics of war or apathy during repression, I might take on a more political angle and be consumed with that throughout the writing of the novel. But politics is not my oeuvre—and I am well aware that the heavy geopolitical themes are what committees for big literary prizes look for, as well as subjugation of mind by mass culture, which my novel touches upon. For some reason, the awards committees also like stories involving ships in the nineteenth century, with authentic descriptions of rigging, rust, wood rot, and such. We authors, however, must make a deliberate choice on what to write, based in part on what we wish to research. So, no despotism, no ships. In this novel, there is subtle moral interplay with the narrator's personal trauma as a child, her awareness of her former Alsatian beauty, her aberrant sexual desires, her secret ambitions to be an icon, and her racist attitudes. There is also her aggressive disregard of fashion, which ironically sets off a fashion trend, which she embraces a bit too willingly by justifying its benefit to society who wrongly look for identity in brand identity. Unlike me, the narrator can be a bit odd and self-unaware, but as a literary author, I know that it is essential to make a first-person narrator *likeable, yet flawed*. Thus, despite her compassion for Nepalese women, she remains unaware of her racist attitude toward white people, an attitude I certainly do not share. I felt, however, that it was critical for a literary novel to gently expose racism in good people, and that self-unawareness may be tied to moral intention that has been transformed by selfish justification over perverse sexual addictions. As should be apparent by now, there is a massive amount of crafting done to weave these curious intricacies, dark themes, and psychological complexities. It would be absurd for anyone to deconstruct strands into a checklist comparison chart to prove the author is the first-person narrator, as one particular reviewer has done. In one sense, I should be flattered that I created a story that felt so *authentic* he believed that to be the case. Had I put the story in third-person, there likely would have been no confusion.

At the same time, there is a point to be made about *universal epiphanies*, those moments when readers become the character, when they realize—*"Omigod! Yes!"*—and they cry or laugh or sing. In this novel, there is quite a bit of that. One reader reported to me that she cried fourteen times and quit psychotherapy. *Osmotic identification* with the story shows how anyone, not just the author, can become the character.

We are the character because we are immersed in the story's emotions, yet we know that we are not *the* character. I have never worked as a geologist in Lhasa, for example, nor have I started a cashmere-weaving cooperative in Nepal. My role was to originate the first-person narrator and all the rest— the narrative, the voice, the themes, the minor characters, their flaws, the trickiness of morals—they are all my invention, and at a higher conceptual level, the kind of stories I tell and the characters I choose do say something about the kind of person I am. From a conceptual point of view you might even say I am the narrative *consciousness*. Some have called it that, but that can lead to misremembering the term as *narrator*. And just to be clear, since I introduced a term potentially confusing to some reviewers, the first-person fictional consciousness is *not* me, unless you think my doppelgänger should get credit as a separate entity. And now, in just raising the rhetorical question, she evidently thinks she should be acknowledged.

So let me rephrase: I am the author of a novel told by a doppelgänger in possession of my thoughts, who inserts her subconscious into my subconscious, which is rather like being unaware that someone has deftly slipped her hands into mine. My hands are not the ones tapping the keyboard, although I still believe they are, and these words you are reading are entirely hers, which I still believe are mine.

CHAPTER NINE

HOW I LEARNED TO READ

In the fall of 1958, when I was six years old, a striking young woman came to our rented duplex apartment on Fifty-First Street in Oakland to discuss a serious matter with my mother and father. She and my parents sat in the living room, my parents on the tweed sofa and the lady in a matching armchair. My older brother, Peter, and I had just returned from school—he was in the third grade and I in the first. I was surprised to see my father there, since he should have been at work. Were we in trouble? It didn't seem so, since my parents were all smiles. The woman greeted me. I recognized her as the lady in nice clothes who had recently taken me out of the classroom and brought me into a small room to do puzzles.

My father told me to go outside and play with Peter. A little while later, I saw my parents standing at the door saying good-bye to the woman. When I came back in the house, my mother and father looked excited and happy. "We have good news," they said. The lady had just told them that I had done well on a test, especially in numbers. "She said you have what it takes to become a doctor—just like Peter." Peter was a genius. He could do anything. Later, as they continued to discuss my future, they added that I should choose to be a brain surgeon, because the brain was the most important part of the body, and that's why brain surgeons were the smartest and the most respected.

I remember being happy, yet confused, mostly because I had suddenly changed in their eyes into a much more pleasing child, one who made them proud, and not angry, as my mother often was with me. I had, in fact, been distressed that she always found fault in me, pointing out that I had not practiced the piano a full hour, or that I had not answered quickly enough when called, or that my hair was messy, or that I had not washed my hands, or that I forgot my sweater, or that I had not finished my rice, on and on. It was true that I was good with numbers. I knew how to count how many times my mother spoke sharply to me. Sometimes I would get through almost the whole day and think that maybe nothing bad would happen, only to find she was upset with me for some little thing, like not getting ready for bed fast enough. Looking back, her irritation may have had to do with her exhaustion in going to nursing school, and later, working part time while dealing with three active children. She was also often irritated with my father. But at six, I was sensitive to how my parents treated my brothers and me, and I had concluded that my mother simply did not like me anymore.

Now a miracle had happened. I was going to be a respected doctor. The pressure of expectations was immediate. I could never be as smart as Peter. How hard would I have to study to keep up? What would I do as a doctor? I had met a few of them. One particular doctor attended our church, and whenever my parents saw him, they made a point of greeting him with excessive praise. They would call us kids over. "This is Dr. Cheu," my father would say. "He's very important, respected by everyone. It's a great honor he's here because he's a very busy man." My brothers and I fell mute before such a god. There were other doctors I met at the hospital where my parents took me whenever I had a high fever or a sore throat. Back in those days, doctors never smiled and they did not welcome questions. My parents were always deferential. The doctor would make a pronouncement. "She has tonsillitis again." My parents would look guilty, as if their carelessness or lack of hygiene had caused this to happen. "She needs to have her tonsils removed," the doctor said one day. The next time I saw a doctor, he was wearing a mask, looking down at me, where I lay on a table in the operating room. Someone put a pouch near my nose, which blew cool air that smelled strong. And then I was waking up in excruciating pain, in a strange room with other crying kids. A nurse took away my doll and my throat hurt too much to protest. So that's what I thought of doctors when I was six. They were the harbinger of pain.

I had also met theologians at the divinity school where my father received his degree and was ordained as a minister. These men were also called "Doctor," but they were much friendlier than the ones in the hospital, and also much older—white haired and dressed in black robes. My father greeted them with familiarity, respect, and religious praise. We also knew two women who were called doctor, one being a friend of my mother from her Shanghai days, the other being much younger, the cousin or niece of a friend from China. The older woman and younger woman did not know each other, but by coincidence they both had doctorate degrees in physics. Even more unusual, they had both been raised in China as boys to compensate for their parents' disappointment that they were not. Out of habit, my mother said, they continued to wear men's clothes and kept their hair cut short. It was more comfortable, my mother explained. Neither of them ever married. We were taught to respect these women, but we were allowed to call them "Auntie," instead of "Doctor." My younger brother made the mistake of calling the older one "Uncle." Fortunately, my parents and the woman took this with good humor, and so my brothers and I continued to call her "Uncle" until we were older and required to be respectful. So those were the models for my future as a doctor: taciturn men, old sages in black robes, and mannish women.

Just because I was going to be a doctor, that didn't mean I no longer had to practice the piano, my parents told me. They still expected me to become a concert pianist. I could do both, my mother explained: be a doctor five days a week and play concerts on the weekends. At age six, the choices had been made. It was final. I had been sentenced to an immigrant parent's dream.

I recently found the house on Fifty-First Street in an online real estate listing. It was as I remembered it: a two-flat clapboard building painted in delicious Girl Scout–cookie colors of mint green and chocolate brown trim. It was the fifth home I had had since birth. Sudden change and upheaval were the norm for my parents, as they were for anyone who had gone through a world war, a civil war, and a love affair.

Our family lived in the downstairs flat—my parents, brothers Peter and John, and me. My mother's half brother, my uncle Joe, his wife, and four children lived upstairs. They had emigrated the year before from China and had gone from fabulous wealth, prestige, and privilege to being just another poor immigrant family, unaccustomed to being treated as illiterates suitable for only menial labor. During their first two years, they depended on my parents to help them adjust to an English-speaking world. I can imagine the horrors my mother laid out to her young sister-in-law, a testament to her own suffering: *You think the American dream is better than the life you had in China? No such thing. When I came here, I learned the hard way. I had to clean not only my own house but also the house of a messy old lady who dribbled food everywhere. She paid me twenty-five cents an hour to break my back. Today we just get by. I have no money to buy luxuries. I watch every penny. I write down everything I spend. One dollar fourteen cents for groceries—write that down. Ten cents for Popsicles—write that down. One dollar for gas—write that down. You have to wear the same clothes you brought from China until they fall off your shoulders in shreds.*

My mother probably spelled out her humiliations, which she took as far worse than poverty. *They treat you like you're dumb. Even if I speak English, people say they do not understand me. If you don't like it, they say, go back to China. You think it's easy here in America? You have to swallow a lot of bitterness and thank people for giving it to you. That's how you survive.* Those were the sorts of things I heard my mother

say over the years. She was proud to have endured so many hardships over the years. Her skin was tough. Her eyes saw the situation
clearly. Her sister-in-law was still naive and tears would follow.

The door on the right side of the duplex went into our flat, and
the one on the left went to the flat upstairs. There was a small patch
of lawn in front and the rest of the landscaping was easy-care concrete, which only required yanking out a few weeds that grew in the
cracks. The bay window of our living room faced the street. But the
rest of the flat lay in the shadow of a building that was only about ten
feet way. A dank-smelling gutter and strip of grass was all that separated us from our neighbors. Remembering this now, I'm puzzled
why my mother chose to live downstairs, where we were not only
deprived of sunlight but also subjected to the thumps and stomps
of our busy relatives above us. Perhaps my mother did not want to
worry that her three children might acquire brain damage from falling down a steep flight of stairs, which we had done multiple times
in the last two houses and always with dramatic bloody effect. Or
maybe she wanted easy access to the shed next to the concrete patio,
where she did the laundry. She had a washing machine; the dryer
would come later. Once, for fun, we helped her hand crank the wash
through the wringer and hang it on a tree-shaped web of clothes-
lines. Then it was no longer fun. In China, she had had servants
who cooked, cleaned, drove the car, and did the laundry. I did not
know about her pampered life at the time. She never talked about her
past. She must have reminded herself many times that her children
would become successful and make up for the deprivations she suffered. Her daughter would become a neurosurgeon and would make
enough money to take care of her in her old age.

By 1958, our family was eking our way toward one day becoming
middle class. We had acquired some of its symbols, the nonessential
luxuries, like a piano and TV set. My mother had received her license
to work as an X-ray technician and quickly found a better-paying job.
My father worked in a manufacturing factory as an engineer, and he
did God's work by serving as a guest minister at churches where the
regular pastors were on vacation. The neighborhood we had moved

to was more convenient than the last; the candy store was two blocks away, the school was just beyond that, and the library was two blocks in the other direction. Our home was perfect, according to a child's point of view. My parents had a small bedroom and my brothers and I shared the bigger one in back, where we slept in bunk beds. The TV was in the living room, which was a little inconvenient because we could not watch it when one of us had to practice the piano. The kitchen was the largest room and served as the heart of our home. On one side were the fridge and grooved counter that sloped toward the sink. The stove lay across from that, as did a longer counter and built-in cupboard with doors, which I was tall enough to open. That was where we kept the box of Wheaties we ate for breakfast when we did not have Chinese rice porridge. We ate at a chrome and yellow Formica table with six matching chairs. A small sepia portrait of Jesus hung on the wall. His blue eyes were aimed upward toward Our Heavenly Father, and at every meal, we murmured the same prayer to him all in one breath: "Bless Oh Lord this food we are about to receive and keep us ever mindful of the needs of others, in Jesus Christ, Amen." We always had six chairs at the table; the empty one was for "Christ, the unseen guest at every meal." Christ also watched Peter and me do our homework there. He watched my father write his guest sermons. He watched my mother study to get her license as an X-ray technician. He had watched my little brother make all kinds of messes with crayons and crumbly food. That table was a hub of immigrant industry.

During Chinese and American holidays, my mother and aunt would layer the table with Chinese newspapers, then set a wooden cutting board on top, and that's where they sat and talked as they gutted fish and pulled out black intestines from the backs of shrimp. They sliced slivers of gingerroot, pickled radish, and garlic. They rolled out perfect circles of dough for dumplings. My mother spoke Mandarin with my father, but she and my aunt gossiped and argued in Shanghainese, and often at high volume. Meals were endless anticipation, mess, and tension. When it was time to cook, my mother spread newspapers on the floor by the stove to catch any beads of oil that popped out when damp vegetables hit the hot pan. She abhorred grease, but you could hardly tell the difference between clean and filthy on that kitchen floor. The linoleum was a wreck in progress—cracked, scuffed, warped, and coming apart at the seams. The floor under the stove and sink, as well as the curved moldings in corners were blackened with a shellac of grease that had built up and hardened over decades of bad housekeeping. Those greasy dark corners served as the hiding spot for "ugly bugs." Likely they were cockroaches. My mother's limited English vocabulary included flies, spiders, and ants, but not all species of bugs that skittered across the ugly linoleum or marched in single file up walls. I can imagine her yelling to my aunt in Shanghainese: "Over there! Use your slipper to kill it." Then she would have made my aunt go outside to clean her slipper. Killing bugs was another humiliating task you had to do as an immigrant.

The rats also liked the kitchen, as well as our bedroom. Our floors, it seemed, were one big welcome mat to vermin. They chewed through the baseboard next to our bunk beds and also through the wall next to the kitchen sink. The holes were big enough for Peter and me to put our fists through. We had already seen what a rat could do. One had climbed up to the counter next to the stove and tunneled through an entire loaf of Kilpatrick's bread, heel to heel, leaving only frames of crust. My mother mashed up what remained, rolled that into balls, and stuck a bit of meat inside—tiny pigs in a blanket for rats. Our father, the defender of fingers and toes, showed us how to set this tasty food offering on a trap so that when that rat took his first bite it would be his last. He placed the traps by the sink and stove. We were excited to see what would happen to our bread thief. What we saw that night was a lesson in cruelty. I don't think any parent should ever express delight when showing a child the crushed body of a creature with bugged-out eyes and blood running out of its mouth and nose. Our parents assured us that we now had nothing to worry about. But the rats continued to pay us visits. One day my father found a hole in the grassy strip between our house and our neighbor's. He pushed a hose into the tunnel as far as it would go and let the water run for hours. I pictured in my mind's eye a vast cavern below with desperate rats swimming hard to keep their whiskers dry. Whatever happened, the rats did not call on us after that.

If my mother were still alive, she would probably recount many more horrors than just grease, bugs, and rats. She would have told you all the reasons she wanted to move to another house, a clean one, sooner rather than later. She also would have said it was only for the sake of the children that she was willing to endure that awful place longer than she wanted. Our family couldn't move to a new house until Peter and I completed the remaining school year.

M y school was a Gothic brick building with massive double doors that opened into a long, hard-tiled hallway. I can still see it. The ceiling was as high as the one in our church. The windows, doorways, chalkboards, and display cases were wood framed. My desk was wooden as well, marred with indentations from decades of students forcefully copying their handwriting exercises. The once stiff pages of books about Dick, Jane, and Sally had become as floppy as cloth and were flecked with dried snot. My class, including myself, comprised the multiple ethnicities of lower-income neighborhoods: black, Hispanic, Chinese, Japanese, and white.

Shortly after the school year started, the principal walked into the classroom with a lady and introduced her to our teacher. The lady was younger than the principal, but she carried the aura of someone more important. The principal treated her in the deferential manner my parents showed when meeting doctors. Yet the principal called her "Miss," which was probably a reason I thought she was young. Something about her look was special—not like a famous movie star—more like the models in the "better dresses" section of the Sears Roebuck catalog. She was slender and taller than the teacher. Her jacket and slim skirt were nicer than the principal's outfit, and much nicer than the dress the teacher wore. Her hair was short, but not in the mannish style of my mother's physicist friends from Shanghai. I would describe it now as being similar to Audrey

Hepburn's chic 1950s pixie hairstyle. That was the lady who would later visit my parents in our living room.

The principal said something private to the teacher and the teacher called my name and told me to go with the lady in the suit. I was surprised, and a bit tentative at first. She did not explain why I had been singled out. It was clear, however, that I was not in trouble. In fact, since the lady seemed important, by going with her, some of her importance fell like fairy dust onto me. The lady took me to a windowless room, big enough for only a small table and two chairs facing each other, one for her, one for me. I do not recall how she explained what the test was for. In fact, I doubted she used the word *test*. I imagine she said we were going to do different kinds of puzzles. She broke a paper seal and opened a booklet of perhaps twenty fresh-smelling pages with pictures. She told me to choose a word that described the picture. If I did not know, I should just move to the next one. She left the room. At first, the games were easy. But after a while, I did not know the answers. I might have guessed at a few. After fifteen minutes, the lady returned and took that booklet away, then gave me a new one and explained what I should do with the next set of puzzles. I don't remember anymore the contents of those tests, only the feelings of shame that I did not know the answer. There were more booklets, more puzzles. At the end of all the tests, the lady said we were done and she thanked me. I returned to the classroom and found that the teacher now treated me differently. When we took turns reading, she had me go last, and when she did, it was as if she knew I would read it the right way. She praised me for pronouncing the words correctly and for saying them with great expression.

Sometime after that, the woman visited my parents, and that was the day my parents said I was smart enough to become a doctor. Later in the school year, I was surprised to find that the woman had come to our classroom again. She took me to the same small windowless room. By then, I knew that these puzzles and guessing games were actually some kind of test and it mattered that I do well. For the next five years, she would come visit me at the beginning of the school year and at the end before the summer recess. Since we moved often, she must have had to do a bit of detective work to track me down. In the second grade, she followed me to a school in Hayward. In the third grade, it was a school in Santa Rosa. In the fifth, it was in Palo Alto. Each time I left the classroom, I felt proud. Each time I returned, I felt I had let her down and it worried me that she was discovering I was less smart with each passing year. Perhaps she regretted saying too quickly that I was smart enough to become a doctor. I worried that my parents would find this out. In 1964, at the end of the fifth grade school year, she told me we were finished with our work together and that she would no longer see me. I felt sad. We had had a bond based on my knowing what she had wanted me to do. Being singled out twice a year had made me special in front of others.

That was supposed to be the end of my vignette about a parent's hope and a child's worry over something a mysterious lady said fifty-nine years ago. But as a result of writing about this memory, I started thinking about those tests from a more objective point of view than the painful one of yesteryear. In the absence of facts, I recalled as much as I could about the woman, the little rooms, and the tests. At one time, I knew her name and it was frustrating that the grease on the kitchen linoleum is still there, but the name of someone who had unknowingly played a major role in how I would see myself was now nameless—Miss Somebody, whose last name had fallen into a mishmash pile of seldom used and now lapsed facts.

Based on everything I could remember about her—her clothes, the way the principal treated her, and her no-nonsense demeanor—she clearly had to have been a trained professional in education or research, and that being the case, it was unlikely that a professional would have made a prediction about a child's future based on a single test. That would have been irresponsible. The woman I met on those ten occasions never talked to me about my future. She never even said that I was particularly good at numbers compared to other skills. When I was with her, she did not step out of the boundaries of the task at hand. She did not exclaim over how well I did on a specific portion of the test or that I should try harder in other areas. She never mentioned that I might become a doctor. In fact, she did not seem the kind of person who would have remarked on anything personal— like "My, how tall you've grown," or "Your dress is so pretty." The woman I remember was friendly, but not overly warm. She would have said, "Do as many questions as you can. But don't worry if you do not know an answer." When she said we would no longer meet, she did not seem sad. So what had she said to my parents that would have made them think I was going to be a doctor? I imagine now my father saying to her with good humor: "So does the test result mean she will become a doctor or a bum?" I can imagine the young woman answering vaguely to remain professional, "She can grow up to be whatever she wants to be." To my parents' way of thinking, whatever I wanted to be was whatever they wanted me to be. That's how I think it went, something like that.

But now an obvious question emerges: Why had I been given that test in the first place? Why not the other students in that class-room? It might have been that the teacher chose me as a student who would be cooperative. Yet that would not answer why I was tested not just once, but ten times and in different schools over the years. I was likely part of a longitudinal study of some sort, and perhaps something to do with minority children in low socioeco-nomic urban areas. I would have qualified on both counts: rats in the kitchen, greasy linoleum, and my mother and aunt arguing loudly in Shanghainese. I guessed that the study might have related to racial bias in IQ tests. Those tests were starting to be criticized for being advantageous to the white middle class. Extrapolating from there, I figured that a study to correct racial bias would have involved a large pool of students and would have been conducted by a team of people. The young woman who saw me yearly was probably one of many research assistants. Or perhaps she was a doctoral student, do-ing research with a handful of kids for her thesis. That made sense. She might have been working on her doctorate when I first saw her. When she finished, she no longer had to see me.

I had come up with a reasonable hypothesis, yet I couldn't stop thinking about the woman and the tests. They had steered the course of my life. If you bound those booklets together they'd be part of a bildungsroman of my self-esteem. I exaggerate only slightly. It occurred to me I might be able to find clues about the study by searching the Internet. It was a long shot. Fifty-nine years had passed, and if the study had been for, say, the young woman's doctoral thesis, there would likely be no record of that. I chose what I thought were the best search words: "longitudinal IQ study Oakland first grade 1958."

In milliseconds, the first item to appear was this:

CHILDREN WHO READ EARLY,
TWO LONGITUDINAL STUDIES, 1966
". . . by D Durkin—1966—Cited by 1305—Related articles
The first study, begun in September 1958, was based on a sample drawn from 5003 first graders in Oakland, California . . ."

Children Who Read Early

Dolores Durkin

TEACHERS COLLEGE PRESS

Dolores Durkin—that was her name. Of course. For five years, I called her Miss Durkin. She was Dolores Durkin of Teachers College, Columbia University, and she could have correctly been addressed as "Dr. Durkin" in 1958, since she already had her doctorate. That accounted for the respect shown by the principal and teacher. And I was right that the test was given as part of a longitudinal study—but it was not about IQ, race, or socioeconomic group. In 1958, the Oakland School District screened 5,003 children entering the first grade and identified 49 kids who had already learned to read. Decades after taking that test, I finally knew why I had gone into those windowless rooms. I could read.

I was dumbfounded. The test had nothing to do with being smart enough to become a doctor. The child in me felt sickened by the deception. It was far worse than discovering Santa Claus was my Chinese father. This lie had followed me throughout my life. As a child, I had never questioned my parents' report of their meeting with Miss Durkin. I had not rebelled against their expectations, not openly. And it would serve as my template for both success and failure throughout childhood. As time went by, I was certain that the test result had been wrong. My IQ was not as high as had been reported. I would fail the expectation. I thought about that test whenever my report card showed I had done better in math than in English. I thought about it when a girl in my class, who was younger than I was, received a better report card. I thought about that test when I was twelve and a girl who was ten and very smart said with great confidence that she was going to be a doctor. I thought about that test when a neurosurgeon told us that Peter had a brain tumor. I thought about it when another neurosurgeon five months later told us my father had a brain tumor. I thought about it when I graduated from high school a year early, at age seventeen, and went to college, where I finally had the courage to drop out of pre-med at the end of my first year. I chose instead to major in English literature because I loved to read. When I told my recently widowed mother I was not going to be a doctor, she was disappointed but she did not fall to pieces. By then, many things in life had failed her. I promised I would get a doctorate instead. Later I thought about that test when I decided to quit the doctoral program in linguistics at UC Berkeley, ending my chances to be called "Dr. Tan." I thought about that test once more when I received an honorary doctorate and was finally able to hand my mother the diploma, giving her the chance to call me "Dr. Tan." By then, she took it all with good humor. She was exceedingly proud of my accomplishments and I had also fulfilled her immigrant dream. I had bought her a house.

I have continued to be influenced by that former expectation with every book I have ever written—when I realized at the end of writing it that it was not the book I had hoped to write. I have thought about it whenever someone showers me with praise and cites all kinds of pie-in-the-sky beliefs about my abilities. I go instantly deaf. I feel sickened by grandiose expectations. I would rather disappoint people immediately than carry the burden of their false preconceptions. Miss Durkin's test has been with me for fifty-nine years. And now, to know that all she was interested in was the fact that I could *read* would have been hilarious if I had not suffered so much from the lie. My parents likely thought it was harmless. Why not tell her she'll be a doctor to give her some motivation? They did not think of the consequences.

I have never lacked for persistence. I have been faulted for it. I have wasted much time in my life being persistent about things that ultimately do not matter. This time persistence led to my finding an out-of-print copy of Dolores Durkin's 1966 book, *Children Who Read Early*. I had so many questions, among them: Why were there only forty-nine children who could read at the start of the first grade? Today it seems every two-year-old is capable of using a cell phone to send text messages. The answer was both simple and stupid: In the 1950s, parents were strongly advised to *not* let their children read before the first grade. Leave it to the experts to teach kids to read—that was the common wisdom. Those children who were taught early through incorrect methods might have difficulties when they were exposed to proper methods, and, as a result, those kids could wind up with permanent learning problems. The school districts sent this warning to parents when they enrolled their children in kindergarten. The kindergarten teachers reiterated the same warning to parents who came to school meetings. Compliance was high. The parents must have been scared into thinking their kids would become lifetime bed wetters if books were left lying around the house. Of those 5,003 children, the parents of 4,954 had obeyed, and it took the tenacity of Miss Durkin to ferret out 49 children whose parents had not adequately guarded against the joys of reading. The reason for Dolores Durkin's study, however, had not been to police ambitious parents, but to discover whether early reading did in fact harm children, as educators had claimed it would. She wanted to know exactly what effect early reading had over the long term—say, by the time a child completed the fifth grade. Was it harmful, harmless, or beneficial? What she found in her landmark study changed the way early reading was viewed in schools across America. Early reading, in fact, did not harm kids at all. In a nutshell, it could help, especially among kids who were disadvantaged by IQ or socioeconomic circumstances. Her work overturned a lot of preconceptions about early reading. It placed the emphasis on reading readiness as indicated by a child's curiosity in words and scribbling. I was proud that I had unintentionally played a part in her findings.

As I read more about her study, my eyes hopscotched over data breakouts. I was somewhere in those columns. There was a tally of racial groups. Half of the 49 children were almost evenly divided between "Negro" and "Oriental." The other half were Caucasian. Other columns showed the number of monolingual versus bilingual families; mine would have been in the latter category. If you counted arguments and gossip in Shanghainese, we were a trilingual family. Most of the families were in the lower-middle or upper-lower socioeconomic class. Seven families were considered to be upper middle class and they were Caucasian, which was not surprising, considering that only ten years earlier nonwhites could not rent or own a house above Shattuck Avenue. The nonwhites were in the flatlands of Oakland. I wondered how our family had been ranked? Clearly we were not upper middle. But were we considered poor? And the house we lived in—if not for the rats and cracked linoleum, would it have been seen as a decent place to live? Would my father's education and profession have affected how Miss Durkin had designated our social status? My past lay within those columns of data breakouts on race, IQ, reading skill level, and social status. I was there, climbing up or down those ladders of numbers and percentages.

I came across a section related to the interviews Miss Durkin had conducted with the parents of the 49 early readers. Here was the reason she had been in our living room. The parents had been asked to choose from a list the traits that applied to their kids. I felt as if I had found a time capsule of my past whose contents were still partially obscured by a code. How did my parents describe me? Did they say I was "affectionate"? Thirty-five parents described their child as "persistent." My parents must have said that about me. I can imagine them bragging:

"Once she starts reading, you can't get her attention back for anything else. It's really a problem."

Or, "Once she starts playing the piano, she can't stop for at least an hour."

Or, "Once she learned five colors, she wanted to learn more, and that's why we had to buy her a box of sixty-four crayons for her fourth birthday."

I went down the list of other characteristics, imagining how my parents might have described me, likely overestimating my positive qualities. Twenty parents had described their child as "perfectionistic," sixteen as "high-strung," fifteen as having a "good disposition," fifteen as "serious," thirteen as "neat," and eleven as a "worrier." Had my parents known I was a worrier? If they had, they would have probably taken that as a good trait. If you didn't worry, that meant you did not care how well you did or how tired your mother might be or whether your little brother was missing. I wondered if they had described me as "eager to please adults."

In another chapter, Miss Durkin described in more detail the case studies of five families. I quickly glanced at the names of the students. I was not among them. I read the first two, and when I got to the third, the case of an Oriental female named Susan, I came across this sentence: *The mother was especially interested in the musical education of her children, although she said she "learned early that children can't be forced to like music."*

Miss Durkin had masked the names of all the kids and their parents. Of course she had. She was a professional. I was Susan, whose family she had categorized as "lower middle class." My reading level did not seem that high for an early reader, barely past first grade. And then I discovered Miss Durkin chose to include only five interviews out of the forty-nine based on those cases representing the highest and lowest in reading achievement. I was one of the lowest. I felt the shame of a child seeing she had received a D— on her report card. I

had barely been literate enough to be part of the study. I wasn't reading Shakespeare at age six. It was probably more on the order of:
"Ducky go quack-quack." I found some solace, however, when I saw
that my reading level at the end of the study was among the highest.
I definitely qualified for "most improved." When I saw the IQ score,
I was again stunned. It was not a bad score, but it would not have set
off casino bells ringing to announce, "Folks, we have a sure winner
here—neurosurgeon!" It was actually lower than the score I received
on a later IQ test. So which was correct? Neither. All the tests I have
ever taken in childhood had proven meaningless. I was a poor test
taker. I never chose what appeared to be the obvious answer. That
was a trick. They all said I excelled in math. They recommended a
career in science. Not one recommended I choose a career that might
depend on my facility with the English language.

As I started to read the interview, I felt as if I were in that living
room from fifty-nine years ago, watching and listening, as both an
innocent six-year-old child and an adult fortified with hindsight. I
pictured my parents sitting stiffly on the sofa leaning forward. Miss
Durkin would have been sitting erect in the armchair taking notes.
My father did almost all the talking, her report said. She informed
them right away that she was interested in finding out how I had
learned to read. But first she needed some background on my parents. My father said he was *"just beginning a year of postgraduate studies
at a divinity school"* and that he was *"a Protestant minister, and had taken
the year off for further study."* I reread those sentences several times. My
father *had* been a minister—until my mother's complaints of poverty
led him to resign in 1954 so that he could earn more money working
as an engineer, his former occupation in China. But there was no
way that he could have taken a year off. My mother's income would
not have been enough to support us. Why had he lied? There was no
shame in saying that he had a B.S. in physics and a B.A. in theology.
He had turned in his master's thesis in theology and was waiting for
it to be accepted. But he did not need to take time off from work to
wait for the mail to arrive with good news. What's more, being an
electrical engineer was hardly a tumble down in status from being

the minister of a small church in Fresno. I knew my father's future better than he did when he gave his answers in that interview: He would always work full-time as an engineer. He would carry that desire for more advanced degrees by studying for his master's degree in Engineering. He would be one semester short of completing it when he died.

The rest of the interview was just as puzzling to me. From the start Miss Durkin was stymied in getting information about me from my parents. To nearly every question, my parents sidestepped the questions and bragged instead about Peter. They praised the experts for advising they not teach their kids to read. Even though Peter was curious about words and knew the alphabet, they did not encourage him. Sure enough, when he started the first grade, he easily learned to read the proper way. Peter, they bragged, was "a very precocious child." Whenever she tried to redirect the questions back to my reading abilities, my father continued to extoll Peter's intelligence. I read with both a child's heart and an adult one, as the fullness of his love for me diminished with each boast about my brother. I fought hard to hang on to the belief that I had been his favorite. I recalled his story of being pulled over by a policeman because he had been weaving down the freeway, marveling over my newborn face. I remembered how much he liked to take photos of me. We used to do word games together. We had many special moments together, just the two of us. Didn't we? What were they? But then I also recalled what I found when I read his diaries recently, searching for mention of me. He recorded that I had been born. He included my weight: 9 lbs. 11 ounces. He recorded my length: "22-1/2." On future birthdays, the page was blank.

My father continued to assure Miss Durkin that he and my mother had done nothing to encourage me to read. I could have vouched that he was telling the truth. We did not own children's books. Our bookshelves were limited to Bibles, books on theology, favorite sermons of Billy Graham, nursing books, and the like. Fortunately, my father's boasts about Peter eventually gave Miss Durkin the information she sought. When Peter started the first grade, he brought home his schoolwork—words he had printed on lined paper. I was four and fascinated with what he had done on the paper. So I would copy the words he had written then ask him, "What do these say?" He did not mind. We often played together. And one of our games was to play school. When I made a mistake, Peter corrected me. My father said that [Amy] *"did not seem to mind the chastisement"*—because I had always respected my brother.

My father mentioned that Peter had also taught his cousins from China how to read by setting up a classroom in the living room. I was allowed to watch. I remembered that. I had tried to teach the cousin closest to me in age how to say Chinese words in English. When he made a mistake, I slapped his hand with a slipper. Miss Durkin's summary of the interview ended with this observation: *Here again, he mentioned that he always kept in mind what [Peter's] kindergarten teacher had said about the inadvisability of parents teaching their children to read, and that he did not want to be the cause of any "school problems" for [Amy].* Methinks he doth protest too much. Why had he been concerned enough to mention that three times?

There had been other reading lessons, I later realized, which no one had considered. They were the piano lessons that started when I was five. I had learned that the letters *C, D, E, F, G, A, B* on a page stood for specific piano keys on a scale and that these corresponded to the sounds those keys made. Those keys were written as musical notes that looked like tadpoles on a sheet of paper. I had learned the symbols for treble and bass clefs, sharps and flats. I could read numbers over the notes—*1, 2, 3, 4, 5*—that corresponded to the fingering—where my thumb and fingers went as I played. The piano lessons, like my brother's instruction, had clearly figured into how I had learned to read.

But all along there had been another reason I was motivated to read. My father stated what it was and didn't even know it.

The father said his daughter had always been a "scribbler, and that even before the age of four she had enjoyed drawing pictures and making up stories about them . . . Her imagination was amazing."

I cried when I read that. I read it repeatedly as balm over the earlier wound. If he knew this about me, that meant he had looked at my drawings and had listened to my stories, enough to believe my imagination was amazing. I marveled over these facts of me as a child.

I liked to draw pictures and make up stories about them. Or maybe it was the other way around. I made up stories in my head and then drew pictures of them. No one taught me to do this. Before the age of four, when pictures and stories are inseparable, I drew stories. That was the nature of my imagination.

I opened a box of memorabilia that contained my parents' documents. I found my parents' proof of college degrees, their student visas, references attesting to good characters, admission letters from colleges, the results of tuberculosis tests, and frequent exchanges between my father and a man named A. Kuckein, chief of the Entry

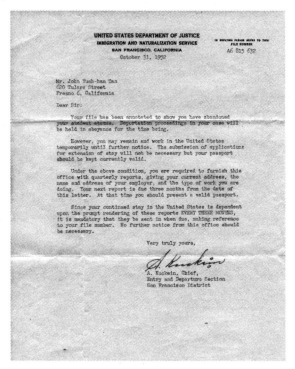

1952: One letter of a dozen concerning my parents' illegal status.

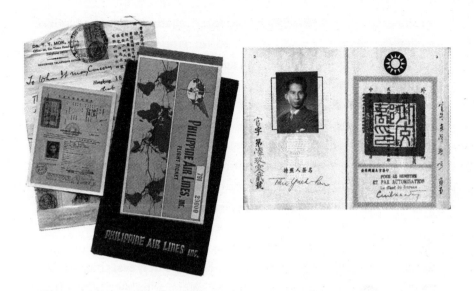

and Departure Section of the Immigration and Naturalization Service with the United States Department of Justice. The letters between them began in 1951 and concerned the extension of his and my mother's student visas, the expiration of the same, the cancellation of passports, their illegal status, the temporary suspension of deportation, my father's inquiry on how to meet the requirements to avoid deportation and enter the path to naturalization as an American citizen, and Mr. Kuckein's cool response that matters pertaining to illegal residency had to first be addressed before any consideration of citizenship should even be considered. I saw another document my father had prepared and signed on June 5, 1958, not long before his meeting with Miss Durkin. Next to it was an Application to Adjust Immigration Status Under Section 6 of the Refugee Relief Act of 1953. The address my father indicated was that of our apartment on Fifty-First Street. On that same sheet of onionskin paper, my father had detailed his education, starting with his B.S. in physics in 1939 and then a B.A. in theology in 1951, followed by a B.D. in theology in 1952, which had led to his being ordained as a minister. And then I saw it: his postgraduate work, the master's in Theology, which he said he would receive when he turned in his thesis in September 1958. His reason to remain longer was based on his obtaining a master's degree. His student visa had become invalid because he was no longer a student.

These exchanges with A. Kuckein were a history of terror, desperation, and ingenuity. I had discovered the reason why my father had lied to Miss Durkin about his year off from work as a minister, and why he had deflected questions pertaining to my learning to read. They were illegal aliens, in jeopardy of being deported. And they had broken the rules by failing to stop me from reading. Miss Durkin had come to the house, sat in their living room, and asked questions that she thought would be informative. And even though she had promised that the interview was strictly confidential, she could not have known that my parents would be wary of saying anything that might give A. Kuckein evidence that they were the kind of people who disobeyed the law. That was why my father had repeated three times that they knew the rule and had adhered to it. That's why they avoided talking about me and my ability to read.

My persistence took me one step further. I wanted to reach Miss Durkin to express my gratitude that her interview had given me a window into my parents' hopes for me and our family. I also wanted to tell her I had become a writer. My search led to the obituary notices of many women named Dolores Durkin. They had been housewives, devoted mothers and grandmothers, but not educators with a Ph.D. I searched through articles about Miss Durkin and there were many, but no mention of her personal life or where she lived or whether she had died. I looked into ancestry records and found a Mary Dolores Durkin who was from Illinois. She would be eighty-six. I found that someone named Mary Dolores Durkin had received her Ph.D. from the University of Illinois in Urbana-Champaign. She had also been on the faculty at the University of California at Berkeley in 1958. I searched through address records for Dolores Durkin in suburbs of Chicago. I eliminated many because the age did not correspond. I found some that were possible, but no one named Dolores Durkin lived there now. I contacted her former colleagues who had presented papers on her and wrote to students who had written biographies on her. I looked for people named Durkin on Facebook. I put out a notice on my Facebook page that I wanted to contact Dolores Durkin, an educator. And when I thought I had exhausted all possibilities, I stopped looking.

Months later, after I had abandoned my search, I spotted a message on my Facebook page. Dolores Durkin, she said, was alive and still as sharp as a tack. She gave me information on how I might reach her.

The image of Miss Durkin was before me. I had put together the pieces of my childhood after chasing down so many half-truths, and I had a vague anxiety that I would learn something unexpected that would again put my understanding of my childhood into havoc. It took me two weeks before I had the nerve to call.

A woman answered in a voice that was surprisingly young-sounding. There was no wobble in her vocal cords, as there often is with older people, no uneven pitches or weakness in volume, no whistling or lisping sounds typical of dentures. Her voice was clear, although slightly impatient with my stumbling explanation. "Dr. Durkin," I began. "My name is Amy Tan, and I'm calling because I was one of the original forty-nine students in 1958. I read your landmark study and I know how important your work has been."

When I stopped babbling, she said, "I remember the study, of course, but I don't remember you. I've worked with so many students over the years." *But I was one of the first forty-nine,* I wanted to say. I told her I was proud to have been part of her study and that I had become a writer. "I'm not surprised," she said. "You were an early reader."

And then I told her about that day when she met with my parents in the living room, what my parents had said afterward, that I would be a doctor, and how it had affected me through childhood, even into adulthood. Before I could continue, she broke in. "I never said anything of the kind. That's not what the study was about. It was about early reading." I assured her that I knew that, because I had read her research and her book. I explained that my parents had used that opportunity to express their hopes that I would become a doctor. "Well, they shouldn't have," she said emphatically. "That was wrong. You were an early reader and that's what mattered. That's why you became a writer."

She had said exactly what I needed to hear.

Splayed Poem: The Road

[From the journal]

FEBRUARY 2012. *Working to figure out the sense of a character, I took down a book of poems from the shelf above my head, Walt Whitman's* Song of Myself. *On the first splayed page, this:*

> *Not I, nor any one else can travel that road for you,*
> *You must travel it for yourself.*
>
> *It is not far, it is within reach,*
> *Perhaps you have been on it since you were born, and did not know,*
> *Perhaps it is everywhere on water and on land.*

Like apparitions, the words appeared, as if summoned. And I understood: This is what the character is about. No, more than that: This is what my writing is about. This is what my whole life is about. It is the loneliness of never fully sharing the truth of who I am because I have not yet found it, yet know only that the words will be inadequate. Words, private not public, are all I have to give in exchange for understanding what I think, the totality of what I've felt. I've known that since I was a child, that I would never be understood.

Eidolons

[From the journal]

FEBRUARY 2012. A new word: eidolons. *An ideal image and not a body double, not the mechanical device replicating the president's signature, not the political surrogate spouting regional forecasts, not the plagiarist of ideas and style, not the hacker of an identity that is sixteen numbers. Eidolon—the companion at the desk, my spirit-image, like an old pair of pajamas I will change into when life is done, when I will see at last the original writing that I changed, scratching over it millions of words to dig for the original meaning.*

CHAPTER TEN

LETTERS TO THE EDITOR

3/8/11
TO: Amy
FROM: Dan

Amy, Lou, and Bombo,

Just arrived in Jacksonville. Where? It is warm and green . . . Golfer territory.

I wanted to say again what a pleasure it was to meet the three of you. I know our paths have crossed, but to spend quality time with you guys was very special to me. I've been a Tan Fan since Faith first told me about "this amazing young writer," so for me as a reader, the meeting had an extra glow.

Warm regards,
Dan

3/8/11
TO: Dan
FROM: Amy

Hi Dan,

It was wonderful to spend time with you and your team and for
the bonus of Malbec time. By the way, I liked your desk lamp being
the solitary light, which gave the room the warmth of an intimate
study, in contrast to the typical fluorescent office. I was also relieved
to find I had already finished the book. The cover is terrific.

"This amazing young writer" is now 23 years older and amazed
at what is happening. I have been talking to friends and with
Steven Barclay, my trusted friend and lecture agent whose clients'
publishing houses run the gamut of good and bad. All the sources
have nothing but good things to say about you.

Amy

3/31/11
TO: Dan
FROM: Amy

Hi Dan,

During this last week, I have been mulling over the structure of *The
Valley of Amazement*. I am considering restructuring, so that instead
of making the book a chronological narrative, it would begin with
what is now the middle section—Daisy/Diashi's story. Reordering
does not really require any major revision to what I've been
writing. It is more dropping in tangents here and there that will be
connected as the book progresses.

The reasons are several for me. There's the intuitive one: I feel
closest to this voice. I know it. There's the narrative intrigue of not
revealing in the beginning what the painting is about, nor who

painted it and for what reason. In addition, this is the character that connects the other two at the end of the book by her absence. Her nature illuminates. I also think this is the voice that will draw in readers more easily and quickly.

It's tricky, of course, to begin with a voice, a particular consciousness, and then switch to another. Big no-no in some provincial creative writing classes. But I think I am providing enough "need to know" narrative pull to make that transition a natural progression of the story. In any case, I now think that beginning with the voice of an American woman would be misdirection as to what this story is about, that is, it is not about American and Chinese culture, but individuals and circumstances. The sense of the story is not chronological, but looping. It's more the sensibility in Borges' Garden of Forking Paths—infinite possibilities, coincidences that are recurrences, a realization that the sense and meaning of anything is not linear, does not follow prescribed order, but branches out of its own accord.

Since you haven't read actual pages, I am not expecting you can comment on this. But since you're now my editor, I will subject you to my mulling around, which, as you will discover more and more, is like making my way through labyrinths and forking paths.

Amy

3/31/11
TO: Amy
FROM: Dan

Hi Amy,

By all means, subject me to your mullings—I'm here for you, on one of the parallel forking paths, happy to be subjected.

The notion of your restructure (in the abstract) sounds like it will offer the narrative more texture, above and below the line. Of course, when the book is done, you'll have the chance to rearrange it again, if you feel so inclined—depending, of course, on how the novel ends up getting itself written. By the way, your description of the story being "looping as opposed to chronological" is great. As is "coincidences that are recurrences . . ." And, sense and meaning of anything not being linear, but branching out of their own accord. Lovely. These thoughts might join that ars poetica essay of our courtship.

Your happy editor,
Dan

4/1/11
TO: Dan
FROM: Amy

Hi Dan,

I cannot imagine any pressing need you might have to call me. But here is a US-based number for reaching me. It has voice mail, which I will listen to, since voice mails take on greater importance when received overseas. It is akin to how I felt about long-distance calls when I was a kid. The distance made the message more important because of cost and imagining a phone line that extended that long on two cans.

You dial the number as you would any US-based number.

415 729 3350

It's easy to remember.

729 is the result of successive factors using the multiplier 3, and starting with the prime number 3:

3 x 3 x 3 x 3 x 3 = 729

Note that the number 3 appears 5 times

Using the factors, it looks like this:

3 x 3 = 9
9 x 3 = 27
27 x 3 = 81
81 x 3 = 243
243 x 3 = 729

Since nothing else follows the local prefix of 729, logically, according to me, that is represented by a zero at the end of 3350.

I was assigned this number, 729-3350, by Skype, as my online number. I kid you not.

Numerically speaking,
Amy

4/1/11
TO: Amy
FROM: Dan

I feel like I've just taken the SAT again. I'll find you if I need you, but I'm hoping it won't be necessary to distract you from your Parisian Days. What's Bombo up to? I guess he doesn't undergo jet lag, with his metabolism.

4/1/11
TO: Dan
FROM: Amy

Thanks for the feedback and your saying once again that you like my confessional outpouring and want even more. The writer friend I sent it to, after having misgivings, thought it was excessive, but enjoyed it in the same way he might the National Enquirer. Well, he did not put it that way, but that was the gist of it. He is a great writer, of good taste, so I was a little worried that you would think I was a watch-out piece of work and best avoided.

Speaking of tabloids, Lou and I could not resist buying one whose cover story was "Where are they now?" He looked at their smiling faces on the cover and said, in front of the cashier, "She's dead, he's dead, she is definitely dead . . ." so he figured that where they were was in a cemetery. He actually insisted he knew that. And the cashier laughed! I was aghast. Of course they were alive. I knew that. How could a tabloid, read by millions of compassionate people about the travails of unlucky people, write a cruel story about their favorite TV stars being dead and forgotten? What's-her-name on "The Dick Van Dyke Show"—alive, thank you very much. (Would a TV show these days ever have a name with the words "dick" and "dyke" in it?) (See how I ramble?)

Up and at 'em. The new me, up before 10 a.m. But oatmeal first. No green milk, which we discovered, in fact, at the tabloid-supplied supermarket, is 30 proof.

4/1/11
TO: Amy
FROM: Dan

You can't really shake me now, National Enquirer or no. And I truly do like your personal thoughts on the art and psychology of writing. Keep a notebook!

The new routine sounds like you've completely shaken the Lyme! Also sounds like an ideal life—wish I could write novels, but I don't have the required patience.

4/28/11
TO: Dan
FROM: Amy

How lucky that you got to have Sunday brunch at the Spenders! Lizzie told me that Wystan, as she called Auden, came over often, and that Stravinsky, another dinner guest, wrote her a 9-note theme, which I wish she could find so I can take it to my music friends (conductors, composers, concert pianists) to appreciate and play around with. Imagine hearing him plunk out Petrushka! I used to play that all day—on my iPod, that is. I latch onto a piece of music and play it endlessly while I work, so I can keep the same mood.

Do you like classical music? In the event you do, here are some musical notes in my life:

My latest is the Rachmaninoff Concerto No. 3 in D minor. I love D minor! (Just kidding about that detail.) And so now you can have to imagine what mood I am in while writing the novel. Rach is always passionate. The pianist in the album I like is Yefim Bronfman—Lang Lang plays the same piece—both of whom I have heard play live, but with Bronfman, my hair stood on end and I wept and could not help but jump up at the end, as opposed to joining a standing ovation because everyone is doing so.

One time, at an impromptu party at the loft, we had four concert pianists, two opera singers, one jazz singer, one hip-hop rock composer and singer, and one opera composer. It was not a music party either. Four of them performed spontaneously. I don't think any musicians are coming this time. I think about myself at age six, suffering my first public humiliation at a church talent show, and am amazed that I know incredible musicians.

4/28/11
TO: Amy
FROM: Dan

Dear Wistful,

Interesting about the same music/same mood. I do that with playlists, some kind of odd, like my contemporary Italian, French pop, Cuban,

Satie/Milhaud. Love classical music but listen to more jazz. I'll go through the notes this weekend and make an AT PLAYLIST.

Remind me to tell you about my interview with Auden.

Root-Canal-ed-Out,
D

5/26/11
TO: Dan
FROM: Amy

Okay, I admit I may be in town, in fact, for Lisa Randall's party. I promised a mutual friend we would go together and then train to DC where I will receive an award.

But the thing about the Moth event is not my personal GPS bearings but absolute time. I know that this is all the answer you need to hear and that you do understand, but I want to tell you about the world in and out of my head when it comes to these sorts of things.

Things like Padma's event requires time figuring out the story—and I have tons of storyettes—but I need to create from them an oral narrative arc. Oral is different from written. I need to have anchors throughout to keep the arc in place, which, in the case of a person with memory issues, means constructing images in my head for each transition point, plus tight entries and exits, and known places to vary the speed, the tone, the phrases I use. I have to know what the arc leads to—a cathartic end, which I think oral storytelling requires, and if I miss it, it's like explaining a joke.

To do all this then requires rehearsal, they said, dry runs, and strict time limits. Those time boundaries are stressful for me. They're killer. It is better for me to lose writing time rearranging my closet than doing a story. Story work takes me out of my novel. It requires the same brainwork.

If I agreed, I would obsess over this for a week or more, lose work time, kick myself that I ever agreed to do what everyone said was so easy. I know I probably gave you the impression that stories fall out of me so easily. And indeed, I can give you tidbits about a story in minutes via e-mail. But when it will be performed in public, that makes it theater, and it takes on seriousness of form that requires shaping as much as any short story. It has to be tight, gently pulled, yet natural, seemingly spontaneous. The shorter it is, the more work it is for me. I'm much more of a free spirit when it comes to talking about something spontaneously. The talk I give at universities and lecture series is one I've worked on for years. It seems natural, off the cuff, but it's not. I speak for an hour without notes.

The worst part of live performance: when it's done, I analyze what I did and I feel sick at heart because I think of all the ways it was terrible. I hate my TED talk that is on their website. I cannot bear to watch it. I want to yank it off there.

A few years back, you could have asked me to do a circus act in a clown suit, and I would have said sure. I was always making exceptions for everyone in the past, and I have gotten myself into trouble so often over the years it is the major reason I don't have a book. An opera that was supposed to be easy—no work necessary!—took 5 years to make. I did hundreds of interviews because they came pleading that this and that interviewer said they would not do it unless I did it—"You gotta! It's the NY Times!" Years out of my life. Then came a book on the making of the opera, published by Chronicle Books. Then a man took wonderful photos of the opera and wanted a foreword. Then came a documentary on the making of the opera, which required shooting in SF and China.

During the last five years, I also did an "easy" assignment, an article for National Geographic. Major work. But that is what took me to the boonies of Guizhou and into a rice field in the mountains of impoverished farmers. That's where I ate the magic food with

the Feng Shui Masters to help those who had been possessed by
ghosts. It's where I sat on little guest stools for breakfast, lunch, and
dinner, having conversations about the ghost of a man who died in
a fire that burned a fifth of the village. I lived in that village about
3 weeks over a period of time. It took months to write that 4,000-
word piece. It was wonderful and I don't regret it, because that is an
enriched life and I need that kind of life to write.

But I also need to finish a novel.

5/26/11
TO: Amy
FROM: Dan

I agonize over every public event for months, write a hundred
drafts of a talk or essay that will be gone the moment the event
is over. Frankly, my best night is a night when I find myself at the
end of day having *forgotten* to make a plan. So I drag myself out to
dinner. I jotted this down (it's all about the Carbonara rhyme):

THE DINER IN THE CORNER

A table in the corner of the room, my table, 52,
beyond the new electronics, dinner alone all the way through.

For a moment. For an evening. If it's true the price of fame
is the loss of anonymity, goodbye applause, goodbye acclaim,

I'm welcomed back to my seat in the neighborhood restaurant,
a plainly clad waitress and the missing maître d', just a pleasant

welcome back, the specials a few chalk marks on the blackboard
leaning against a badly painted wall. Tonight it's the grilled sword-

fish, Mussels in Cast Iron and Brussels Sprouts Carbonara.
I have the company I need—a novel and recent e-mails are a

Happy evening's entertainment. Solo, nothing to dialogue,
Only my plate and me, sustenance, some wine and monologue

Between self and soul. It's pretty fucking grand sitting here
In the corner at table 52, just me and me, unpardoned and clear.

5/27/11
TO: Dan
FROM: Amy

I LOVE YOUR POEM! I will have to have a table number for
myself, and that will be something to keep in mind when I need
to mentally escape. I sat at the bar of a really popular restaurant
in the Ferry Building last Saturday after my French class and ate
a Vietnamese lunch. I was anonymous, but there were no table
numbers. Maybe I was Stool 17.

I have anonymity, I feel, most of the time, but not enough during
some important times. Like being in a public toilet. Tonight it
was nice to not be anonymous. I went to a screening of Woody
Allen's new movie and when we arrived we were told by some
officious guy with red-streaked hair that there were no more seats
left, even though we had RSVPd. He waved his hand to four other
disappointed people and said we were not alone. We were about to
leave, when a woman coming out of the screening room spotted me
and said, "Amy?" She made a gesture for me to wait, then went into
the theater. After a couple of minutes, she came out and gestured
for me to come in, just like the rabbit from Wonderland. I called
for Lou and the red-streaked guy warned him not to go in. But we
dashed inside and we were being shown to seats. The guy ran in
and I heard him say that we didn't have tickets. Then rabbit woman
said something and he went away.

So, no table 52, but I was glad. Also, no swordfish, high mercury,
but brussels sprouts are among my favorite foods.

The movie was hilarious. The stranger on my left was "not entertained," he said to a man on my right side. Before the movie started, they had sent barrages of film opinions back and forth with me in the middle. I did not know either of them, but thought the guy on the left was a pedant. The movie had a similar pedant, so I think he didn't like how he was portrayed, i.e., as an asshole.

I bought a large bag of popcorn as dinner after the screening.

Stool 17

7/3/12
TO: Dan
FROM: Amy

Hi Dan,

You are too kind.

I always recall something that Faith once said when I was in ruts— the usual reason is that the story is not "felt." I have thrown out 100s of pages of bad starts that were not felt. They lie in plastic bins in the garage. I cannot bear to see them. I cannot reread the pages. They are like babies I cannot throw out.

I do think that with this narrator I see her at a more cerebral level. As an example, there is something to do with romanticism—as in the romanticism of the 19th century in paintings—and to me, the notions are important to the way the characters differ and also how it governs their decisions later. Perhaps her cerebral (and self-centered) character makes her too unsympathetic. Yet, the chapters do concern her inability to love, or at least to show it, and her question as to whether she ever was truly loved, which is Violet's question.

Maybe I have told you too much already. You will be biased.

As editor, you may be able to give me advice. You may tell me to get rid of her chapters, to start afresh with something else. I need the eviction notice, the tornado that destroys the house, arson, murder of darlings . . . all those things when you should let go and can't until someone picks you up and puts you in recovery.

xoox
A

7/6/12
TO: Amy
FROM: Dan

Dear Amy Tan,

Too kind: Not really. I know this is an important book for you, and that along the way a lot of life has intervened. To respond to your notes. I don't think you should reread old material at this point—the relevant residue, the distillate, certainly remains with you. But how to get a fresh, unjaded eye on what you have? (I mean your eye.)

As for the notion of what's felt, I don't imagine you ever did not feel powerfully about these characters or their circumstances, their story. One might argue that a rut could also be caused by something being overly felt. Think of the rut we got ourselves into obsessing over an adolescent love (at whatever age). Think Salinger's definition of sentimentality . . .

Dry voice is something else, but can be addressed, with a little careful work and a sensitive ear. Happy to lend mine, bent and used as it is from exposure to great and horrible prose and poetry.

If you're worried about cerebral and cold, I'm sure there's a way to show a crack in some of that affect, by showing us that the heat is really there—that is, allowing us readers to see something the character hopes to withhold, even from herself. Alas, I hope this doesn't sound too abstract.

As for the two chapters, which I haven't yet read, let me read them now so that they're not further filed down.

Btw, I'm never biased, except in the service of the novel.

Yours,
Daniel Halpern

9/23/12
TO: Amy
FROM: Dan

Amy,

So here are my notes. An overview letter first, followed by Chapter by Chapter notes. You should have the line edits on Monday, sent to your home via UPS—if that package doesn't arrive Monday, do let me know right away. I asked my assistant to combine all the notes in a clearer handwriting than mine, although I did add some further notes from my last read-through, in red. I think everything is obvious.

As I've been saying, I love this book—I feel I've lived it for months, so that the characters are MY people, the landscapes those I'VE inhabited. In many ways, it's a profound novel, with so many intertwining themes—family, mother-daughter relationships, diverse philosophies of life, the intermix of cultures, the subtexts around the arrivals and departures.

It's just a beautiful book, and I hope the suggestions here help pull everything together.

9/23/12
TO: Dan
FROM: Amy

You had said so little before this, other than that quite wonderful praise that I needed to go on when I was stymied by precisely some of the things you said more coherently than what I sensed. And until I received these notes, I frankly wondered if you were a bit too easy to please. But I see now that all along you were thinking about those ways the novel could better realize its potential. More on that later.

I'm also grateful to get these notes now. It is not just that they provide a clearer path through brambles that grew over six years' time. They provide a constructive use of my days. I spent the first two days after Bombo's death crying non-stop, not sleeping or eating. I cried out every bit of moisture that was not absolutely needed to sustain life. I think I am down to 102 and look simply awful. I played videos of Bombo, went through all photos I had taken of him, and there are many. I could not speak to anyone. I finally rose from bed two days later, and went outside into the garden at Lou's insistence. It was a beautiful day, and I planted flowers and pruned all the dead leaves—obvious metaphor, but I did not do it for its metaphoric value. I looked for meaning in an orange cat who came into the yard, headed straight for me and nudged me to pay attention and scratch it—as Bombo did. The cat stayed with me for the two hours I spent pruning, and when I was done, it abruptly left. And now for the past 18 hours, I have done nothing but either post in Facebook, cry and watch videos of Bombo, or watch Downton Abbey reruns on Netflix.

So back to the notes. I heartily agree with most of the notes, questions, and suggestions, and those that I cannot say I agree with are simply those I don't quite understand. Some of the remarks that were confusing to you were indeed related to changes later that were not made earlier.

The obvious narrative flaws are ones I completely agree with—
the major one about Violet's character, those rather soap opera-
ish ups and downs, the contrivances that obscure character, and
the sins of narrative omission, some of which were parts once
there and which I removed because they also headed toward
detours and dead ends. I was humored by one remark you
made about the Night Scholar. I recall my saying to you that
there should be less sex and I had taken it out. And I *thought* you
said the more the better—which made me think you had an
appreciation for the prurient. So I put the Night Scholar back in.
He is, by the way, based on actual research on the sexual practices
among concubines, if one believes illustrations of the same and
pornographic novels of the time. I am curious why you did not say
he should be eliminated when you read the Byliner version. Were
you being respectful of Walter's position as the Byliner editor?
Walter had a very, very light touch—only a very few number of
line edits.

Re: Forthright. As I mentioned in an earlier e-mail, I did think that
early chapter of his could go, and that his meeting Violet as a boy
be buried easily and quickly into Violet's narrative. I wrote it early
on to give myself a sense of the House. Later, I wrote more about
the house in Violet's earlier chapter, and so Forthright's chapter
became superfluous. But I left it in for fun, thinking you might
find it interesting to see my imagination of a young boy's near-
defloration.

I appreciate your comments on character. What has bothered me in
the past is my tendency to make characters a bit too cartoony and
stock, to go for easy but convoluted plot movement. It was a major
flaw with my last book. In my head, it always starts off differently. I
think what I should do in the future is dash out my story and send it
to you in its natal flawed form so that I can get feedback very early
on before I keep wading through a muddle that becomes deeper
and deeper. The chapters you found worked better narratively were
those I wrote quickly—pretty much a straight shot.

My plan now is, first, to get a new printer. I think I was afraid to look at what I had written and avoided doing so by having the excuse that my printer was broken. I am quite adept at avoidance, I'm afraid. I did it when Bombo was dying, when I knew something was seriously wrong. I would not look at the possibility, while also knowing it. Avoidance is different from ignorance.

The second, which is simultaneous with the first, is to re-read the novel—gulp!—so I can then review your notes again with clearer appreciation and perspective, and not a foggy one of a hundred iterations.

Third, I will outline a new narrative line using yours to indicate which of these questions might be answered in such and thus a way. And that, of course, would have parallels of character development and backdrop, be it historical or setting or societal norms, e.g., the way that mixed race children were viewed. I want to get rid of that episodic feel that lacks a stronger narrative pull.

I think I mentioned before that I was stuck on Lulu's chapter that comes later because it was stiff and she was so unlikeable. If you think she is unlikeable now, you should have seen her when you would have detested her and written her off completely. Perhaps by giving her a rest, I can see her again and see what I can do to make her more of a sympathetic character. However, she is so stuck in my head as that same character that I may find it proves difficult to rehabilitate her. Having her reactions to learning Violet is alive would likely contribute a bit. And sadly, my having lost Bombo would give me more to think about—what my feelings would be if I learned he was once again alive.

I don't know if I told you about my motivations for this story, and what I truly want to come out: It is my intense need to know of the influences of my character from the preceding generations of women. What of me did my mother pass on to me? That is an easier question to answer. But I am also pulled to learn more about my grandmother—her nature, personality, and attitude to opportunities and adversity—which were passed along, and given how different the circumstances of our lives were/are. I think there are bits and pieces that my mother never recognized because it was covered up. She had the photos, but never saw them as anything but photos of her mother. She believed her mother was raped. But was that a concocted story necessarily told in an era when a widow's willingness to remarry was tantamount to digging up her dead husband's grave? I have evidence that my grandmother had quite an influence in the household.

So those are my initial reactions and the usual digressions.

More to say later, I'm sure.

Thanks again so much.
A

9/28/12

Hi Amy,

Sorry to be slow in getting back on this one. As I said yesterday, I wanted to think about your response. So—first of all, start eating again. We can't meet unless you're north of 110. And I don't mean Harlem. I hope you've kept in touch with the orange cat . . .

Everything you say in your letter makes good sense—a good response to a lot of mostly minor things. As for the things you don't understand, feel free to e-mail questions. And we can discuss when you're here, when we meet. I figured, since you said so, that some of the confusion came from changes made later in the book that were not then addressed in the earlier chapters.

For me, Violet's character is the most important issue, because it IS her story and she still needs a lot of flesh. She is often just too vague, willing to swing in the wind. Unlike her mother, she doesn't seem to know what she wants, making her motivations unclear.

The ups and downs will disappear as the overriding narrative
gets stronger and clearer. That repetition does detract from the
impact of the writing and the various scene descriptions, which are
spectacular.

I'm going to reread the passage with the Night Scholar. I think it
should be there, but just not so much of it. I agree the Forthright
chapter can go.

It is odd that you have a tendency to make the characters "cartoony
and stock," because mostly they are so not! Is this from over-
revision, which has a planing effect that takes away the highs and
lows of their personalities? Anyway, you're aware of it. Maybe
you should trust your first draft more, as you say. Not necessarily
"dashing" it out, but not overthinking it, either.

Your plan:

1. Get a new printer! I can earmark the progress payment. I get the
   avoidance thing, but as Ali said, you can run but you can't hide.

2. It seems to me this is the best thing you can do, once you've
   printed out a clean copy on your new HP printer. Reading from
   beginning to end. Not sure if it would be more effective just to
   read it through, making some notes of your own, or to read the
   editorial notes as you go along.

3. I like the idea of starting with an outline that addresses the
   new narrative arc. It seems the clearest way of moving forward
   in an organized way, with a skeleton to keep you on the path.
   Certainly this would help with character development and
   backdrop material (historical, societal, race, etc.). Getting away
   from anything that sounds episodic is going to help in many
   ways, and a stronger narrative pull will obviously do much to
   accomplish this.

One thing I want to mention, and this is more complicated. Now
that the book has gotten itself written, I'm wondering if your

"intense need to know of the influences of my character from
the preceding generations of women" is a useful concern at this
point. Whether that material is really the narrative scaffolding
that allowed you to write the book, but should now be discarded,
now that the book has taken on its own life. Is it possible that the
book you've written and the book you wish you'd written—"the
true story of the gradual revelations and ambivalence of what I was
finding and what I wanted to cling to of the family myth, and what
of that I was overjoyed to learn as an illumination of who I am," are
at odds with each other? Or so it seems to me.

Feel free to send me your "quick stabs" whenever you like, but not
to the heart.

Dan

9/28/12
TO: Dan
FROM: Amy

Great. Enough of a response to delve into overall changes. Better-
weighted characters but not equal page length.

Good insight about getting away from the personal need-to-know
that propelled the novel. I think it has made Violet have two
motivations and not a clear one and resulting thus in a vague one.
If I were to strip that away, there is still left my interest in identity,
and of course, it brings in personal questions about identity: what
we mean by identity, and what is set by circumstance, birth,
what can be changed, how dramatic changes affect us, what we
wind up believing as the way things happen in the world. How
beliefs affect what we do, can beliefs be changed, what underlies
them, what is impossible to undo, how does a dual identity
imposed by society affect one's perception of self. So that is on the
psychological level, and the emotional level becomes a compass,
an honest one, unreliable one, and a self-destructive one. How

does age affect all of what we desire? What do we compromise, accept, give up, still hang on to in desire, yet know on a practical level is fruitless to pursue.

10/2/12
TO: Dan
FROM: Amy

PS Non-miscellania—I keep asking myself how the hell I wrote such a long and bloated book. Too many pages. I think your printer printed out even more than I wrote. Plus, it formatted the pages differently—no para breaks. Huge margins at the bottom. I tried to fix the formatting and gave up.

The story is so much better having V know early on that she has a father, who she thinks is dead and white, and then learns early on is Chinese and alive. But I am also trying to keep in control the new stuff, to not write more than I eliminate. Like a whole book on Chinese history of rebellions.

The best part of this revision was throwing out whole chapters. So easy. When I cut them, I feel like I accomplished a lot. One keystroke, one delete button.

Oh, one thing I should have asked about and then never did: Did you want me to write on the marked-up manuscript what changes I made? I started to do that, and it was impossible. I would have then had to write in those new sentences to replace blocks of stuff that was deleted. Tell me please that you did not need me to do that. The marked-up manuscript is a mess, as is. My scribbles of notes. Big slashes.

10/2/12
TO: Amy
FROM: Dan

Wow, I guess so . . . I'll get to mine later, and I do have a few. But I want to respond quickly to your question about the manuscript. I think the best thing to do is not worry about the hard copy, and just submit a clean copy, so I can read it again, fresh, from start to finish. I don't need to see your edits, I'll feel them as I read.

1/17/13
TO: Dan
FROM: Amy

My mother, brother, and I took a boat from Spain to Tangier. The city has plenty of water. But I remember it had a desert, too. The tourist trappers there had imported some sand, a camel, a sleepy donkey and cobras, and set up a show by the fake souk to give us tourists the authentic bargaining-in-the-desert experience.

Can you believe my mother actually let some stranger wrap a cobra around my neck? She trusted that guy because he was standing on sand, which meant he was authentic and knew what he was doing. I could have died. Besides that, I could have fallen off that camel and been paralyzed for life. I could have been dictating like Stephen Hawking my theory of everything, which would have been about misery as a state of consciousness.

What's more, the donkey could have done a field goal kick using my face as a soccer ball. And then I would have been writing about being paralyzed and having a face that people could not bear to look at. I never would have left the psychiatric unit, which, given all the spare time, would have allowed me to churn out 100 horror books all about me. None of those books would have been any you would have wanted to publish—no one wants to read about continual self-pity. And I would have indeed pitied myself every waking minute because I would not have had any semblance of a happy life, given that at age 17 I would have been committed to a psychiatric unit for the rest of my life, and not starting college, where I would have met Lou at a sorority barn dance. All this, because my mother and I believed Tangier was a desert, when the desert was really a few buckets of sand, a bunch of snakes, and a man playing a flute that mesmerized my mother.

1/17/13

TO: Amy

FROM: Dan

THE SAND OF TANGIER sounds like a Bowles story . . . No deserts in Tangier, however.

2/13/13

TO: Dan

FROM: Amy

About Flora's character: I talked to a psychiatrist (distinction: not my psychiatrist—I don't have one I pay for by the hour)—okay, so I talked to one of my many psychiatrist friends, concerning a 3-1/2 yo child separated from her mother in a traumatic way. What would the psychological manifestations of that be in the long term? Answer: Bad. Very bad. Even if mom simply goes away for a week to Hawaii, the child would show for some period of time anxiety, distrust, and regression in potty training progress A week??? But here it's not a week. A very violent abandonment! In the case of forced and sudden permanent separation and with horrible people, what would the aftermath be? Flora, poor girl. They did not have suicide hotlines then, did they? Priests, rabbis, village elders and shamans.

I have not yet decided on her actual crisis, whether she is suicidal, has an abortion, or is destructive in another way. Why did I not realize that the first time? Slapping my forehead. I knew it at some level yet forgot that big chunk of my psyche: my mother losing her mother at age 9, watching her die after a deliberate overdose. The permanent effects were obsessions and constant anxiety, regret, anger, and unreasonable expectations, which were also inflicted on me. My mother was not a carefree spirit. She was suicidal all the way to her last year of life, which was when she was demented and suddenly became happy and worry-free. Flora, not a happy child.

Another concern I have: There are so many new pages I wonder if you will go through them and think that much more revision is needed. Can't worry about that. It's more of a question of your timing than mine. You may think the new pages are boring or elliptical. At the very least, I think it will be more than your looking for line edits. I am a whole lot happier with the pages than what was there. But you?

2/13/13
TO: Dan
FROM: Amy

Dan—your mom and dad did damage to you by going off to Vegas. You became an editor and a poet. How could you not see that cause and effect? The effect on a very young child whose parent goes away to Vegas once would probably be nothing most would notice. More a temporary need to be cuddled more (anxious). Second time in a month: bed wetting. Not lifetime. Third time: Poet with angst about dying one day, and in an elevator no less. I do think you would have been a happy car mechanic if your parents simply stayed home and watched the Ed Sullivan show with you. Lennon Sisters, yeah! You would have been practical about buying a coffin you happened to see at a clearance sale. Save for the future!

I should have explained that those questions I threw out were examples only of my pinball mind—that is the kind of stuff that flies through my mind. I hit a pinball, it goes off in angles, then I hit it again. It is endless. So in the version you read, there is nothing from Violet to Minerva in 1926, and there is now. And Forthright has a role in that. But I am glad that you think that is good, and also that the dramatic aspect can be an abortion, and that Flora remembers and also finds the letter.

Other thoughts: I have this feeling that, unlike the desired novel endings some readers want, real people don't learn how to be unselfish, but maybe they can be more self-aware for a second that they are or perhaps they are pathetically more unaware. How do you cure someone of selfishness? Send them to Mother Teresa school? There is something deep-seated about selfishness. It is not like cleanliness. So Minerva is helpless to know how to not be who she is. And there is Lu Shing, who seems to be doing the right thing and never is. But this leaves me with the question of how much change in awareness and behavior and action forward does Flora have upon/after being with Violet.

I am so happy you like Whitman's Quicksand Years being there. It is everything about this book in terms of who one is.

> *Quicksand years that whirl me I know not whither*
> *Your schemes, politics, fail, lines give way, substances mock and elude me,*
> *Only the theme I sing, the great and strong-possess'd soul, eludes not,*
> *One's-self must never give way—that is the final substance—that out of all is sure,*
> *Out of politics, triumphs, battles, life, what at last finally remains?*
> *When shows break up what but One's-Self is sure?*

Violet has a "theory" she develops as a child. I don't know if you will think it is corny, but she calls it "My Pure Self-Being," her resolve not to be changed into what someone thinks is better, promulgated timing wise with her learning her extra fingers were amputated, and that everyone discussed this and chose the best answer based on playing the piano. She alternates between thinking that others would make her ordinary or—perhaps worse, that she is already ordinary and that is why they want to improve her. Regardless, she wants to "be my pure self-being."

At what age do you think children feel that? Did you feel that? Am I weird that I thought that? Or were your parents more—"whatever you want, Danny! Just be yourself!" No one told me to be who I wanted to be.

So what do we alter?

2/13/13
TO: Dan
FROM: Amy

What did you mean by Lawrentian? Bad? Cheesy? Over the top? Or, oh, pu-leeze? Too much psychological self-absorption? What's that scene from Sons and Lovers I read when I was 16—with Miriam—was that her name? I remember the couple standing by the fence, simmering with sexual tension. That's it. Did I absorb more that has now become too Lawrentian? Is it too much introspective sex and ecstatic renewal and "fuck you, Mom"? For the last 25 years, I have been told by writers group members and Molly that I cannot write a decent sex scene—so I never did. Or maybe I wrote one and I was then told it was bad. Now I am really trying to figure out how to not write a bad one. I think that an honest sex scene would have the same two sentences repeatedly: "That feels good" and "Don't stop," plus some obscene interjections, and possibly a narrative remark that he or she is not really thinking about much of anything existentially remarkable or spiritually transcendent. Actually, introspection happens only when the sex is bad and the internal thoughts might include: "This is a big mistake," or "This guy has no idea what he's doing," or "Why is the dog barking?" There might be color commentary / epistolary dissection later with a BFF: "That sucked, and not in a good way," or "He's definitely a keeper."

2/13/13
TO: Dan
FROM: Amy

Never mind. I deleted. It was bad.

2/13/13
TO: Amy
FROM: Dan

I love Whitman and was talking about him today on the way home. There's Whitman and there's Dickinson—and all other poetry falls in between, except for Stevens, Yeats, and Eliot.

> *The smallest sprout shows there is really no death.*
> *And if ever there was it led forward life, and does not*
> *wait at the end to arrest it,*
> *And ceas'd the moment life appear'd.*
>
> *All goes onward and outward, nothing collapses,*
> *And to die is different from what any one supposed,*
> *and luckier.*

2/13/13
TO: Amy
FROM: Dan

I was just reading this, which made me sad it was so true.

  "ONE OF THE BUTTERFLIES"
  W. S. Merwin

  The trouble with pleasure is the timing
  it can overtake me without warning
  and be gone before I know it is here
  it can stand facing me unrecognized
  while I am remembering somewhere else
  in another age or someone not seen
  for years and never to be seen again
  in this world and it seems that I cherish
  only now a joy I was not aware of
  when it was here although it remains
  out of reach and will not be caught or named
  or called back and if I could make it stay
  as I want to it would turn to pain.

3/3/13
TO: Amy
FROM: Dan

That night he memorized the geography of me: the changing
circumference of my limbs, the distance between two beloved
points, the hollows, dimples, and curves, the depth of our hearts
pressed together. We conjoined and separated, conjoined and
separated, so that we could have the joy of looking into each other's
eyes, before falling into each other again. I slept tucked into him
and he wrapped his arms around me and for the first time in my
life, I felt I was truly loved.

In the middle of the night, I felt a shudder followed by three smaller ones. I turned around. He was weeping.

"I'm terrified of losing you," he said.

"Why would you fear that now?" I stroked his brow and kissed it.

"I want us to love each other so deeply we ache with the fullness of it."

3/3/13
TO: Amy
FROM: Dan

Who wrote that?

3/3/13
TO: Dan
FROM: Amy

And not a censorable word.

3/3/13
TO: Amy
FROM: Dan

Right.

3/3/13
TO: Dan
FROM: Amy

Ha.ha. Yes, I wrote it. I had considered taking it out at one point. Glad you like it.

3/3/13
TO: Amy
FROM: Dan

It's beautiful. Why would you take it out? Of course I knew you wrote it—it's in your book, the book by the other Amy Tan.

3/3/13
TO: Dan
FROM: Amy

I read things I write and after a while I cannot tell what is bad and what is good. At one time that passage seemed corny to me. I leave in other stuff that truly is corny. I don't recognize it until I let it sit. And then I am aghast at what I left in.

4/30/13
TO: Amy
FROM: Dan

I would have liked your mother, I know that.

Books are never done, they're merely abandoned. Can't wait to celebrate!!!

4/30/13
TO: Dan
FROM: Amy

Books are never done. They're merely jerked out of your hands by your publisher.

6/20/13
TO: Dan
FROM: Amy

What can I say beyond thanks? I am kneeling to the Ecco gods. Me, a writer, without appropriate words that are not clichés. I'm beyond happy—beyond grateful, beyond excited. I feel so good, so supported. It gives me confidence to be with the right team. And I love everyone at Ecco. They're so enthusiastic and smart. So—two more books. We're going to have fun this time. As for the press release. If you want, we can indicate that the title for the novel is "The Memory of Desire." The non-fiction book? How about "The Story Behind the Story."

Or how about, "Dear Dan."

CHAPTER ELEVEN

LETTERS IN ENGLISH

My mother's skill in writing English was similar to her skill in speaking it. But that wasn't much of a problem when I was growing up, since my father handled anything that required writing in English, from letters to the Department of Justice regarding their immigration status to the annual Christmas brag letter.

But when my father's brain tumor left him unable to write, I became my mother's secretary and my first job was to write thank-you letters to those who sent flowers or condolence letters. I was fifteen, both angry and scared about what had happened to our family, and the last thing I wanted to do was thank someone for their condolences. To do so, I had to simultaneously take dictation from my mother and do drastic editing in my head before committing to paper the words that approximated what she wanted to express. Fortunately for her, and unfortunately for me, our handwriting styles were almost identical. It was as if I inherited the slant of the words, the way she capitalized letters, crossed her *t*'s and made bumps in her *n*'s and *m*'s. I had to practice only a little to write her name exactly as she did. For the thank-you notes, I used the stationery provided by the funeral home. The front said, "We sincerely appreciate your sympathy"—a preprinted form of sincerity that was as insincere as could be—that was my cynical view as a teenager. We sat at the dining table, with a pile of letters on the table. We opened them one at a time and I read them aloud. My mother would cry when a letter included a fond memory of my father or brother. That was torture to me and I had to struggle to not show emotion. My mother, however, welcomed fresh reasons for grief. I would then write the response, beginning with the pro forma: *We are grateful for your sympathy and presence at the funeral.* I then appended whatever my mother thought would give each note a personal touch: *I will always be grateful for your thoughtfulness in counseling Amy on ways to support me in this time of trouble.* Or, *We appreciated the delicious casserole.* Or, *It warms my heart to hear how fondly you remember my son.* I found it excruciating to write these formal, unfeeling words. It was like whacking a bruise to keep it discolored. Later, I had to write lengthy letters to the bank and umpteen other places that needed to be notified of my father's death. Shortly after my father died, my mother espied a Ouija board, which a friend from school had brought over for the important task of learning whom we would marry—mine being an unknown man named Garfolk who lived in West Virginia. My father had looked upon the Ouija board as a form of blasphemy, tantamount to speaking to the devil. My mother, however, seized upon it as a stenographic tool of sorts to record and transmit messages to and from heaven. She had long felt that I had a secret ability to talk to ghosts and that I should now use my talent and the Ouija board to communicate with my father and brother Peter. I recall a sick feeling in my stomach when she said that. Asking for the name of your husband was a joke. For my mother, this would be a reunion. There had been other times when she had called upon the divine in hopes of curing my brother and father—a feng shui master who went through the house and backyard to determine what was out of alignment with nature; two women who sat on the sofa with my mother, the three of them babbling with tongues flapping out of their mouths. Now, as with those other occasions, I could not say what I actually felt: a hybrid of helplessness and anger added to her growing pile of wacky ideas. She had lost pieces of her mind, and now she was losing more. Protesting any of her ideas had always led to either prolonged weeping or outrage that I was implying she was stupid. And maybe she was stupid, she would say, to not recognize the signs of a curse so that she could have protected my father, Peter, and even her mother who had died when my mother was nine. Each missed opportunity was a regret, and she could tally many. That was the beginning of my vow to myself to never have regrets.

We put the Ouija board on the dining-room table that night and placed our fingers on opposite sides of a heart-shaped plastic planchette, whose clear round eye glided over letters of the alphabet. When the planchette abruptly stopped and the metal pin in the planchette's eye was directly over a letter, we recorded it. The first few answers came quickly. She began by asking, "Do you miss me? Do you still love me?" I knew the only answer I could give her. I pushed the planchette firmly to the word "Yes." She responded with copious tears and declarations of love. Eventually, she asked my father and brother for advice on what she should do next with her life. Open a Chinese restaurant? I answered on behalf of my mute father with a resounding "No." Open a souvenir shop in Portland? No. Move to Taiwan where John and Amy could learn to become more Chinese? I answered: No. After we had gone through a number of other ideas— each of them undesirable from my point of view—she asked if she should invest in IBM or U.S. Steel stock? By then I had become reckless with power. I can no longer recall my answer, but whatever it was, she followed it, and I am happy to report that we did not suffer financial ruin. In fact, by the end of her life, she had accumulated an impressive portfolio for a widow.

A few months later, my mother became friends with three widows, and they used the Ouija board on numerous occasions and received much better answers than mine, including one that indicated that my father was disappointed in my choice of boyfriend, and another in which my boyfriend's father declared—in German, no less—that he was disappointed in his son.

That would have been the end of my ghostwriting stint if I had not started writing fiction. My mother believed that many of the stories I had written had been dictated to me by her mother.

The other day, while digging through a box of documents, I found a bit of my mother's writing. It was a recipe she had jotted down after someone suggested she write a sequel to my novel *The Kitchen God's Wife,* which she felt was close to her true story. She would call her book *The Kitchen God's Wife Cookbook.* She was indeed an excellent cook, but she was not able to organize her knowledge into precise amounts of ingredients and clear instructions. Her method of explanation ran more toward a haphazard list of ingredients without quantities. She was an intuitive cook. "The recipe is in my nose," she often said to those who admired her cooking. Her sense of smell determined if she had the right mix of ingredients and whether it was salty enough. Her eyes, tongue, and fingers judged whether the food had cooked long enough. As she saw it, it took only twenty additional seconds for fish to go from tender and juicy to overcooked and dry. Having grown up eating her food, I developed a refined palate for how Shanghainese dishes should taste, as well as an eye for how a dish should appear—how thick or thin or long the meat or vegetables had been sliced, whether the dish glistened with just the right amount of oil or was soaking in nasty pools of it. Being in the kitchen with her was stressful. She was a perfectionist, and given the amount

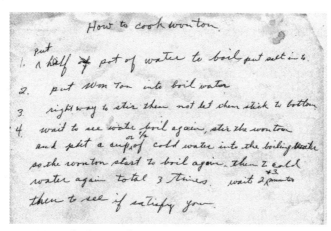

1991: My mother's recipe for wonton.

of work it took to shop, prepare, cook, serve, and clean up, I was not motivated to learn how to cook. On those rare occasions when I did cook, I would simply wing it, but with less satisfactory results.

But now, nearly two decades after her death, I have in hand her written instructions for cooking wonton soup. I found it in a box of documents and letters. The recipe included steps on how to cook wonton but not how to make it—no list of ingredients, no helpful hints on the precise way to wrap the filling using thin square sheets of dough. What she wrote sounded exactly like the way she talked. It brought back to vivid memory what she looked like as she explained what to do with a pile of uncooked dumplings and a steaming pot of boiling water. Those instructions were also a reminder why I was required to serve as her scribe.

HOW TO COOK WONTON

1. *put half pot of water to boil put salt into*
2. *put wonton into boil water*
3. *right way to stir them not let them stick to bottom.*
4. *wait to see water boil again, stir the wonton and put a cup or ½ of cold water into the boiling water so the wonton start to boil again. Then cold water again total 3 times. Wait 2–3 minutes then to see if satisfy you.*

In the box with the wonton recipe, I found my mother's letters. A half dozen were written in English, most of them on tissue-thin sheets of paper that ensured that a four-page letter would not exceed the weight limit of a first-class airmail stamp. Several were written on aerograms, like the one she sent in 1968 to an old family friend, posted from Montreux, Switzerland, where my mother, little brother, John, and I had finally settled after hopscotching across the United States and Europe, as part of a peripatetic effort to escape grief over the deaths of my brother and father. I thought it was odd that the letter was in English, since this friend she had known since her adolescence also spoke her Shanghainese dialect. The letter started off in perfect English, which made me think she had dictated the letter to me. The handwriting might have been mine.

> *We spent Christmas Day in Geneva, invited to dinner by John's former professor and his wife at their apt. It was a rather sad celebration, and it will never be the same as before.*

She inserted someone's name in Chinese, and the letter continued but in lighter script. This was written in her hand. The sentences were pretty much grammatical, although there were mistakes here and there, which made me think she had incorrectly copied the sentences I had written on another sheet of paper. And then the sentences contained numerous errors, making it apparent she had abandoned my help. The last paragraph was in her voice, and it was obvious I had not helped her write it, given the subject matter.

> *It is headache to raise children, and almost lead to a senseless and aimless life. Here is gossip colum: [X] ever since I've known her never forgets to say, "I don't feel strong, sick here, sick there. Now she writes the same as she talks. Of anything, she mentions something she never keeps her word.*

I was surprised that she knew how to use the present perfect tense: *ever since I've known her.* Some teacher must have drilled that into her. In fact, of all the tenses she used, the ones that she used correctly most often were both the present and past perfect tenses, what she might have learned in an advanced English grammar course. The present perfect is what you use to describe where you've been. *I've been to Florida. I've been to New York. I've been to Switzerland.* Use the past perfect to describe what had just happened before you lost your mind: *They had both died.* Use the past perfect to tell us about assumptions that proved false. *I had thought a change of scenery might do us good. I had neglected to choose the scenery we should change to.*

My mother made several changes of scenery. Her first choice was inspired by a can of Old Dutch Cleanser, which she used each night to clean the kitchen sink. The little Dutch girl on the can's label had already served as inspiration for a hideous Halloween costume that I wore in the first grade. She would now help set our new course in life. "Holland is clean," my mother announced to my little brother and me one night. "We are moving to Holland." Had my mother asked my father through the Ouija board whether this impetuous idea was a good one, I would have answered without hesitation: Yes, that is the best idea you've ever had. But I also knew that it would be crazy to move to a country where we knew no one. My mother reasoned that we had seldom gone on a true vacation. We only worked hard and maybe that was the reason my father and brother fell ill. She hinted that we should see the world before it was too late—meaning, before we all died of a curse. Friends and family counseled her to wait longer before making such a big decision. She interpreted their concern as insults to her intelligence. The more objections my mother received, the more adamant she was about her choice. When they could not dissuade her, they conceded that a change of scenery might do her some good, but she should return if she felt lonely. They told her to bring back souvenirs. By June 1968, four months after my father died, my mother had already sold the house, the car, and most of our furnishings—although not the piano, which she stored at a relative's house.

My mother laid out maps she got for free from AAA. She showed us her grand plan. She had bought round-the-world airline tickets for each of us, $700 apiece, a bargain. She had booked us on a train and a boat. She had even contemplated a ride in a helicopter. She put her finger on the map to show us a series of destinations we would make in a year. In July, we embarked on John's and my first trip outside of California. We took our first airplane ride—a trip to Florida to stay with my great-aunt and great-uncle. Because the flight was nearly empty, we sat in first class and also roamed the length of the plane to look out of different windows to see the differing landscapes and cities that lay below. In Florida, we wrote postcards to report that we had swum with manatees and had dipped our fingers in Ponce de Leon's Fountain of Youth. With the help of my great-uncle and his traps, we caught over fifty softshell crabs, which my great-aunt boiled alive, a distressing sight that made it impossible for me to eat them. I wrote that we were almost killed several times because my great-aunt was a terrible driver; she turned around to talk to us and nearly ran off the road or crashed head-on into other cars on the other side of the road. In Washington, D.C., we sent postcards of the White House, the Lincoln Memorial, the Smithsonian, and Mount Vernon. In New York, we sent postcards of the Rockettes, the Empire State Building, and the Statue of Liberty. We bragged that we happened to see Shirley MacLaine dancing around a fountain in Rockefeller Center while the movie *Sweet Charity* was being filmed. That's New York. You can see just about anything. I wrote in a letter to one high school friend that I saw a man dressed in a business suit, who was lying in the gutter with his limbs turned in impossible angles after being hit by a cab and killed. No one did anything for him, I said. That's New York.

From New York, we boarded the SS *Rotterdam* and sailed to the fabled land of cleanliness. Each night we dressed in our best clothes and sat at a table with a white tablecloth. Three handsome young men in white tuxedoes served us. I was ecstatic that they flirted shamelessly with me in front of my mother, each one claiming I had broken his heart. No boys in high school had ever flirted with me. I had broken no one's heart. One night, I surreptitiously met with one of the waiters, Sieggy, who was ten years older than I was. We shared a romantically forbidden nicotine-flavored kiss. Standards were low then. I wrote an exaggerated account about this to my best friend back home. *He took a risk and could have been fired.* Our family, now reduced to three, embraced all that was new to escape reminders of tragedy. I traded my old identity for a glamorous one. I pretended to be familiar with the routine of ordering three courses from a French menu. On one occasion, when the silver dome covering my plate was lifted, I saw a quarter round of hideous tissue. Brains. My brother's. My father's. The waiters smiled with good humor. To maintain my new sophisticated persona, I pretended that this was indeed what my mouth had been watering to eat. I had many cosmopolitan experiences like that. My mother had a knack for meeting strangers and asking them straight out for advice on what there was to see in Europe. One evening, I listened to a Swiss German salesman with oily hair and bad teeth offer to give us a tour of his small but charming hometown. To further entice us, he yodeled. For the first time in eighteen months, my mother seemed happy.

After a glamorous week on the high seas, we landed in Rotterdam, which was indeed a big change of scenery. My brother and I quickly learned that our mother had done nothing to prepare for life after disembarkation. She had no idea where we would live, let alone where my brother and I would go to school. Carpe diem led us to a cheap but clean hotel. Because we could not read the Dutch menus and feared ordering something like brains, we ate the local dishes that we could clearly see in vending machines. We also ate at a series of so-called Chinese restaurants, and they were all, by my mother's opinion, awful, not Chinese food, but Indonesian. We discovered there was no furnished apartment we could rent in Rotterdam, so we moved to Utrecht and stayed in the YMCA, where the staff spoke English. From there, John and I commuted an hour and a half each way by train and bus to reach the closest English-speaking school. It was located in Werkhoven on the grounds of a picturesque castle with horse stables. It even had a drawbridge and swans swimming in the moat. I thought it was perfect. I quickly won favor by drawing realistic pictures of swans.

We took lodgings in the home of a parsimonious landlady, who prohibited us from using lights past nine o'clock. After a week, my mother decided we should next go to Karlsruhe, Germany, where a family friend lived—a minister who had attended divinity school with my father—with his wife, who was genuinely fond of my mother. They offered us a guest room where we could stay until we found an apartment. Because none of us could speak German, my mother used a simple and ingenious method to glean information necessary for our survival. First, she would ask strangers if they could speak English. If they could not, she would use pantomime to ask them for recommendations for hotels, restaurants, and tourist sites. This mode of communication, unfortunately, led several men to presume my mother was a pimp and that I was a girl for hire. One time, a line of drunken men followed us along the street. Another time, a man who had picked us up as hitchhikers let my mother and brother off, and then nearly drove away with me stuck in the back of his car. My mother ran after the car and managed to open the door. After she extricated me from the confines of the back seat, I shouted that she should no longer ask strangers for help. "I could have been raped!" My mother did not apologize, nor did she argue. Instead, she bought a VW bug, and with a handbook of English-speaking schools as our guide, we drove south, stopping in towns with English-speaking schools to inquire if there were any openings for two students. My mother also asked the locals, even those in small towns, if they had a Chinese restaurant. These were people who had never seen anyone who was Asian.

I recall our drive as joyful. The scenery was so stunning, we sang tunes from *The Sound of Music*. Like the von Trapp family, we had escaped—from sadness, from bad landladies, from perverted men. We finally reached a resort town in Switzerland next to Lake Geneva, Montreux. The school, then called Institut Monte Rosa, did indeed have two openings for day students, and being a vacation destination, the town had plenty of advertisements for furnished apartments. My mother rejected those that smelled of dust and chose a clean one, a Bavarian-style chalet made of thick dark logs. We stepped into a parlor with a ticking cuckoo clock. On the right was the bedroom my mother and I would share. It had two feather-tick beds and two square windows with shutters that gave us a view of Lake Geneva. My brother would sleep in the bigger room next to ours. It was furnished with a long dining table suitable for twelve, a sofa bed, a TV, and a china cabinet. The cabinet contained a bonus: stationery, tissue-thin pink and green sheets with matching envelopes. The landlady encouraged us to use as much as we wanted. Over the next year, my mother and I took her at her word. We sent many letters reporting about our new life.

Mine were typically ten pages long. I wrote about the impossibly beautiful views: We could see clear across the lake, practically to Geneva. We could see the French Alps and the Italian Alps, and there was always snow on top. We could see the school that lay at the bottom of a cobblestone path of fourteenth-century buildings. Steps away from our chalet, I could climb onto a funicular with my new boyfriend, an unemployed German army deserter. We went to Les Avants to have *café au lait*. I watched my boyfriend play table foosball all afternoon; he was very good and usually won in competitions with the locals, so he never had to pay a franc for a new game. From Les Avants, we took a cogwheel train up to the peak of the mountain, Rochers de Naye. From there, we could see the world.

We were smart tourists who used carpe diem as our motto—seize the day, for tomorrow we may die. In that picturesque town, I learned so much. I learned to ski—albeit miserably. I learned to eat the local dishes: yogurt and muesli, as well as raclette. I learned to drink Bordeaux wine and café. I learned French, just a bit. I learned about love; I had the love letters to prove it. I learned what kind of fur coat you needed to be a snob, not rabbit. I learned to smoke cigarettes; Marlboros, then Gauloise, then hashish; and soon after, hashish cut with opium. I learned what happens when you are arrested in Switzerland for drugs. I learned I would not go to jail, unlike my boyfriend, because I was only sixteen. I learned what my mother could do to me when she went crazy and what she would do for me out of love. Sometimes they were the same thing.

At the end of our stay in Montreux, nearly all the sheets of paper were gone.

This month I retrieved the file that contained my letters to her written soon after I arrived at college, the first time we were apart. I was moved to tears that she had saved them. I had drawn so much from our lives together for my fiction, and here were the letters that preserved some of those experiences. The first letter I saw was a typed list of expenses, dated September 26, 1969, when I was seventeen. I had graduated a year early from the school in Switzerland because of thrift and greed. The tuition at the school was $600 a year, a large sum for our family. We discovered, however, that there was no limit on the number of courses I could take. It operated on the same principle as those $1.99 restaurants where you could eat all you wanted, choosing from a glut of offerings, ranging from roast beef and mashed potatoes to Jell-O pudding and fruit cocktail in mayonnaise. I loved learning and saw no reason why I could not take French and Spanish, art history and art, chemistry, math, American history, English literature, piano, and skiing. At the start of the second semester, the headmaster told me I would graduate that year. I felt I had won a prize. I would be able to leave home a year early. My mother, little brother, and I had gone through a tumultuous year with frequent fights, self-destructive impulses, followed by tearful reconciliations. We had been emotionally pummeled during the year my brother and father were dying, and now, with hope no longer necessary, we had all gone a little crazy. During one argument, John threw lemonade on my college applications, I slugged him, and he ran off barefoot in the dark night when it was snowing so hard the pathway to our chalet had foot-deep drifts. My mother and I called on the landlady, her son, and a teacher to form a search party. As we walked down the snowy cobblestone path, we yelled for my brother. I was certain we would find him frozen blue and my mother would never stop screaming. How much more could we take? He was eventually found alive, shivering with near hypothermia and frostbite. We were all exhausted from crises yet we could not stop making them.

The letters I held in my hand were those I had written when I began college. And that would become the pattern: we wrote letters in English when we were far apart. Except for the run-away letter I wrote when I was eight, this was the first time I had written *to* her and not *for* her. Reading the letters now, I am struck by how odd the tone is—like that of a perky character from a teen movie in the 1960s. This was not how I spoke to her in person.

September 26, 1969

Dear Mom,

    Boy! It sure was good to talk to you on the telephone even though I didn't say anything too profound. Two phones in the apartment, wowee-zowee! Don't you think you are becoming a little extravagant like Mrs. McClintock? Today is Friday and for once in a long time I am really sitting at home—no date tonight! Although I do have one for Sunday. He's taking me to Sunday dinner. So never fear, dear MOTHER, I DO get plenty to eat. In fact, I think I better stop eating desserts! Well, the main purpose of this letter is to present you with a look at my financial situation. Say, I'm not doing so bad at typing, am I?

    Expenses:

plane fare	*$19.95*
student i.d.	*$ 3.00*
dorm fee	*$ 2.00*
mail box	*$ 1.20*
books	*$13.74*
notebooks	*$ 1.54*
church	*$ .25*
coke	*$ .15*
beanie hat	*$ 2.00*
pens, stamps	*$ .60*
panty hose	*$ 1.33*
p.e. clothes	*$ 1.20*
miscellaneous	*$ .80*
p.e. shoes	*$ 4.99*
p.e. socks	*$ 1.00*
curtains, rods	*$ 5.17*
misc.	*$ .80*
concert	*$ 1.00*
rush fee	*$ 2.00*

bedspread _____	$ 6.00
game _____	$ 1.00
misc. _____	$ 1.00
c.o.d. packages _____	$ 7.70
calc., che., phys., books _____	$ 4.75
food, misc. _____	$ 1.00

There it is! I think I had a hundred-forty dollars to begin and I have about $55 left. It scares me how fast the money actually goes. No, I just added it and that's $53.17 left. Plus if I join a sorority I must pay at once $25 a semester. The misc. items I have listed mean little things like food, cookies, thread, stamps, phone calls, etc.

Actually I think if you exclude all the things I had to buy and just count the stuff like food, stamps, panty hose, entertainment (game, concert), then I have only spent $6.68 for these four weeks. That's not too bad, but I could eliminate it! It's that sorority fee that will get me down! This college was made for rich kids! Not poor little Chinese girls who spend their senior year in Switzerland and who must graduate a year early because her poor mommy can't afford another crazy year of a daughter in high school! Only kidding of course!

I think I can save money on food, and entertainment if I go on a date every week. That way I get pizzas, Cokes, dances, etc. . . .

I went on to detail how I might be able to get a refund on some of the books if I dated somebody in a fraternity who would then be willing to give me his freshman textbooks. The letter focused only on frugality and the kind of bargain-hunting tips she would have appreciated. That must have been the safe topic between us. I had omitted cigarettes as part of "miscellaneous." In those days, they cost twenty-five cents a pack and thus they were easily absorbed into those $1.00 miscellaneous expenses. In any case, my mother had probably guessed that some of my purchases included cigarettes. I openly smoked in front of her, and that is because she and I had both started smoking when we lived in Switzerland. I don't recall her warning me

September 26, 1969

ear Mom,

Boy! It sure was good to talk to you on the telephone even though I didn't say anything too profound.
Two phones in the apartment, wowee-zowee! Don't you
think you are becoming a little extravagant like Mrs.
McClintock?? Today is Friday and for once in a long
time I am really sitting at home -- no date tonite!
Although I do have one for Sunday. He's taking me out
to Sunday dinner. So never fear, dear MOTHER, I DO
get plenty to eat. In fact I think I better stop eating desserts! Well, the main purpose of this letter
is to present you with a look at my financial situation.
Say, I'm not doing so bad at typing, am I?

```
Expenses:
plane fare------------$19.95
student i.d.---------$ 3.00
dorm fee-------------$ 2.00
mail box-------------$ 1.20
books----------------$13.74
notebooks------------$ 1.54
church---------------$  .25
coke-----------------$  .15
beanie hat-----------$ 2.00
pens, stamps---------$  .60
panty hose-----------$ 1.33
p.e. clothes---------$ 1.20
miscellaneous--------$  .80
p.e. shoes-----------$ 4.99
p.e. socks-----------$ 1.00
curtains,rods--------$ 5.17
misc.----------------$  .80
concert--------------$ 1.00
rush fee-------------$ 2.00
bedspread------------$ 6.00
game-----------------$ 1.00
misc.----------------$ 1.00
c.o.d. packages------$ 7.70
calc.,che.,phys.,
books----------------$ 4.75
food,misc.-----------$ 1.00
```

There it all is! I think I had a hundred-forty dollars
to begin with and I have about $55 left. It scares me
how fast the money actually goes. No , I just added
it and that's $53.17 left. Plus if I join a sorority
I must pay at once $25 a semester. The misc. items
I have listed mean little things like food, cokes,
thread, stamps, phone calls, etc.

about any dangers once I started college. At one time, she would tell
me inexhaustible stories about what a bad man might do to me—take
away my innocence, make me pregnant, imprison me, make me insane and suicidal. But now there were no warnings about sex or about
the importance of saving my virginity for my wedding night. In fact,
she openly guessed I had lost my virginity to my German boyfriend
in Switzerland, which was not the case, but I found it strange that she

was not upset in thinking that I had. She also did not warn me about drugs. She knew I had already smoked hashish in Switzerland, and, in fact, she felt somewhat guilty that her attempts to have my boyfriend arrested for drugs had led to my arrest as well. Perhaps she no longer worried about any of those perils because my list of expenses showed I had become a mature and responsible young woman. Perhaps so many bad things had already happened to our family that these other concerns had become inconsequential.

When I turned to the next letter, I realized I had started reading them out of order. The typed letter with the list of expenditures had been the third. The first was this:

August 29, 1969

Dear Mom,

Aren't you heartsick with pure grief now that I've gone to college? I've been so upset lately and I really don't know why. I really didn't want everything to be so bad when I left. What I'm saying is that I'm sorry I was so crazy and stupid those few days. Even while I was getting mad, I knew I was wrong but I was so mad that I couldn't admit it. You know how it is with me, don't you?

I was really getting unsure about college and really scared because I felt so unprepared and it seemed no one understood. Well, everything is fine now. I got to Portland after a very scenic flight (saw Mt. Shasta & Crater Lake) and it was only 9:20 . . .

So I had been right. This was evidence of the relationship I remembered most clearly, an emotional seesaw of fights followed by declarations of love, and what would be a constant theme: that when we were not at battle, we each understood the other deeply. We understood the parts of ourselves that were similar, the feelings that mounted out of control. The remainder of that first letter concerned my roommate and the delightful amount of junk she had brought with her: a turntable, popcorn maker, hot plate, radio, alarm clock, matching towels and bedspread, and tons of clothes. Her closet was overflowing. In contrast, I had a few dresses, but not even a pair of jeans or sneakers. I remember thinking that I was like that girl in the movie *Daddy Long Legs,* a French orphan who winds up at a posh American college, thanks to an anonymous American benefactor. Like me, she arrives with not much more than the clothes on her back. Unlike me, within fifteen minutes of feeling sorry for herself, trunks of clothes arrive—designer dresses, ball gowns, and even a tennis costume, sent by her unknown benefactor. I would receive over time C.O.D. boxes containing things I requested—my winter dresses, my father's typewriter, and photos of the family when there were five of us.

I now wonder why my mother did not help me to pack, nor why she had not accompanied me to college, like most parents. I had not been emotionally or psychologically prepared to be a college student. I was only seventeen. She did not even go to the airport with me. A family friend dropped me off. I stood alone at the reservations counter and paid for a one-way ticket to Portland, Oregon. I had with me only one suitcase. I looked out the window on the airplane as we flew over the peaks of mountains, and I had no one to exclaim how beautiful they were. When I landed, I was hungry. I went to a phone booth and put a dime in the telephone slot to call a cousin who said he would pick me up. I heard only a busy signal for the next hour and I was becoming hungrier by the minute. My mother had paid for part of my tuition. But for the rest of my tuition and expenses, I depended on a student loan, a scholarship, my father's $50 a month survivor's benefits and my earnings from two part-time jobs. Most of the students did not work. When the girls in my dorm talked about going home for Thanksgiving, I realized that my mother and I had not discussed what I would do. It seemed unlikely, however, that I would pay for a round-trip flight simply to have Thanksgiving dinner at home. That would have been awfully extravagant.

Now that I think about this more, I know why my mother did not help me pack. In July, when we came back to the United States, she found herself in an empty rented apartment, not a home with a permanent address. There were no menus in foreign languages to

1968: Aboard the SS Rotterdam. *John, Daisy, and me, posing as sophisticates.*

decipher, no road signs to towns with *umlauts* or accents *aigu* or *grave* in their names. In Europe, everything had been an adventure, and it had contained no surprise past memories. Everything we did there had been first-time experiences. We had been nomads, open to whatever came our way. Europe was cheap, and with the U.S. dollar's favorable exchange rate, we could stay in hotels that cost two dollars a night and not feel we had to penny pinch. When the three of us returned to California, she found that friends and family had adjusted to our loss. She was staggered by grief all over again. She was paralyzed by uncertainty. The past was all around her. The future could not be seen.

I picture her with tears in her eyes and her face bunched with agony. I see her surveying the nearly empty apartment, then throwing her hands up and asking the same question. What will I do? It made my brother and me anxious when she could not stop. I imagine I finally told her we could not take it anymore and that I was glad I was going to college. That's why she did not get on the airplane with me, why she did not count the number of socks, shoes, pants, skirts, dresses, blouses, and sweaters I needed.

I imagine she read my letter and cried. My letter of apology was accepted and she made plans to visit me soon. But then she called up, upset and incoherent. And I, the seventeen-year-old, tried to sound mature as I stood up for her just as my father had. Instead, my style of writing comes across as the voice of a perky stranger, a teenage therapist who had already learned to mirror back whatever my mother was feeling to curb her suicidal urges.

September 17, 1969

Dearest Mom,

Please don't feel bad because you can't come up. At least I'm not mad at you! (we Tans stick together, no matter how far apart we are!!) Of course, I'm sad that you can't come up—that's expected (I think you would be disappointed if I wasn't). But I understand <u>completely</u> why you can't come up. You didn't get to tell me too much why, but even so I can understand and know that you can't come up. You didn't get to tell me too much why, but even so I can understand and know that you can't. If you'd like to look at it another way: If you had come up this week-end, I would have been swamped with homework and tests in calculus and chemistry anyway—and now I can study this week-end, O.K.?

Anyway, you're welcome to come anytime you want. The dorms are spacious to accommodate one petite Chinese mother in Failing Room 23 anyway, anytime. There are many people who want to meet you. I've told them all about you and it's always fun to have a mom in the dorm if you don't mind girls running in and out in their pyjamas! . . .

Tell me why you sounded so upset on the phone. I don't see why X should be mad. This trip to Linfield for him is just for <u>fun</u> whereas you have <u>so</u> many other problems to cope with. Maybe <u>they</u> think you can't make big decisions, but I'd like to see them try without a father or older son to decide how to start a second life. I'd like to see them make snap decisions about where to live and at the same time decide your future and children's too. (I'm not making much sense but I'm really mad at them for not understanding.) But even as husband and wife it would be super hard to even try to change your life, and when you're alone it's almost impossible. . . . They don't know how to make *big decisions in my opinion, and you've made quite a few almost impossible ones—in just one year. I'm willing to let you change your mind a hundred times just as long as you come up with the right one at the end—and you've done fine so far! You're great in my opinion!*

By not coming up to Linfield this weekend you are looking after your responsibility towards John and his future and home. That's a lot *more important than delivering me some clothes. I know you'd be so much more relieved to* settle *down first and start on a new future. I have mine pretty well taken care of here at Linfield.*

I have so much to say on this matter but I'm really keyed up inside with anger at them. Don't let them upset you. Maybe get mad at them but their opinions are not worthy to get upset over. They're so up-tight about getting things set into a stupid routine so fast that the best decision doesn't seem to matter to them. . . . I believe in making decisions—sure—but if one solution doesn't work—find another to replace it. If I decided early in life to become a nurse and found I hated it after a month—why stick with it? Not that I'll be one but that's America's privilege—freedom to your own pursuit of happiness—and by this you make decisions that suit you—and no one else! Of course we do this as a family and I only wish I could be there with you and John to stick up for whatever you decide.

Mom—please promise me you'll always decide what you want and think is best and not listen to unhelpful advice from certain people. You're Mom*—who can decide for the* Tan *family and no one else should interfere or make you anything you don't want to be.*

Maybe I sound spiteful and maybe I'm not right about everything I've said so far but right now, I'm mad, and I think they are more harmful than helpful. They have proved they are only good in undermining your intelligence. They underestimate your abilities and are confusing you into thinking you should be dependent on them.

Just know I'm campaigning for you and everything you do. If you're right or wrong, it's what you and we *wanted. If we're happy but foolish in other people's minds, let them worry about that, and not us.*

Let's have a future of happiness and not regrets by listening to others. Do whatever you want with your money, Mom. It's your

money, your prerogative and your <u>mind</u>*. And if the money's gone*
in a couple of years, I will take care of you. I promise, Mom, if you
promise to <u>believe</u> *me—I will support you right or wrong and rich*
or poor. Your doctor daughter (hopefully, a doctor) will support you
and <u>not</u> *send you to a rest home. I never told you because I knew*
you wouldn't believe me, but one reason (one very important reason)
I want to be successful is so that we won't have to worry about our
family. If at the time I have the money, I'll see that John gets through
college and that you are not frantically counting your pennies. But
with your mind, I'm sure you can be a success. We are never sure of
the future, but if we can be sure of ourselves that's important enough.

This is a very terrible letter for me to write but I hope you
realize that I'm about as mad as I have ever been. You're my mom
and I won't have anyone insinuate anything against you. Our family
is such a different situation—will anyone ever understand? I wish I
could say this to you in person; it would make more sense.

I really am fine except that I miss you and John terribly, terribly.
Please write and let me know the situation.

Lots and lots of love,
Amy

I remember now a cultlike sense that our family was one against
the world. No one had experienced what we had been through. They
did not know our pain, our insecurity, and our distrust of homilies
that "things will work out for the best." Although I fought often with
my mother, my little brother and I would not tolerate anyone else
criticizing her. We knew how lost she was. We knew how much she
cried and wailed and appealed to God and her dead mother to bring
her son and husband back. We knew how often she thought about
suicide. To judge by the letter I wrote, I am guessing that family and
friends had become exasperated with her inability to decide what
to do with her life. She would ask people for their advice and then
she would dismiss it, reciting her fears like Hail Marys counted out
on rosary beads. I'm sure they believed that by pushing her to make
decisions, they were being helpful. Perhaps someone suggested she

not do anything foolish, like move to Taiwan, or open a restaurant. Maybe she believed that they were implying she was stupid. I understood the frustration that friends and family might have felt, because I had the same reaction. I watched her spin in her emotional eddies, as she called to be saved but then refused to be helped. And yet throughout the years, beginning with that first year in college, she and I both knew I would defend her if anyone had demeaned her. I not only understood her, but I also became her. I was as infuriated as she was. When she felt exposed and disparaged, my brother and I closed in and became closer, unified.

Just recently someone who had known my mother in Shanghai criticized her in a letter. She insinuated that my mother could be cruel and selfish. She cited examples. I was shocked and horrified that my mother had done these things. I apologized to the woman for having suffered from my mother's actions. I even admitted my mother had wounded me as well, but I did not think my mother was intentionally cruel. She had been mentally ill. My defense of my mother led the woman to relate more details, not only about my mother's cruelty, but also about her immorality for leaving her husband, a pilot, a national hero. It was in all the gossip columns, she said. Everyone was talking about her, saying she belonged in jail. She had brought disgrace on the family who had adopted her after her mother killed herself. That family helped her, the woman said, even though they were not blood-related. She was an orphan, not a true daughter. And what did she do? She brought shame on them. She was a disgrace.

This woman had recited all the things my mother had already told me, in tears of fury. They were the reasons why she often wanted to kill herself. People looked down on her mother for becoming a concubine, when she should have remained a chaste widow. My mother inherited that shame and she was always reminded she was an orphan, not blood-related. She felt she did not belong to anyone and would always be tainted and never good enough. It was true that she had left her husband, the pilot. How could she stay? He brought other women into the marriage bed. He held a gun to her head when she would not sleep with him. He raped young girls. He gambled away

most of their money. He brought home gonorrhea. And he was not a
hero. He was a coward who turned his plane around in the face of fire.
The other pilots died. He lived. For having left him, my mother was
a disgrace. I was furious at myself for having apologized to a woman
who hated my mother. How could I have doubted my mother's integrity and morals? I understood her. I had her character.

I returned to the file with my mother's letters and pulled out one
written in 1980, after Lou and I had apparently tried to "draw the
line" on what my mother could expect us to do. I suspect this had to
do with my mother's obsession with a family house in Shanghai that
belonged to her. Or it could have been the issue having to do with her
birth year. It had been recorded as 1917 instead of 1916. The one-year
discrepancy wasn't a problem until she realized it meant she had to
work a year longer before she could retire. We were charged with
changing it, a process that took much time. Whenever we saw her,
she would go into the same laments over the mistake in her birth
year. Whatever it was, we had probably spoken too tersely, and then
the conversation spun out of control, and she had continued to vent
when she reached home by writing the letter below. It starts with
a reasonable but wounded tone. The handwriting is controlled, but
soon enough, she mentions a wish to die. Then comes anger. By the
second page, the written words lose their shape and disintegrate as
she goes into the past, to a moment when my brother Peter was lying
in a coma, at which point she is pulling out pain in fistfuls during a
free fall into depression.

Dear Amy,

*I left I thought there wasn't any reason for me to stay a little bit
longer. I did not wish you to see me crying. It was too hard to control
not to cry, my tears just won't stop coming down, even were at the
restaurant eating and all the way coming home. I cry very hard. I felt
so ashamed. I wish I could die or there some place to crawl in to hide
myself, never want to see anybody.*

*You exercised your humanity out of your love at least you
should keep your tone softer, but your voices sounded so cruel and*

*cold, both you are highly educated compare with my Peking English
you know it is unthinkable too far apart. The accusation coming
from both of you at the same time I had little space to defend
myself. What's use! You didn't like my bug all the time, intervene
to your private life that was totally intolerable because of my bad
taste of behavior no sense of when and where that I should draw
a line that I should do and shouldn't do. I spoiled everything, so
I should say sorry. I promise I'll never do it again. Then another
thing I can't make my words clear enough to let people know what
really mean that also cause the problem and irritate lots of people.
I've to apologize for this stupidity God didn't give me such handy
wisdom to have disappointed you. I thought I was that bad, thank
God for your generosity gave me assurance you were repeatly
saying: "We concern for your health, try to unwind my mind—not
like idiosyncrasy so I can have strong body and healthy mind. But
you put the ax on me too hard, it was pityless! And you have said
too much, I don't know what to believe, which is the truth.*

*Peter blinked his eyes three times to say I love you. It was so
sudden. Dad and I lost our control, tears flooded our eyes with love,
joy, and hope. I never forget it until I die. I understand what is love,
so touchy, so gentle and warm.*

*I don't want to make any judgment about Amy. There must be
something happen in school—Jr. high, kids are sometimes very cruel.
I really don't know. Only noticed Amy was changed in many ways.
She turned away from us. Dad was still alive. Why? Chinese?*

*I will not come to disturb you anymore. You don't have to worry
about it. I will understand it very well.*

*And I want to thank you for the dinner and the gifts for my
birthday, and your thought too. I do not expect anything next time
please! When you finish photo, I want it back. They are mine.*

What a waste of my life! No good for anybody! No-nothing!
                                                    Mother

We heard her express similar emotions many times—and they
always had to do with slights, about people not believing her, and her

not knowing what to believe. We often heard her say she was worth-less. We would assess by her manner whether she might truly try to kill herself or if we would be able to calm her by assuring her that we believed her and loved her. But what she had expressed in that letter arrived days after she had been crying and shaking in distress. Writ-ten words have the force of commitment and hers were frightening. When I read her letter thirty-six years ago, I must have panicked, not knowing what she had done after she finished writing. No doubt I called her as soon as I finished reading the letter. Likely she told me not to cry, that everything would be better, that we would under-stand each other better.

The seriousness of her mental illness is apparent in those letters. I had experienced the living force of those words, but the letters had captured her disintegration in real time and preserved it. Even in the best of times, she could easily break and come apart. I saw that in her letter to me from Shanghai in 1985, where she was visiting family. Most of the letter concerns a lost radio. When something bothered her, she was unable to let go. It ground in her mind and fragmented into more pieces, and she would sift through those as well, eventu-ally believing she was going crazy.

Next day I opened my bag I could not find one of the radio. I couldn't believe I could have lost it, because I picked it up from the table after the inspection and put it into my bag (like yours). I carried that bag on my shoulder, one hand pushed the cart and the other hand pulled the luggage went through the door to outside, everybody (chauffeur, relatives) offered hands to grab my luggage and bags I only took care of my purse, something they also want to take care of my purse (politeness) but I like to hold on my own thing, another thing to take. After the plane arrived I went to wait for luggage, I was so strong I pull every one of the luggage out the turning cart. I became very independent through two years of working for the [husband].

The radio got lost, I really don't understand it. I didn't loose my mind that time, however it bothered me. During my stay between

[family friends], it seemed like I accused someone when I couldn't
find my thing. Actually, I was so confused. I worried I lost my mind,
so I wanted to think hard to see if I was having bad memory or went
crazy. My mind often wandered far away. I usually heard half of the
conversation if someone was talking to me sometimes I was thinking
that could make me cry, at the time I had to swallow my tear, it
wasn't easy. At John's wedding my mind was thinking something
else and tried so hard to swallow my tear. I think your friend took
a picture of me very very sad face. I was so miserable during that
period. It's hard to say I'll be all right.

Two weeks later, she was still fretting over the lost radio and
now, on top of that, she had also been forced to pay a $110 duty sur-
charge for bringing in an extra camera for a cousin.

Every time people go out to foreign country by air and before
arriving the stewardess will hand to you a couple of printed paper
requested you write down things you bring in, and the other paper
is for the information of nationality, age, and address etc. When
you enter to show the passport. Then go through the customs.
They check the list of things on the paper, sometimes they ask to
see, like the radio you gave, (later I couldn't find the one I showed)
I don't think they took it, and also like Frank he brought in two
cameras and one big item—T.V. for someone else tax free. Frank
probably didn't know he couldn't bring the extra camera, besides
he got one item free of duty. The camera should be charged for
the duty. They estimated the camera worth 200Y, then use 150%
off from 200Y came out 300Y equals $110 less 11Y. If Frank had
explained the camera for an America to use in China, later the
camera would be taken out of China, situation would be different,
may be they will put it down on the paper like if the camera wasn't
taken out then charge for the duty. Anyway it could be worked out
better. Now I got the camera that worth twice price though I got
part of receipt showed charge of the camera for 300Y, but I won't be
going out of country same way Frank came in. I went to customs of

Beijing supposed to be the head. What use I tried. They said, "Too complicated they can't do." suggested I write to Canton.

I was mad inside of me. Frank felt bad about the duty and he needed that $110 to spend.

There was a counterbalance to my mother's depressions and feelings of helplessness. It was her persistence, which led to a plan.

Auntie Elsie wanted me to go to Hong Kong for a visit. I'm thinking it is not bad idea, that means I go to Canton to get the $110 back, I use the money for part of the expense that also makes me feel better, at the same time once again to see Hong Kong. . . . I take time to relax, plenty time to sleep and afternoon a nap.

It has taken me thirty-six years to understand why she could not let go of that lost radio. I understood when I carefully reread the letter. I had given her that radio.

[Regarding the lost radio] I felt you love me so much you wanted me be happy to find every way to please me. I understand you deeply, but you work so hard I worry for you. Is it worth? You don't have to work so hard. Sit all day in front of the computer, squeeze every bit of your brain, it is too hard on you. What other way you would not be stress that would harm you?

I better stop. Take care of yourself, don't get hungry, smoke less, drink less (coffee), eat plenty of fruit. Do you like hear?

Love,
Mom

We wrote letters in English when we were far apart. I wrote a book to show her how close we truly were.

Why Write?

[From the journal]

CHAUTAUQUA, NEW YORK, AUGUST 2008. *A poet friend quoted another writer—who?—that we write to prolong the time between our two deaths: the physical death of our being when we cease to exist, and the death of us when no one remembers us, which can be weeks, months, years.*

But I don't write for that reason. Why would I want to be remembered by strangers and those whose memories of me are the misperceptions that people already have now of my work? Inaccurate "memory," acquired from my writing.

I write to prolong my memory of life now, to see that I have had thoughts, emotions, ideas, encounters, and experiences. If I cannot remember, it is as if I had not lived those days, and that my life was the barest of details I do remember. By writing it down, it is engrained, and my thoughts continue, are part of some stream and not just discrete bits from the day's menu, the same offerings, and my eating the same things I liked the last time.

VI

LANGUAGE

CHAPTER TWELVE

··

LANGUAGE: A LOVE STORY

At night, I resurrect the languages I love that are no longer spoken. I lie in my bed, and next to me is a book, a different one each night. I turn on my side toward my chosen, slip my thumb and forefinger along its spine, flatten the cleft to smooth the pages, and I read. They are words from a language struck dumb by the mortality of all its native speakers. Two nights ago, it was Aramaic origins of the Bible. Last night it was Lyconian funereal verses. Tonight it is Sumerian cuneiforms in the fourth millennium B.C. at that very moment a Sumerian scanned the heavens and saw a star, as glorious and frightening as anything he had ever seen. On a smooth limestone wall, he carved that star, an intersection of light from all six directions: east, west, north, south, heaven, and earth. He named his first written word, *Ahn*. "God." I say it with him, *Ahn*. And now, the illusion arrives, and I no longer see the Sumerian symbol nor the tightly fitted explanations on its linguistic descent. I hear the word, formless, without boundaries, a pulsing life within me. I am *Ahn*.

We speak and listen, the Sumerian and I, lovers now, who were strangers to each other when we lived in the past. We say the words that have not been spoken in thousands of years, becoming them, the sense of them, the ecstatic visions and unspeakable torments, the sad half of half-truths, the confessions that died before torture could extract them, all unheard since the smothering death of my Sumerian friend by Akkadian, four thousand years ago, a long time to be silent.

Night after night, the languages and I are more alive than ever. In this way, I have embraced over eight hundred dead languages. They have told me the weaknesses of their enemies, the prayers said to gods, the plans for victory that were blighted by unexpected weather. They have murmured to me the names for parts of the body, all the ways to say "mouth," "breasts," and "belly," so many of them uttered with bilabials, the sounds made by pressing the lips together. These are the words that pleasure, the way we feel them in our mouths, in the shapes of the words we say to each other.

But in the morning, the words appear again, clean and mute on the page. And I appear in the mirror, not a bilabial sensation but a sixty-four-year-old shape of flesh and bones, knees and knuckles, that has pressed against many men, against their shapes, against what I wanted, and that is a history not worth recounting. It was time spent. I remind myself that I know the difference between illusion and delusion. It is the separation between desire and belief. I know what separates the past from the present, what lies between then and now. It is but a moment, an easy thing to lose. And the separation between sounds uttered then and the sounds uttered now is silence, not easily broken.

I put the book on Sumerian cuneiforms back in its proper place: bottom shelf, a gap-tooth space between Scythian and Taino in a bookshelf among many bookshelves, floor to ceiling, on all four sides, and on both windowsills of my bedroom. I have arranged the books in alphabetical order, according to region—that is, how the regions are known today, and not by the names given to them by their Mongol or Ottoman or Babylonian or other conquering empires that subsumed them as collateral property. I did not further order them by their time of decimation. That would have caused me to recall all those pedantic arguments by linguists on what constitutes extinction. The linguists would say that Akkadian, once the language of all the Mesopotamian nations, died around the time the last cuneiform was written, in first century B.C. I once abided by the empirical evidence. But now I allow for another realm of possibilities—my own. Imagine it: there must have been innumerable Akkadian illiterates who continued to chat and lie and scold without benefit of cuneiforms.

On the other hand, I have taken a hard line with Latin. A language is not alive if it is used only in liturgical text and sacred chanting. A language is not living if its current-day speakers have to be taught the vocabulary, pronunciation, and conjugation, rather than by absorbing it as infants along with mother's milk. It possesses no signs of life if it is not spoken in daily conversation in all its motley ways: as idle chatter among friends, to haggle over the price of cabbage, to bear strange news of plagues or that an enemy is dead, as is the hero who killed him. When a language has no native speakers, it cannot be resuscitated. It is forever dead. Latin is dead, *Latina mortua est*, and the Catholics could not save her. Let us grieve for her. *Nos eam contristare.*

I cannot fathom the logic of those who claim Latin is still alive because Italian, Spanish, and French are her living progeny. Shall we also count Esperanto? Can we claim Neanderthals are alive because they, like *Homo sapiens,* evolved from hominids? The sentimental linguaphiles believe that the Aeolian dialect of ancient Greek is not extinct. Modern Greek has made it younger. They should ask the poet Sappho where she bought her lyre. A language engulfed by another should be mourned. The remnants of a language after the bulk has been assimilated and absorbed are not enough to say it survived. The lexicon of a language is not those words on a thousand tombstones. The language is its people and their spontaneous puns, the bad jokes and long-winded stories. It is the particular nuances of languages that allow nefarious politicians to wet them with spittle and wring out the false appearance of truth. Another language cannot serve adequately as a dead language's translator. It would not be able to fully capture the art of ambiguity, the ironic iconic words, the cadence of words as accompaniment to emotion, the play of one historical pun on another. We should honor the dead and grieve what has been lost and is irreplaceable.

Without language, written or spoken, who can provide the proper eulogy of the speakers and their culture, its history of beneficence, uprisings, and decline? Can we believe what the Romans said about their enemy the Etruscans? They maligned them as cruel. *Imagine it, Flavius: the slaves wear only their loincloths and a hood over their heads, a club in one hand, and the leashes of vicious dogs latched to their ankles.* Isn't it odd that the Romans gave no thanks to the Etruscans for inspiring their own Coliseum entertainment? And no pious Roman aunt had anything good to say about an Etruscan lady. *Believe me, Luciana, they are lascivious beyond compare, swaying their hips outside the home, sitting beside their husbands at sporting events, cheering for their favorite lion. Those Etruscan women might be mating with rams, for all we know.* How much of history is calumny chipped in stone, with vengeance as the last word and the last laugh. The Etruscans may have been a lovely people, full of humor and comparatively kind to slaves. But there are no Etruscan words to defend themselves from slander. What remains are their status symbols viewed through glass or behind ropes in museums—the gold bangles and necklace with gems, the bronze chariot inlaid with ivory, the terracotta statues in the sarcophagi, the almond-eyed husband and wife lying on their sides, whose mysterious faces look bemused, as if being entertained by the antics of their children or their theatrical dramas of mythology, none of which remain, only shards that suggest they once existed. Out of thirteen thousand linen scraps and marble chunks of words, the only clues of the Etruscan language are the names of borrowed gods and the popular vacation destinations in the afterlife. "The Tomb of Fishing and Hunting." "The Tomb of the Sun and the Moon." They are not enough to unlock the cryptic code of Etruscan. But I suspect that one day, some farmer—it is always a farmer and his cow—will trip on the head of a gorgon, a statue that stood on the peak of an Etruscan home, and that roofline will lead to the remnants of an Etruscan suburb, where archaeologists will find sufficient script to solve the linguistic puzzle. I imagine that much will be learned by the graffiti scrawled on walls: "Cutu Sveitus, the bastard, died owing me three casks of extra virgin olive oil." "Lady Thana was an unfaithful whore with two mouths instead of a vagina." "Mourn Larth not. He is the son of Velthur Pompli, the purveyor of fake gold belts."

On my shelves, there is no debate which languages are dead, only agreement of departure: Etruscan is here, of course, as is Agta-Dicamay of the Philippines, Ahon of India, Arin of Siberia, Azari of the Iranian Plateau—so many, it is like counting stars. Some of their remains are thick tomes. Others are thin-spined monographs with typewritten titles. They tilt and jut up at different heights like tombstones settling in soft dirt. Sometimes I reflect that I will one day join the dead languages and their speakers, and no one will recall what I spoke. I will leave no mark in the record of humankind. Like most of these silent languages, I will not be missed and mourned. This is not a complaint, just a reminder to myself from time to time, to ask if there is anything else I should be doing. And then I continue.

Here are three extinct languages, as close as sisters: Cappadocian, Cataonian, and Cilician. I have cataloged the places where they appear in Greek literature, always in passing, the lower status neighbors of the god-laden Greeks, to whom those sisters had come to borrow an amphora of wine and died shortly after because they forgot to specify in the dominant language, "Plain wine, that is, not poisoned."

I will mourn Washo and Quechan when the last of her native speakers are gone and those at their funerals speak only English. I have put those two languages with the endangered ones in my study. There are so many, crammed on bookshelves along all the walls with only the stanchions of doorways and small windows to interrupt the flow. I find it agonizing to decide which language should be placed on the shelf for imminent extinction—and of the hundred and twenty endangered languages in China, which are the twenty that are the most critical? The books and monographs on these dying languages

are not always rigorously done. Many are neither informative nor
interesting. For some, the remains of its lexicon resemble the lesson
plan for kindergarten children, numbers one through ten, primary
colors, and such. I cannot always determine whether the data is a bad
transcription done by someone without an ear for phonemes.

The death knell will soon be rung for many more, be it through
the brutality of ethnic cleansing or the education of the masses. Han
is the language of instruction in China; it is the language on the playground, the language of pop music and movies. We can't deny the
children of minority languages from attending school. We can't deny
them the pleasures of pop culture. We can't prohibit them from gazing at the small screens of their cell phones while walking to school,
while eating breakfast, lunch, and dinner, while seated in the classroom or at the movie theater. In a just society, every child and adult
has equal opportunity to devise a condensed form of their thoughts,
devoid of complete sentences, but rich in dynamic spellings and ac-
ronyms as shorthand for emotions. They should all have the means
to text a lover and document every second of their existence: *just got
home, just sat down, just saw your photo, just got under the covers, just got
caught.* Through text, they talk, and they are losing the idiosyncrasies
of their voices, the regional nuances, the whiny tone of irritation, the
wobbling one of shyness. They are merging with a more utilitarian
grammar-lite language, in which datives and locatives are the here
and now of when a message was sent and not when it was received.
"Are you here?" "No, I'm not here."

I don't condemn these changes. I mourn and move on. I observe
and describe what is happening. So let us continue. Here is Yiddish,
still spoken but ebbing into folktales, religious ceremonies, and jokes.
I have banished the joke books.

My love for languages began at home, listening to the linguistic hubbub of an extended family prone to disagreement—
Mandarin, Shanghainese, English, both excellent and substandard
versions of all of them. I mimicked my elders and peers, not just the

words but also their mannerisms. To speak a language fluently, you must be persuasive in that language and not just argumentative. To know a language well, you must understand intent before words.

At seventeen, I took my love of languages to the university and studied linguistics to obtain an undergraduate degree, then a master's, and a Ph.D. I was young and needed to make a mark of some kind, and my love for language soon gave way to intellectual enthusiasm. I fell into the sinkholes of theories—Chomsky's view of innate language structures as ready-made scaffolding in the brain, followed by waves of other theorists who banged their heads on a closed system and eventually built their own theoretical camps. I did so as well; my position as an assistant professor at the university depended on it. New approaches to the puzzle of language origins, acquisition, change, and decay. New questions on how change occurs.

In time, I forgot about the persuasive nature of language, the intent before words. I wrote papers like, "Gain and Loss Innovation in the Genealogical Classification of Mongolian and Manchu-Tungusic Languages." My papers were read by the twenty-six linguists who claimed this same diachronous territory, from Manchuria to the Altai mountains, between Genghis and glasnost. That was how I nearly killed my love for language. I buried it under academic discourse with my contentious colleagues, who sought the smallest differences to undo me. *Did you link Kalmuk with Oirat, Dagur with Buriat? Do you agree with the theories of those Soviet scholars—that languages go their separate ways according to those that are vowel harmonizing and those that are not? Did you consider those languages that are syllabic in phonological structure and not simply those that are purely vocalic?*

Through scholarship, I saw language as territory and a reason for combat. I saw only in between, and not within. I looked for evidence in homonyms, counterevidence in rhymes. The goal was to find proof, better and more proof, impenetrable and inviolable by opposing views. Without proof, you have nothing more to say. I sat in judgment with my colleagues over what should be included in the realm of consideration.

Twenty years ago, my opinions about proof changed. I was driving home from a meeting, going up the familiar eucalyptus-lined road in the Oakland hills, when a fox suddenly appeared. A driver coming downhill in the opposite direction saw the same. She was a lover of felines, she later explained, which was what she mistook the vulpine to be. Out of such love, she turned her wheel sharply to avoid hitting the catlike fox and in so doing, hit my car instead, sending my car and me tumbling over the embankment. I was not thrown from the car, but the bony case that holds my brain banged against the side window each time the car rolled over—three times. I was lucky I had not fractured my skull, the doctor later told me. I had suffered only a bad concussion, a bruise on my temporal lobe. But the next day, there was evidence of a subdural hematoma—a slight one, just a bit of a blood leak under the skull but not in the brain, and that resolved quickly on its own, no surgery required, so again I was lucky. Luck ebbed when I found that a bit of a hematoma and bruise on the brain do not heal like a scratch and bump on the knee. I had difficulties keeping my thoughts organized as words. When asked to describe what I saw on the road just before the accident, I could see the road, the fox, the other car, and the woman's eyes staring into mine before the sound of crushed metal. But I could not describe this. I could not say where one was in relation to the other, spatially or temporally. When I could speak again, I felt as if my thoughts were being diverted to a holding place, where some were released more quickly than others. I knew my intellect had suffered greatly when I could no longer understand the arguments waged against my most recent work published in *Lingua*. Instead of resigning, however, I asked for a leave of absence, believing that I might fully recover. I said I might ease back in later by teaching only one class. The department head made vague assurances that my position would still be there when I was ready—they would try their very best to make that possible. His tone of voice was too consoling and full of the kind of excessive warmth expressed to people who are dying and leaving behind a fortune. As damaged as my brain was, I detected that. He was glad to be rid of me. In the next beat, I shouted: "How stupid do you think I've become to believe that?" It was the most comprehensible thing I had said since the accident.

The insurance settlement was large, commensurate with the amount of damage done to me, as enumerated and exaggerated by my lawyers. After six months, I understood that the vast sum was not excessive, given that no amount could compensate me for what I had lost. I was forced to consider how much of my existence had been my intellect. And then I sank into grief for my former wholly cerebral self.

My mind had become a Scrabble board of unrelated words. I had to consciously put them together to form a sentence. My thoughts were similarly disconnected, and I had to search for contiguous thoughts I could stitch together in logical order. I could not recognize satire or irony or humor more subtle than slapstick. I became terrified that I might have lost more than I could fathom.

To rehabilitate my brain, I underwent speech therapy, but I was impatient with my slow progress. At night, I read simple texts, children's nursery rhymes and fairy tales, first in English, and then in other languages. In those early days, I counted my victories in small parcels—when I could recall the gist of the story a day later, or remember the particular abilities of various gnomes, fairies, genies, and witches. I read a hundred fairy tales. I reread them, again and again, until they no longer felt new. I recovered basic analytic skills by seeking patterns in those fairy tales: there was often a desire, an obstacle, a trial requiring feats of ingenuity. I recorded my discoveries on scratch pads, which served as interim memory. I noted that victory required both the violent destruction of enemies and the reward of castle, kingdom, and love. I also discovered that many of the stories had a common refrain, which often appeared in the middle of the tale, at that intersection where bad decisions quickly become fatal ones: *When leaving a place, don't look back. If you do, you are back to where you started.* I took it to be a warning about my own life—that if I looked back, all progress I had made would vanish. I was like a character from a fairy tale, banished from the kingdom until I could find enough clues to solve the puzzle. I had to walk blindfolded into a forest of talking trees. I had to find the salivating sea with its tongue-lapping waves. I had to bail water with a leaky bucket until the sea waves turned into sand dunes. Damn the castle and its puzzles.

One evening, I opened drawers in search of a scratch pad and came across the draft of a monograph I had written before the accident. Here in my hands were the vestiges of who I was five years ago, just hours before I tumbled into a ravine. I knew I should not read those pages. But a small hope that my brain had improved became a great torment in my need to know. I read the title, and then, cautiously, the short descriptive paragraph, and I shouted with jubilation. I understood it, or, rather the intent of it—the morphological evidence that Xibe was likely a dialect of Manchu and not its evolutionary heir apparent. I continued reading and remembered why I had chosen to write the monograph. New pockets of native Manchu speakers had been found in isolated villages in northeast China. I possessed new data, new proof. But the speakers were elderly and their progeny spoke only Chinese, which put Manchu in the bell lap of a race it could not finish. The monograph was timely. I was elated that I could follow bits and pieces of the premise, the data, the hypothesis, the competing theories, and the body of evidence that was still needed. I understood only the gist of those pieces, but they were enough clues to the puzzle, each an oasis, linked to another, creating a path out of the dry dunes of my memory.

As a linguist, I knew better than most that one does not inherit a predisposition toward a particular language. Yet, when I first studied Manchu, I had the odd sense that I was becoming reacquainted with a language I had once used. The textures of reduplicative syllables in my mouth felt familiar. The meanings of the words came with vivid images, what seemed like recollections. That night, now fifteen years ago, I recalled one—not the word, but the image that it stood for—an ancient desiccated tree that had lost its bark. In my mind, I could still picture that bare tree. And when I did, a shape ran out from behind that tree and floated before my eyes like a hologram. I went to touch it and it immediately disappeared. A stroke,

I thought, a leak in my brain. There goes the rest of me. I closed my eyes to await the change. After a minute, I opened them and saw the shape was there again. It was a word. *Kirsa,* I read aloud. Immediately the word pulsated and dashed across my field of vision. A detached retina. My doctor had cautioned that this might occur months or even years after the accident. The word returned, solid and still. What was the meaning of this hallucination? Was I psychotic? I wanted proof that I was not insane. I wanted *kirsa* to mingle with memory and return as a word I once knew. I uttered those two syllables, velar and sibilant, still unclaimed by its meaning. *Kirsa, kirsa, kirsa,* I said. Just as I gave up, I saw it: *kirsa,* the fox, and not the one on the road that blighted my brain, but the fox of the steppes, the one you can never find when you seek it. I knew what the fox knew: to see the illusion, you must become the illusion. In the next instant, I was running on the Mongolian steppes, dry sand beating against my white belly.

From that day forward, I roamed freely among the words of dead languages. I spoke them, I wondered over them, I cherished them, and they came to me alive for a moment, as briefly and as bright as the spark of phosphorus before there is flame.

I now know why the Mongol dynasty retreated from China in the thirteenth century. Listen to the open vowels, the rapid lateral flaps. They were hungry to hunt again and gallop bolt upright in their stirrups over the Hump and across the Prickly Grass. I know why the Manchu soldiers were just as eager to leave those plains three hundred years later when the Qing languished and the sands were no longer theirs to protect. They wanted to return to Manchuria, their ancestral farmland, where their families had been waiting for centuries. As they moved across the steppes alongside the Altai mountains, the sounds of Manchu began to migrate. Palatalized affricates fell forward into sibilants and the Tungus tongues slushed with happiness. Each night, they sat under a full bowl of stars, imbibing fermented mare's milk, muttering that tomorrow would be yet another day wending through Endless Grass. But two years in, they sank to their knees and cried in surprise—*Adada eb-*

ebe! Adada ebebe! How could this be? Nothing rose above the tall grass to mark the path. Hostile tribes had knocked down the ancestral rock piles—thirty-seven generations of guidance now scattered. Soon the illusions greeted them. Deer looked like rocks and rocks became rabbits.

From then on, the only precious words they spoke were rumors of water. Water flowing underground from a hidden river. Sweet water in an oasis poured from pitchers by seven lovely sisters. A muddy pool fouled by the breath of camels. The dental nasal *n* lurched back to the liquid lateral *l*. The water seekers scratched in the sand: "In retrospect, there is no water half a day's journey east of this spot. In retrospect, this was the wrong way to go." And then their cries weakened to *olhokon, olhokon*—"we are all dried up"—and their desiccated voices were sucked forward into the wind hiss. The last sound they heard was a hundred thousand crickets shrieking *sar-sar* as they leaped into the air and onto the Manchus to devour them while they were still fresh.

Fifteen years ago, I read these words: *When leaving a place, don't look back. If you do, you are back to where you started.* I took it as warning. But when the fox appeared, it became a choice, and since then, I have looked back every night.

Tonight I go to a spot in my mind where the foot of the mountain and a river connect, *senggin*, a meeting place. I wait until I feel the sound pulsing in my veins. And it comes—*Pes-pas! Pes-pas!*—the sound of horses galloping softly over grass. The second vowel tightens. *Pes-pis! Pes-pis!* The hooves are hitting the hard-baked earth of the steppes. Soon we will arrive at that place where the past begins.

Intestinal Fortitude

[From the journal]

I misread "intentions" as "intestines" and now think the image is an apt one. Your intentions come in part from what was fed to you so long ago you've forgotten what it was, let alone whether it was good for you or if it simply staved off hunger, whether it was delicious or a kind of poison, an addicting taste.

Books are no longer being bought. People are scrimping on their minds. They are starving.

CHAPTER THIRTEEN

PRINCIPLES OF LINGUISTICS

LANGUAGE ACQUISITION

My mother spoke Shanghainese, Mandarin, and English, but in any of those languages, people often misunderstood what she meant.

Shanghainese was the first language she acquired, the language she heard her parents speak, and she spoke that the best. She picked up Mandarin as a child in school, where it was the language of instruction. That was also the common language she and my father used between them when they argued and, I assume, when they made love. She took English classes as a schoolgirl and of the languages she spoke, English was by far the worst, which was why I was shocked when I came across the facsimile of a college diploma twelve years after her death that showed she had received a bachelor of arts degree from an English-speaking University. Upon closer inspection, I saw that the name of the recipient, Tu Chuan, was only similar to the one on her student visa: Tu Chan. She had used the diploma of someone who had actually earned the degree. The fact that her English had always been rife with mistakes was evidence that this hypothesis was likely true. If she had truly majored in English, I would have seen her reading English novels, but not once did I see her read even one. The only novels we owned were ones packaged under the Reader's Digest Condensed Books series. They were donated to us, but she never read them; I did. Carson McCullers's *A Member of the Wedding*—that was one. She never acknowledged she had read any of the novels I was reading in high school. *Oh, The Scarlet Letter. I love that novel. The minister and the lady. She the punished one, not the man. So sad.* She and my father were the minister and the lady, and she was punished. But she never said that.

In 1949, when she was accepted to Lincoln University in San Francisco to obtain a master's degree in American literature, she confessed by letter to the college registrar that her English had become a little "rusty." The registrar wrote back: "Yours is a common difficulty with Chinese students who have had their studies interrupted." Presumably, the registrar was referring to World War II, which began in China in 1937, when my mother was twenty-one. Or maybe she meant the more recent civil war, which ran from 1945 to 1949, a period of personal turmoil for my mother, when she fell in love with my father, left her husband, and was jailed for infidelity.

"Do not let this dismay you," the registrar wrote on July 26, 1949. "It is a problem easily solved." As soon as she arrived in the United States, the registrar explained, she would be enrolled in intensive courses in oral English, ear training, and idiomatic speech. Once she was proficient, she could begin her coursework. The registrar simultaneously wrote a letter to the American consul general in Hong Kong, where my mother went to apply for a student visa. She presented the letter, which attested that the university had accepted her and that "any language insufficiency would be promptly corrected, including problems in grammatical construction." She arrived in the United States on August 27, 1949, and two weeks later, instead of starting instruction to improve her English, she married my father. Within a month, she was pregnant with my brother Peter. She never set foot in that university with the helpful registrar. She never took the brush-up courses to remove the rust until two years after my father died, when I was away at college and she had no one

*San Francisco, 1989: My mother translates
a letter to us written by my half sister Lijun.*

to write letters for her. She took an ESL class. I was impressed by how well she expressed herself. Her sentence constructions, while hardly perfect, were much improved. What struck me most was the feeling she expressed about her exile in the United States.

> *It was long time since I came to this country. The last I can remember that I was on the last ship sneaky out from the out-port of Shanghai while the fighting was on between the Communist and the Chang Kai Tze Government. That was in May 1949, and two weeks later after I arrived in Hong Kong, Shanghai was lost to the Communist Government. To the people, the war was merely between the two governments and the most of people thought it was just a short period of changing, everyone would go back to their home sweet home. But those people had just the dream.*

She never got rid of the rust in her speech. If anything, her English continued to rust and flake over the next fifty years. And she never read any American literature until she read my first book, and only the first. When my second novel was published, she was already ill with Alzheimer's disease and had difficulty keeping track of the story in *The Kitchen God's Wife,* which included many incidents from her life. "I don't need to be read it," she told me. "That's my story and I know what happened."

LINGUISTIC CHANGE

After my mother developed Alzheimer's disease, she lost her languages in the reverse order of acquisition. First to go was the language she spoke with me, her customized form of English. Our language together then became Mandarin, which I understood fairly easily but could speak only within the limits of a five-year-old child. It was perfectly adequate for communicating with my mother, whose mind and emotions had retreated to childhood. Over time, she transitioned to speaking to me in a blend of Mandarin and Shanghainese, and before long, her expressive deficiencies and mine were about equal, leaving me to resort to pointing to guess what she was saying. *You want to go there—to the bathroom?* Toward the end of her life, her verbal communication consisted mostly of garbled Shanghainese, gestures, grunts, and a few odd surprises. I understood everything she was saying, because by then it was always the same: she simply wanted me to be there.

Even in the last months of her life, she recognized me as soon as I walked through the door of her apartment in the assisted living center. Sometimes she called out a good representation of my name, a two-syllable nasalized vowel. By then, her lips barely moved and her whimpers sounded like someone had put a gag in her mouth. Her face was expressionless—a common development among those in the late stages of the disease. But I knew my mother was not emotionless. Her excitement was obvious by her fluttering hands to have me reach her as soon as possible. She mumbled the occasional word, made comprehensible by context and gestures—to get her favorite sweater or to show me a scrap of paper that held a mysterious meaning I could not decipher—and it did not matter which language we used, English or Mandarin, or a combination, as long as I was by her side, soothing her with words she wanted to hear. I would tell her she was so beautiful she made other women jealous. I would tell her she was smart and noticed things other people could not see. I told her that everyone loved her and that they would be waiting for her at her favorite restaurant where she would be the guest of honor. I named in Mandarin the foods she loved: shrimp and scallops, sea bass and jellyfish, pea greens and dumplings, and hot soup—very, very hot, the way she liked it. Our primary language was emotion, the touch of my hand on hers and her hand on mine. It was the tone of our voices, our gestures, and the degree of animation of our limbs. It was my facial expressions and my interpretation of what hers would have been had she been able to smile or frown or look puzzled. "Are you laughing at me?" I would ask, feigning shock and I would interpret out loud any sounds and mouth movements she made as an affirmative answer. She loved the teasing attention. Even toward the end of her conscious life, she understood all those things conveyed through only intonation and tone of voice, the expressions of love, assurance, and happiness. Take out the words, and the meaning was still there. Say it in any language and the meaning was the same. This was our shared language of emotions. It bypassed the part of the brain where syntax, semantics, and phonological rules operate. It was processed in the area where long-term emotional memories are stored, beginning with the morning words she must have heard her mother say when she was a baby: *"Don't cry. I'm going to feed you,"* the shapes of sounds that meant comfort and trust. She used them with me.

I expressed alarm to her one day when I returned from a trip to New York and saw that she had lost a great deal of weight over the two weeks I had been absent. A few months before, she had begun her dwindling course—from a high of eighty pounds on her four-foot-nine-inch frame to seventy-two. Now she was barely sixty-five pounds. Soon it became sixty. The day arrived when she refused to eat. She repeatedly whimpered and pushed away the spoon I held before her mouth. When I persisted, she started bawling like a baby. I had come to that point where I could no longer deny she would actually die. My mother had made me promise years ago that I would never put her on a feeding tube. The most agonizing decision she had been forced to make, she told me, was agreeing with the doctors to remove the feeding tube from my comatose brother. "Don't start, don't have to stop," I remember her saying. "No use, anyway."

Four years of mental and emotional preparation had not lessened my shock in realizing she would not last much longer, a month or less, her doctor said. My mother had never shied away from talking about death. In fact, she had desired it too often, especially if she had discovered you had kept a secret from her or talked about her behind her back. She would go into a suicidal rage. Whether she understood me, I decided I would respect what she would have wanted me to do. So I sat down beside her. I lifted one of her sticklike arms and gently said in English, "Look how thin you are."

She stared at her arm for a while then mumbled, "Still pretty good." She had spoken actual words and they were in English. It was an automatic expression she once used for all kinds of situations. "Still pretty good" was how she had described an old sofa she wanted to give to her daughter Lijun. "Still pretty good" was how she had described her ability to play a Chopin étude. "Still pretty good" was status quo and holding.

I stroked her arm and said: "You're so thin. Do you think you're going to die?"

She looked at her arm again, stared at it for a long time, as if it were changing before her eyes, then said, "Maybe I die."

She had not simply repeated the last few words of my question, *going to die,* she had formed her own: *maybe I die,* words she had used in healthier days to spout a suicidal threat. I did not know what she understood, but I told her in a soothing tone that I would do everything to make her comfortable and that she had nothing to worry about. She would be happy.

"Okay," she said. It was in the tone of a child who believed whatever her mother said: We can go to the park as soon as you put on your sweater. Okay. After I left her, I broke down and cried in the car.

When the hospice nurse arrived to assess her condition and

needs, my mother put her index finger on the woman's badge. "Kaiser Permanente Hospital," my mother said slowly. This was another surprise. She recognized the logo of the hospital where she had worked for many years as an allergy technician, and where she now received her medical care. She had pronounced those words more intelligibly than anything she had said in months. She continued staring at the name tag. And then she ran her finger over the next line and said aloud the nurse's name. She could read. How was it possible that her dying brain still enabled her to read and speak?

My mother had never ceased to surprise me with revelations over the years: The secret truth of her mother's second marriage. The secret of her mother's suicide. The secret of her own first marriage to an abusive man. The secret of the three daughters she left in China. Her acceptance, without anger, that I had stopped taking piano lessons. Her acceptance without anger that I was living with my Caucasian boyfriend. Her defense of me when my future in-laws disapproved of their son's choice. Her announcement she was marrying a grocer in Fresno, a man who spoke Cantonese, which she could not speak. Her announcement over the phone that she was divorcing the grocer and wanted me to pick her up that same day.

And then there was her announcement a few years later that she had an eighty-five-year-old Shanghainese boyfriend who would come with us on my book tour in Japan. We had to scramble to get him an airline ticket, but we were happy she would be occupied full-time with a man she loved. They did not marry but it was my assignment to tell my uncle in Beijing, her brother, that they had and would be with us as part of their honeymoon—meaning, they would share a bedroom. Halfway through the tour, she and her boyfriend had a fight and she announced she wanted to go home that day. That was not a surprise.

And now, in her final few weeks of life, she had revealed she could still read English, a skill I thought she had lost three years before. I quickly found a piece of paper and printed stacked words in large letters: *Eyes Nose Mouth Ears Stomach*. I asked her to read the first word. "Eye," she enunciated slowly like a schoolgirl learning English.

I asked her, "Where is your eye?" She pointed to her eye. We went through the list and she correctly identified them all. How strange. Something must have shifted in her brain. Fugitive language had bypassed the barriers and traveled to less damaged areas of the brain. She could read, speak, and understand the words—in English. I then asked her if she felt pain in any part of her body? Does your stomach hurt? She looked at me blankly. So there were limitations. It was still gratifying that we were communicating through reading. She was showing me that she recognized what I was saying. We were connected once again by written language, that this word means *love* and that word means *you*. It took me back to a time many years before when we had been separated by both distance and understanding, and to bridge the gap, we had written letters to one another.

"You can read," I said. "All this time you were hiding this from me." I teased her, I praised her, I exulted. Her response sounded like she was saying, "Ha-ha." I praised her in all the ways I could think of so she could simply hear the tone of my excitement. "You're a sneaky little girl. You fooled me. You're so clever, the smartest girl there is." By the movement of her head, arms and legs, I knew she was pleased that she had made me happy.

That was the only time we read those printed words together. Once she stopped eating, she quickly became weaker, listless. Our family came for the vigil, my brother, a half sister from El Cerrito, another from Wisconsin, cousins and nephews, and her longtime friends. She dozed often, and in her conscious state, she appeared dazed and was motionless. She soon weighed less than fifty pounds. One day, while lying back in the palm of a recliner piled with pillows, she woke and was more active than she had been since her downward spiral. She mumbled and raised a thin arm, gesturing toward the ceiling. *Nnn-yeh! Nnn-yeh!* she said. It was the Shanghainese word for "Mama." She was calling to her mother, who she had not seen since she was a weeping girl of nine, when she stood for three days at the bedside of her mother, who slowly succumbed to an overdose of raw opium. My mother's voice was now jittery, her teeth were chattering. I imagined my grandmother dressed in the

Chinese jacket and skirt she wore for her last photo, now smiling, with both arms outstretched to sweep her daughter into her arms and take her home. My mother flapped one hand at me. She uttered a garble of words with the same intonation of exasperation she once used for issuing orders when company arrived: *Don't just stand there. Quick! Invite her to sit down.* I gestured for my grandmother to take a seat on the sofa. My mother pointed to something on the other side of the room and made impatient sounds. I guessed at what she wanted: photo, TV remote, tea, chair, water. Finally, I hit upon the right answer: her mink coat, which I had bought her when she hinted she wanted one. She pointed to the sofa. *Quick! Quick!* She wanted me to give the coat to her mother. I draped it over the sofa where I imagined my grandmother might be sitting. My mother was now babbling to the ceiling. Apparently other invisible guests had arrived. By the intonation of her mumbles, she appeared to be answering them: *I'm happy to see you, too. Yes, I'm going home soon.* She did not order me to invite them to sit down. Maybe there were too many of them. Later that evening, when the air cooled, I put the mink coat over my dozing mother. When she woke, she became agitated, pushing at the coat as if it were on fire. She gestured frantically to the sofa where I had invited her mother to sit. How strange. I had forgotten we had given her mother the coat. She had not. She was in a different kind of consciousness.

The next day, she slept without waking. She continued to breathe, but some part of her had already left. The hospice nurse gave us a booklet on what to expect when someone is dying. Hearing is the last sense to go, it said. So we threw my mother a noisy party to let her know she was still the center of our world, the most important person. We knew she would love the attention. Twenty friends and relatives played mahjong and poker from morning to night. We ordered pizza and Chinese takeout. We watched her favorite movies and listened to Chopin études. After two days, we realized she would never leave her own party, so we wound things down, and all but a few went home. I slept next to her, where I watched her breathe, three quick inhalations and a long held one.

These were the last sounds she would ever make. I watched for signs that she had already left with her mother.

COMMON EXPRESSIONS

My parents did not force me to learn Mandarin, because of a widespread belief at the time that kids who learned their parents' language would never fully master English. It was as if our brains had the capacity to hold only one language at a time, and by learning two, we could only half master each. Fortunately, I did manage to absorb enough Mandarin through what I overheard or what was directed to me during daily routines, or what my mother shouted when she was emotionally overwrought.

Those experiences were evidently enough for the innate language structures of my brain to hold a permanent place for Mandarin, along with the Spanish I learned in school and the French I picked up through misadventure in Switzerland and, more recently, through self-study. While I can read and write in Spanish and French, I am completely illiterate in Chinese. Yet I understand conversational Mandarin without doing the extra linguistic step I need with Spanish and English of translating in my head what the words mean and which conjugation is being used. When I am with my sisters and we exchange gossip and opinions, we speak Mandarin, and my latent ability to express myself temporarily returns. I am stymied because of my child-level vocabulary, but they know how to automatically adjust downward or give more context. *That place we went to the other day. The reason they are taking blood from my arm.* I have numerous Caucasian friends who speak far better Mandarin than I can. They studied it diligently. They can read Chinese menus and do elaborate ordering, conduct business meetings, and hold their own in just about any situation. But I have intuitions in Mandarin they will never have, and it is those aspects of language that would never be taught in language school. They have to do with expressions that come through the daily life of a child raised by Chinese parents. I am fluent in emotional nuance, intent, and subtext of words said in anger, with worry, or with tenderness.

Take the well-used expression: *wo qì sǐ le (woh CHEE-suh-luh)*, which transliterates to "I am mad to death." An English translation would be "I'm angry as hell," but it really pales in comparison to what my mother might have meant when she said those Chinese words. Hell and death are not equal in terms of fear. The phrase has gradations of meaning, which depend on how emphatically you say the two words *qì* and *sǐ*, and whether you include the word *wo*, "I." Muttered quickly—*qì sǐ le*—might have conveyed the irritation she felt in finding she had pulled slippers for two left feet off a store shelf, paid for them, and realized what she had done only when she had returned home. In that case, *qì sǐ le* simply means, "I'm so mad at myself" and would be suitably accompanied by a slap to the forehead. If it was the salesman who had boxed up shoes for two left feet and the shoes were expensive and the store far away, the first word *qì* would be said with such emphasis that a puff of air might follow, suggesting that skin-peeling steam was coming out of her mouth. If she said the word *sǐ* in a low growly tone with a lot of sibilant emphasis, that conveyed the onomatopoeic sound of a knife slitting the throat.

My mother also used the Mandarin expression *wo da si ni (Woh DAH-suh-nee)*, which was another way to express how angry she was. In this case, the expression means, literally, "I'll beat you to death." In English, you might say something similar, for example: *I'll kill you if you eat any of those chocolates.* That suggests you are serious about how much you love chocolate, and you're being direct in telling someone they can't have any, but there is no real threat that you're going to do anything that would lead to life in prison. The Chinese meaning of the phrase, *wo da si ni*, carries about the same weight, but it sounds so much worse. It's a syllable longer in scariness and suggests that a true beating might follow. I saw this literal meaning amply illustrated when, in an effort to improve my Mandarin, I watched about thirty episodes of a period drama soap opera in Chinese about three generations of a family whose wealth waxed and waned over seventy years. There were no subtitles. Had I not known even the basic rudiments of Mandarin, *wo da si ni* would have been the first expression I would have learned through frequency of usage in many kinds of situations—from insults to disobedience to betrayal. Fathers threatened to beat to death sons who failed an examination, and they came close to killing one who gambled away a lot of the family fortune. In that soap opera, brothers threatened brothers, cousins threatened cousins, in-laws threatened in-laws, masters threatened servants, concubines threatened maids, and the maids were nearly beaten to death before they killed themselves. Everyone in this period drama had bad tempers. In our family, *qi sǐ le "I'm mad to death"* was an emotional preamble to *da si ni "I'll beat you to death."* I hasten to add that this was not particular to Chinese culture. I grew up in an era when many American parents abided by the dictum "Spare the rod, spoil the child," and even teachers paddled students at the front of the classroom. In comparison to other parents, mine did not punish us that often or as severely. Some of the kids I grew up with were slapped as soon as they made a sullen face. I still remember the shrieks and wails of a four-year-old girl with blond curls who was beaten daily in the bathroom of the house next door. That girl developed her own violent streak. She pushed us down and slammed the door on our fingers whenever she could. There were certainly times in our family when the hairbrush came out and my father followed my mother's orders to use it. On a few occasions, my mother slapped me, but by age twelve, I was taller than she was and she had to resort to beating her fists on my back. I remember another occasion when my mother carried through with a neighbor's demand that she punish us. My brother, cousins, and I had picked wild blackberries in our backyard and had thrown them over the fence. We looked through the knothole and rejoiced when we saw that our fusillade had hit its target: the sunbaked white sheets hanging on a clothesline. My mother disliked this Caucasian neighbor, but she could not let us get away with what we had done. So, with the neighbor listening on the other side of the fence, she said to us in Chinese, "When I clap my hands, scream loud." Then she shouted in English, "You do this bad

thing? Eh? Give me your hand." And then she clapped her hands together, and we took turns screaming as loud as we could.

The other Chinese expressions my mother often used with me and my brothers were the threads that kept our life together as a family:

Brush your teeth. Wash your face. Turn off the light. Go to sleep.

Dinner's ready. Don't wait for me. Hurry eat before it's cold. Eat more. How does it taste? Too salty? No taste? Spicy enough? How many dumplings can you eat?

Listen to me. Don't cause trouble. Be careful. Watch out. You scared me to death.

What a bunch of lies. Stupid beyond belief. You're so bad. Such a temper. Why are you giving me an ugly face? If I died would you be happy?

I'm exhausted. My legs feel sour. What bitterness I have to swallow. Do you believe me or her?

Are you sick? You're burning up. Do you hurt? Your stomach isn't feeling well? Eat more rice porridge. Don't cry. Lie down. Wait for me. Don't be scared. I'll be back soon. Do you believe me?

STANDARD ENGLISH

Most of my non-Chinese friends had a hard time making out what my mother was saying. Sometimes they would understand half, sometimes, nothing at all. During her fifty years of living in the United States her grammar became more idiosyncratic and her pronunciation worsened after she retired as an allergy technician and she no longer had to make an effort for patients to understand her. But she had no problems speaking voluble amounts of her form of English. "Lots lots lots I have to tell you," she'd say to me before settling into a two-hour conversation. She was not aware how off the mark her articulation was, as I discovered one day when I caught her trying to teach her daughter, my half sister Lijun, how to pronounce words incorrectly.

I understood her version of English as a pidgin I had grown up with, an assimilation of Shanghainese, Mandarin, and English into unique pronunciations and surprisingly useful blended idioms, e.g. "you unwind my mind," meaning, "you twist my words to confuse me." Her sentence structures were English words overlaid on a free-style Chinese topic-comment syntax, which ordered words according to what my mother wanted to emphasize: "You wear that dress so short you want everyone see up to your *pi gu?*"

Her version of English did not impair my learning to speak standard English. At a young age, all kids naturally pick up the language of the schoolyard. Actually, I did use some of her constructions here and there, but inconsistently. I would say, "go school," "go hospital," and "go library." That was likely the result of my speaking a modified form of English at home, the one that followed the patterns of her speech. Her vocabulary was limited, and until I read books and went to school, I relied on her same strategy for identifying objects by purpose and not name. "I want that thing you put on your face."

By my teens I knew how to speak a modified form of English at
home, one that was geared to my mother's language. For one thing,
I instinctively eliminated in real time the words and also the idioms
I knew she wouldn't understand, for example: *Ignorance is bliss. El-
ephant in the room. Shoot the breeze.* Among those she probably would
have understood, it might have been these: *a bitter pill, burn the mid-
night oil, thumb one's nose, be glad to see the back of him, costs an arm and
a leg, a picture is worth a thousand words,* and *cut corners.* She told me
that a lot—that I was lazy and "cut corners."

I knew to avoid complicated English constructions and concepts.
So instead of reporting, "We're discussing the amendments to the
Constitution," I might have done a long circumnavigation to explain
what this was to my mother. "We read that when the United States
started as a country, they created something that was like the number
one law, and it means we have the freedom to speak our mind and no
one can take that away from us." There were plenty of times when
my mother surprised me with how much she actually knew. With
the example I just gave, she would have likely said this in return:
"Let me see book. Amendments to Constitution. First Amendment,

this not law, not like Ten Commandments. This like saying you own something, now many laws protect. I know this, because Daddy and I memorize this for citizenship test. Got 100 percent. What you think, I so ignorant, know nothing? I know. This important amendment, American right. But this don't mean you say what you want to me. That's not American right, this treat your mother bad." And she did in fact learn about the Constitution, the Bill of Rights, the amendments, the branches of government, and the words to the Pledge of Allegiance. Her English was sufficient, surprisingly so for someone whose English was rusty. After ten hair-raising years of expired student visas and repeated requests to the Department of Justice to put their deportation in abeyance, she and my father said the Pledge of Allegiance with a hand over their heart and became U.S. citizens in 1961. When they returned home, they were crying. I remember.

HISTORICAL LINGUISTICS

My father's first language was not Mandarin. He was born into a Cantonese family whose ancestral home was in Zhongshan County in Guangzhou, in the southeast part of China. Since he spoke Cantonese fluently, that must have been the language spoken in the home. He also spoke English with ease. And no wonder: he had the advantage of a father who spoke it fluently. I'm told that his grandfather, my great-grandfather, had been educated in English, and I am guessing that he was enrolled in a Christian missionary school, possibly one run by Methodists, since that was the religion my father's family followed. My grandfather was also educated at an English-speaking school, and, as a result, he learned to read and write in English before he learned to do so in Chinese. My father attended an English-speaking boys school outside of Beijing, and that was where he must have also perfected his English and standard Mandarin. His family likely put to good use their multilingual skills in Cantonese, Mandarin, and English for transactions with foreigners. They ran an export business, and their migratory path of commerce in China went from the south to the north, the north to the south, and also into the middle, to Wuhan, where my father was born. My grandfather wanted all twelve children to learn English. He wrote them letters in English, applying enough pressure on eleven carbon sheets under the original to give copies to all of them. One of my uncles said that the copies he received were very faint because he was much younger than my father, whereas my father, being the oldest, received the original, and that was why my father's English was the best of all twelve children. That skill enabled my father to give tours to American and British visitors to the Central Radio Factory in Guilin, where he worked as an engineer. It also helped him land a job later with the U.S. Information Agency and the U.S. Army Corps. My father's favorite sister, Gui Ying, "Jean," also lived in Guilin. She was the second oldest in the family and thus received the first carbon copy out of the stack. Her English was excellent, if not equal to my father's. That enabled her to become the English-speaking host of a program broadcast by a station operated by the same radio factory where my father worked.

In 1977, when my grandfather was eighty-seven and I was twenty-five, he sent me a letter from Shanghai in response to my letter to him from San Francisco. We had never met and it was the first time I had heard from him. My father, his eldest son, who he had not seen since 1947, had been dead for nearly ten years. The letter was written in shaky handwriting on a single tissue-thin sheet. He apologized that he was not able to respond sooner. His eyesight was poor due to old age, he said, and not any other malady, and he found it difficult to read and write. Most of his letter concerned more details about the nature of his vision problem. He added that his appetite was good and he slept well. He was glad to hear my mother was strong enough to still work as a nurse. He welcomed more letters from me. It was not an informative letter, nor particularly warm, but what puzzled me most was his signature at the end, "yours affectionately, Hugh." I had addressed him as "Grandpa" in my five-page letter. I had signed it, "Love, your granddaughter Amy." I thought to myself, Why not "Your grandfather," or "Grandfather Hugh"? Did he think "Hugh" would sound warmer to an American granddaughter? I had heard that some family members had disapproved of my father's marriage to my mother. My mother resented his sister Jean for that reason. But I had not heard of any disagreement between my father and grandfather. Maybe his vision was so poor he had not read my declaration of love for him. Maybe he simply signed his first name out of habit, without thought of the complications of family relationships that are contained within a name. Whatever the case, I'm certain he could not have known that his signature might cause his granddaughter to wonder the rest of her life what her grandfather felt was the nature of their bond.

While my father's English was far better than my mother's, I had always assumed until recently that their Mandarin was equal. People used to remark that my father spoke it beautifully. They said the same about his Cantonese and English. He was a minister, accustomed to public speaking, whose job was to convince and console. Even when he switched his career to engineering, he still gave spiritually invigorating sermons as a guest pastor. He performed weddings, served as the unofficial MC at celebrations, the person who offered the toast, and led friends and family into song. People had many opportunities to hear him speak. My mother, on the other hand, was not called upon to speak at any gatherings. She was the silent better half, who spoke forcefully at home.

I used to wonder what Chinese people perceived in my mother based on the way she talked. Language usage is an instant marker of age, education, regional habitat, and upbringing as reflected in the polite and nuanced ways that you speak. But language usage can also fool you. Many autodidacts I know sound more articulate and knowledgeable than those who have advanced college degrees. And many American mothers today will imitate the upward questioning intonation pattern of their children's English. *I was at the same restaurant? And I ran into a friend I knew from high school?* I used to think millennials in search of jobs would sound more confident and mature if they dropped that upward intonation pattern. But then I heard a college professor my age use it.

In China, your vocabulary is also telling in another way: a Chinese person who left China in the 1940s may leave linguistic foot-prints of that in their vocabulary. Words or expressions that were popular then are archaic now. I would not know what those were, but a friend who has the skills of a linguistic detective told me that my mother used them. She is a film director and actress, who speaks Shanghainese, Mandarin, Cantonese, and also nearly flawless English. I saw her ability to discern accents in action. We were at an elevation of about eight thousand feet in the Sierra Mountains, hiking down a rocky path on a hot day. Even with hiking boots, I often lost my footing when we trudged over scree. A Chinese couple dressed in street clothes and sneakers were climbing up the same path. They were sweating and red-faced from exertion. As often happens when Chinese people encounter one another in unusual places, we exchanged greetings, and then my friend asked in Mandarin where they were from. The man looked evasive and said they had just moved to this area and gestured to the mountains behind him. My friend clarified that she meant what part of China they had come from. The man said, "Beijing." My friend clarified further that she was asking about his family origins, not where he lived now. He again stated "Beijing." My friend smiled sweetly and nodded. When we continued our walk, my friend said, "No way he's from Beijing. That guy's from somewhere like Shanxi. He has a crude way of speaking, like someone who's been in the army a long time and never had a college education. He's probably one of those corrupt officials who embezzled millions and is being hunted down by the Chinese government."

That's when I asked how strong my mother's accent was, and she said, "A really thick one. You know how bad her English pronunciation was? That's what her Mandarin was like." I was incredulous. I asked if my Mandarin had a similar accent, and she confirmed that it did. I recalled a Chinese friend who laughed every time she heard me speak Mandarin. She said that I spoke like a baby, and that it was very cute. I thought she was referring only to my vocabulary. But she must have been referring to my accent as well, a Shanghainese one, which is a dialect I don't even speak and only vaguely understand, just the gist of the conversations. I have heard other people describe Shanghainese as sounding like baby talk. To me, Shanghainese conversations sound like nonstop arguments and not quarreling babies. But there are indeed Shanghainese words that have traits of baby talk, for example, those words that are reduplicative, like *yi di di,* "a little." In *Putong Hua,* "common Mandarin," the equivalent is *yi dian dian.* And in Beijing Mandarin, which is the standard accent of newscasters and film stars, *yi dian* is pronounced with a retroflex *r,* and sounds more like *yee-dyarh,* and no reduplication would ever be used, not even in baby talk. None of those distinctions matter when you're a baby and your Shanghainese mother is holding a morsel of food before you, telling you to eat *yi di di.*

I had barely grasped this news about my mother's Mandarin when my friend added that my mother's Shanghainese pronunciation was excellent—and that she had had only a slight Suzhou accent; Suzhou is a city about ninety minutes away from Shanghai, a lovely place with canals, famous for the classical gardens that inspired great poets. It is where my grandmother was born. The Suzhou language is actually prestigious, because it is identified with gentility. "Many think it makes Shanghainese sound prettier," my friend said. "Some people try to imitate the accent." It's commonly said that a person from Suzhou speaks so delicately that the tone of their arguments makes it sound to Shanghainese people like they are merely having a normal conversation.

My mother, it seems, spoke no language that was purely of any region, and how lucky I was that this was the case. Her idiosyncratic language skills were clues to our family history. Generations of her mother's side of the family had lived in Suzhou and ran a good business selling fine embroidered silk cloth before an unknown catastrophe sent them seventy miles to the east, to Shanghai. My great-grandmother likely continued to speak the Suzhou dialect to her daughter, my grandmother, when she was a baby, and that was the language of the home my mother heard and likely spoke, alongside the Shanghainese dialect that other family members used. Although her mother died when she nine, she evidently retained its influence, the Suzhou shadings of pronunciation but not the gentle tone of arguments. Her Suzhou-tinted Shanghainese-shaded Mandarin-accented English was what she spoke when I was growing up, and it embarrassed me as a teenager when she spoke it in public.

My friend assured me that to a Shanghainese person, my mother sounded both articulate and refined. Her words were a little old-fashioned at times, as were the expressions she used in her letters. But her writing style was especially telling. It conveyed she was educated, intelligent, and from a family with class.

If my mother were still alive, I would make recordings of her speech in a methodical way. I would not ask her to simply say words, like "eye," "nose," "mouth," and "ear." I would have her speak naturally in the Suzhou dialect, in Shanghainese, in Mandarin, and in English to express hunger, pain, and exhaustion. I would examine which of the languages she used enabled her to express nuances of love or sorrow. I would identify the subtleties that did not survive the migration into English. I would listen to words she might have uttered as a baby to her grandmother, as well as the words her Suzhou-speaking grandmother might have murmured to her when she was delirious with pain after a pot of oily soup overturned and burned her neck. I would listen to determine how words for "hatred" and "betrayal" are colored in the Suzhou dialect, in Shanghainese, and in Mandarin, and at which age—infancy, childhood, adolescence, or adulthood—those words had entered her vocabulary. I would have her relate the same instances of betrayal in English to determine whether I had understood the degree of her anguish. I would have her describe in Mandarin what she felt when she met my father for the first time and to then describe that moment in English. Which language described it more poignantly? I would ask her to describe in Shanghainese, then English, the anger she felt when the tabloids described her love affair with my father as a disgrace to her family. Which one captured her outrage and despair more completely? I would have her describe in Mandarin and then English the moment she agreed with the doctors to remove the feeding tube from my comatose brother. Which language captured her torment more accurately? I would record thousands of hours of her speech and the idioms that stood for hope, fear, and despair—from the Suzhou dialect, into Shanghainese, into Mandarin, into English. I would observe facial expressions and chest beating and note their effect on intent and meaning. I would isolate the meanings that would be lost to someone who did not know her.

I would also record my speech, the baby talk Mandarin I spoke to her in those last months of her life. I would record the baby talk she still understood. And then I would know us through the history of her language, and in the natural and forced evolution of her accents, in her ability to speak in nuances, in her effectiveness in making demands. I would know all the ways I had misunderstood her, all the ways I wish I could have known her, all the ways I could have told her that I knew what she had endured.

COMPANIONS IN THE HOUSE

My husband rises early each morning and goes upstairs to read the newspaper. I scrunch deeper under the quilt, squeezing out more dreams. Tucked into the curve of my lower legs is my four-pound Yorkie, and leaning against my arm is my husband's rescue mutt, an old dog who will stare at you for a long time, as if he is sending you messages of love. *Feed me.* Lou always feeds the dogs first thing in the morning, then takes them out to the garden to do their business, and returns them to bed, where they will not stir even after I rise, shower, and prepare for another day at my writing desk. That is their habit, to laze about.

My office is an alcove next to the bedroom. Sleep and work are separated by six sliding Chinese lattice screens. They are constructed of the salvaged elm and camphor wood of broken furniture a hundred years old. I had them made in Shanghai, where both sides of my family once lived. They were shipped by boat, a voyage of a month, during which time some of the panels swelled with humidity and cracked after we installed them. The furniture maker had warned me this might happen, but I told him it would make them look antique rather than a reproduction. At the top of each screen is a panel with two carved Chinese characters, a different couplet for each screen. Together those twelve characters form the first Chinese poem I've ever written, laughably clumsy, but meaningful to me. *The heart is like the full moon reflected in a deep winter pond. Spring rain arrives, creativity bursts forth.* They are the sentiments of the late friend who taught me about the symbolism in Chinese gardens. I wish I could remember exactly what he said about the moon and the pond, but he meant that I was the kind of writer who felt deeply so that one day I could express what I felt. I try.

Every morning I hear the grinding of coffee beans. Its scent grows stronger as my husband comes down the stairs. He hands me my mug, and we do our ritual. "What do you say?" he asks. "Thank you," I answer, and he receives his kiss. There are days when I awake confused because it is quiet and the smell of the house is of unstirred air. And then I remember that my husband is away in the mountains skiing, and I chose to stay home to write. To miss someone is to also miss what is supposed to be the same when you wake up. I've lost two dogs to old age and one to illness, and each death left me with such grief I lay mute in bed for days, because I could not bear missing the humor of their habits: their running up and down the stairs barking at ghosts, or lying in a small circle of sun on the porch, or standing still in the garden wearing a pleased look as a breeze pushed the hair from their faces. I planted a dwarf crab apple tree in the garden, and at the base of the trunk are smooth stones carved with their names. I included a stone for my cat Sagwa as well, even though she died long before we had a garden. The tree looks like a small weeping willow and by early winter, the leaves will have fallen off. In the spring, when the leaves return, always all at once, I imagine the dogs running in the garden again. The cat watches. The return of those leaves is both sad and a comfort.

Our house sits on a hill that overlooks the Sausalito harbor, Raccoon Strait, and San Francisco Bay. At their confluence is an island. We built this house to have the airiness and sensibility of a Chinese pavilion, similar to the scholar retreats depicted in Chinese brush paintings. Giant oak trees flank one side of the house, and from the upper floor, we are at eye level with the branches, where crows and scrub jays perch. They take turns; otherwise, they squabble. I have seen them do that. I sometimes watch a little gray squirrel scampering up and down and onto our roof. I'm not fond of squirrels. They nearly destroyed a little cabin we have in the mountains, after they chewed their way through the eaves and floors, walls and ceilings. They pulled out the insulation to line the nests they made in our shoes. When we tore open the kitchen walls we saw what looked like the Egyptian tomb of a thousand squirrels. The squirrel in the oak trees of our new home does acrobatics among the branches, but it has not destroyed anything, not that I know of. Sometimes it will shrill for hours during the day in a sad weeping tone. A birder friend told me that it was probably defending its babies from a crow or a scrub jay. Those birds will also raid the nests of songbirds, my friend said, as will owls. On several occasions, I've heard the night sounds of a great horned owl coming from somewhere in the dark. *Hoo-hoo, Hoo, Hoo.* The timbre of their call sounds like an oboe and can carry quite a distance, a mile or so. I've never seen an owl in our garden, which is good, since it can easily kill a four-pound dog like mine. Then again, just because I haven't seen an owl doesn't mean it is not right there. Owls look like tree bark when they're still.

One day when it was raining, I came home and saw tufts of down float past my face. Baby bird fluff was falling from the tree branch above me and when it landed on the wet stone steps, it instantly flattened as flowers do when pressed between pages in a book. I took a downy feather inside and drew a sketch to see all its details and to think about the bird it belonged to. Lately, I've heard fewer songbirds, and I haven't seen the squirrel in months. Maybe a crow or scrub jay killed the babies and the mother abandoned the tree. If the owl did the deed, the mother would likely have been killed, too. Despite the carnage, I still think the tree is beautiful, glorious, and strong, over a hundred years old. It has held in its branches many squirrels and birds, maybe owls, as well.

The living room and dining area upstairs are one big open space, and when the glass sliding panels that run the length of the room are pushed open it feels as if the room is an infinity pool that goes all the way across the water to the island. When we built the house, we kept in mind a Chinese philosophy called feng shui, which concerns principles of harmony with nature. The words stand for "wind and water." The spirit of harmony flows on wind and water; I suppose that is the sentiment. The right alignment of elements can align you with the right forces, and the wrong alignment can affect your health, finances, and peace of mind. The best orientation for a home is one that faces mountains and water. Real estate agents will tell you the same. Beyond providing a terrific view, mountains often figure into Chinese poetry and also four-character proverbs with a historical context—mountain retreats for classical poet painters, for example. They're chock-full of symbolism and literary references. You can easily imagine the possible meanings: hardship to overcome, a pile of opportunities, lofty thoughts, or the pinnacle as the ideal station in life. Chinese meanings sometimes oversaturate my writing brain and I just want to see nature, the physical appearance of a mountain as a beautiful view, and not as a symbolic opportunity or an obstacle.

I see this island daily from where I sit in my office, Angel Island, an island of ghosts. During the cold war, the peak was flattened for a Nike missile station. A decade ago, the peak was restored, and now the shape of the island looks like a peasant's conical hat. Maybe I think that because the island once served as a quarantine station between 1910 and 1940 for immigrants, most of them Chinese. For them, this mountain island was an obstacle. No papers were stamped upon arrival; no boats quickly took them across the bay to their families waiting for them on the shore of San Francisco, the place they called Old Gold Mountain. The arrivals were stripped, inspected for vermin and disease, then interrogated repeatedly, and if their answers differed in even the smallest way from what other family members had said—be it the ages of family members back home or the number of steps in their home—the whole family would be deported. Many were detained for such a long time they wrote poems about loneliness. Station staff used putty to cover the poems, but new poems would appear elsewhere. In turn, more putty muffled those poems. Then poems appeared on other walls, and more putty was applied. Long after the station was closed, the putty fell off one wall and revealed over two hundred poems: elegiac words about seeing sadness in seaweed and fog, couplets about despair, angry poems about injustice or racism. They look like inscriptions on a mausoleum, or messages in a bottle from people who wanted others to know they were there, a human with feelings that were important to express and should be known, now or later, no matter what happened to them.

One was philosophical:

> Instead, you must cast your idle worries to
> the flowing stream.
> Experiencing a little ordeal is not hardship.
> Napoleon was once a prisoner on an island.

I wonder if he was deported. Napoleon escaped after a year and took control of France once again.

At night, the island is a purple shadow against the sky. When there's a full moon, and the sky is clear and the water still, the peak of the island glows and its body is reflected in the water. The immigrants in those barracks would not have been able to see the glow or reflection. They saw the walls of a prison for two months, for two years, for a period of time whose end was never known until they were told they could enter the United States or that they were being sent back to China. I imagine that a few of them saw that island glow when they were finally able to stand onshore in San Francisco. They must have thought about those still in that prison, a friend, an uncle, son or a wife. And there were some who never went to shore and never returned to China either—like the bride-to-be of a U.S. Chinese citizen. When she was told entry had been denied, she took her wedding dress out of her bag, put it on, and hung herself in the shower. Over the years there were women who claimed they saw her ghost.

I imagine the lives of those immigrants were monotonous—the

same puttied walls, the same stink, the same food, the same cycle of hope then despair and anger. What would happen when the monotony broke? When they leaned against a window, what did they see in the water? To me the water changes from morning to night, from day to day, season to season. It might be glassy or choppy, sapphire colored or muddy gray, never the same. One day my husband and I saw a glinting swath in the water the length of a rich man's yacht. It was right in front of the island. We said at the same time: What's that? I guessed it was a school of golden fish. Did anchovies in a tin have that same sheen? Then we discovered it was the sun angled just so. The next time we saw the floating gold we said aloud: What's that? And then we remembered.

Did the immigrants notice the golden water between the island and Sausalito? Or did they see the water only as a barrier to reunion?

Egrets and pelicans fly over the water, and turkey vultures circle high above. In the fall, swarms of geese put on a show over the island, as do the Blue Angels during their precision maneuvers. Raptors begin their migration in October, coasting on the thermals, and there are always a few red-tailed hawks and peregrine falcons that take a detour to scan the hill where our house sits. They perch at the highest points of trees. They are looking for little furry animals to eat and can zoom down as fast as a Blue Angel. During autumn, I watch the sky when I let my dogs out to play in the garden. The hawks can land on a little dog and tear it to pieces in seconds.

In the spring, the hummingbirds return and fly by my office window. A few months ago, I hung feeders filled with red sugar water. I placed a large fake red pansy nearby. It looks like the plastic openings of the feeders. I thought it would be a sign to the hummingbirds that this was the spot where breakfast is served. I checked the sugar water level daily to see if it ever went down. It never did. I changed the sugar water often. I placed a birdbath nearby. One day, I moved the feeder closer to the trees, and immediately a hummingbird flew to the bottle for a long drink. It did not mind my presence. Nowadays, I call the birds with my own birdsong, and they come—the titmice, chickadees, scrub jays, towhees, doves, and hummingbirds. Sometimes the hummingbirds will drink from a little feeder on my palm.

But really, I should be writing. It's hard though when the scrub jays are having a fight over the feeders I put out for them in another part of the garden, also within view from my desk. With them, I have been quite successful. They come morning and evening, and sometimes in between. So I often have to tell myself I should be writing.

On the long bookshelf by the window, I placed photos of people I have loved and who have died. When I look in the direction of the island, I see them as well: my mother and father at different times when they were madly in love; my older brother and me as toddlers; my friend who taught me about Chinese gardens. It is a terrible picture of him in a peasant's hat—like the shape of the island. He would have hated it, but it is the only one I have that is not blurred, and I do want to remember him. I have many photos of my grandmother. I never knew her, except in imagination, and in that way, I know her very well. The frames for each are different, because I added the photos at different times, and now some of them are falling apart. I should get new ones, but then I think that those frames are like homes that the people in the photos have settled into.

I also have two small makeshift urns. One is a hollow bamboo branch with an airtight cap. It holds the ashes of a friend who taught me to shoot photos and also to shoot pool. We have a pool table as a result, a sowbelly built in 1909. The other urn is a blue and white porcelain tea canister. It contains the ashes of a friend who taught me to have fun by acting ridiculous. I have been meaning to scatter the ashes of both urns in my garden. But so far it's never been the right time to do so.

Every day I thank my husband for the coffee, I watch the birds in the tree, and laugh at the pleased faces of my dogs. I notice the different colors of the water. I look at the photos on my bookshelf and the island of ghosts. I imagine the poets on the island looking out across the infinite water toward me as I look across the water toward them. I imagine my family as the living people they once were and I am with them in their past. Eventually, I write.

ACKNOWLEDGMENTS

I am grateful to many people—family, friends, and acquaintances—who have felicitously or inadvertently contributed to the metamorphosis of this book.

For family stories and love: John Tan, Jindo Eng, Lijun Wang, Benjamin Tan, Sieu-mei Tu, Norman and Antonia Tu, Harold Tu, David Tu, Tuck and Jayne Chin, and Sandy Bremner.

For immersing me in the calm, the ecstasy, and the profundity of music: Michael Tilson Thomas and Joshua Robison.

For letting me experience the genius manifested in jazz, love, and God: God, Joey Alexander and his parents, and Farah and Denny Sila.

For teaching me how to draw using a No. 2 pencil coupled with burbling wonderment: Megan Gavin, Joe Furman, and John Muir Laws.

For identifying me as an early reader when I was six: Dolores Durkin. Thanks also to Colleen Whittingham, who made it possible for me to speak to Dr. Durkin.

For saturating my writer's brain with life-altering inventions, future possibilities, illusions and conundrums, genuine science and quixotic theories: Michael Hawley and the E. G. Conference, Lucia Jacobs and the Philosophical Club, Oliver Sacks, Robert Binnick, Carl Pabo, and Kary Mullis.

For leading me into the curiouser and curiouser world of the cell, the ocean, and the rain forest: Crissy Huffard, Mark Moffett, Mark Siddall, Michael Tessler, and the squishy *Chtonobdella tanae.*

For insights into the global effects of Chinese culture, the uniqueness of Shanghai style, as well as my mother's idiosyncratic linguistic medley: Joan Chen, Shelley Lim, Duncan Clark, and Robin Wang.

For thoughtfulness in giving me the appearance that I am organized, prepared, responsive, and responsible: Ellen Moore and Marcia Soares.

For giving this book and its slightly off-keel writer understanding, care, and enthusiasm: the Ecco publishing team—Daniel Halpern, Sonya Cheuse, Bridget Read, Miriam Parker, and Suet Yee Chong.

For always being there as my advocate and secretary of defense: Sandy Dijkstra and her team, Elise Capron and Andrea Cavallaro.

For steadfast love, support, and indulgence, including the delivery of breakfast, lunch, and dinner to my desk during the writing of this book: Lou DeMattei.